Cisco Networking Academy Program: Lab Companion, Volume II

Jim Lorenz

CISCO SYSTEMS

CISCO PRESS

Cisco Press
201 West 103rd Street
Indianapolis, IN 46290 USA

Cisco Networking Academy Program: Lab Companion, Volume II

Jim Lorenz

Copyright © 2000 Cisco Press

Cisco Press logo is a trademark of Cisco Systems, Inc.

Published by:
Cisco Press
210 West 103rd Street
Indianapolis, IN 46290 USA

Printed in the United States of America 1 2 3 4 5 6 7 8 9 0

ISBN: 1-57870-235-6

Warning and Disclaimer

This book is designed to provide information on Cisco internetworking fundamentals. Every effort has been made to make this book as complete and as accurate as possible, but no warranty or fitness is implied.

The information is provided on an as-is basis. The author, Cisco Press, and Cisco Systems, Inc., shall have neither liability nor responsibility to any person or entity with respect to any loss or damages arising from the information contained in this book or from the use of the programs that may accompany it.

The opinions expressed in this book belong to the author and are not necessarily those of Cisco Systems, Inc.

Trademark Acknowledgments

All terms mentioned in this book that are known to be trademarks or service marks have been appropriately capitalized. Cisco Press or Cisco Systems, Inc., cannot attest to the accuracy of this information. Use of a term in this book should not be regarded as affecting the validity of any trademark or service mark.

Feedback Information

At Cisco Press, our goal is to create in-depth technical books of the highest quality and value. Each book is crafted with care and precision, undergoing rigorous development that involves the unique expertise of members from the professional technical community.

Readers' feedback is a natural continuation of this process. If you have any comments regarding how we could improve the quality of this book, or otherwise alter it to better suit your needs, you can contact us at ciscopress@mcp.com. Please make sure to include the book title and ISBN in your message.

We greatly appreciate your assistance.

Publisher	John Wait
Executive Editor	Dave Dusthimer
Cisco Systems Program Manager	Jim LeValley
Managing Editor	Patrick Kanouse
Senior Editor	Jennifer Chisholm
Copy Editor	Krista Hansing
Proofreader	Bob LaRoche
Associate Editor	Shannon Gross

About the Author

Jim Lorenz is the lead instructor and coordinator for the Cisco Regional Training Academy at Chandler-Gilbert Community College (CGCC) in Chandler, Arizona, where he is a full-time faculty member. He also was a lead instructor for the Microsoft Certified Systems Engineering (MCSE) curriculum. He has 20 years of experience in computers and information systems with companies such as Honeywell and Motorola, and he has held various positions ranging from programming and database administration to network design and program management. Jim has taught computer and networking courses for both public and private institutions for more than 15 years.

Jim is a Novell Certified NetWare Engineer (CNE), a Microsoft Certified Trainer (MCT), a Cisco Certified Network Associate (CCNA), and a Cisco Certified Academy Instructor (CCAI). He holds a bachelor's degree in computer information systems from Prescott College.

Acknowledgements

Brad Niesluchowski has been a great help in putting together these labs and reviewing them for technical accuracy. Brad is a network administrator with Higley Unified School District in Arizona and is a graduate of the Chandler-Gilbert Cisco Academy. Ray Moore, director of technology for Fountain Hills School District in Arizona, has also been a big help as an author and a technical reviewer. Ray is the president of the Phoenix NT Users Special Interest Group and is also a part-time Cisco instructor at Chandler-Gilbert Community College.

I would like to thank Cisco Press Executive Editor Dave Dusthimer, Cisco Networking Academy Editor Vito Amato, and Academy curriculum specialists Kevin Johnston and Dennis Frezzo for their support as well as their guidance.

I would also like to thank the administration of Chandler-Gilbert Community College for their tremendous support of my efforts and the Cisco Networking Academy Program. Most importantly, I would like to thank my wife, Mary, and my daughters, Jessica and Natasha, for their patience and their understanding.

Table of Contents

Semester 4: Wide-Area Networking

Introduction

This manual was developed for use with the Cisco CCNA online curriculum and *Cisco Networking Academy Program: Second-Year Companion Guide* for semesters 3 and 4. These labs coincide with those in the current Cisco Networking Academy Program (CNAP), with some additional information added. Most of the labs are hands-on and will require access to a Cisco router lab, a simulator, or software such as Cisco ConfigMaker. Additional paper-based labs are included to supplement the online curriculum, which are practice exercises for complex topics.

All labs and exercises are comprised of three main sections:

1. **Overview Section**: Includes objectives, background information, and a "Tools/Preparation" section to help students, instructors, and lab assistants prepare for the lab. This section also includes web site resources and references to the corresponding chapter(s) to read in *Cisco Networking Academy Program: First-Year Companion Guide* and online curriculum. For planning purposes, each lab indicates the approximate amount of time it should take. This may vary depending on the number students working together on the lab and the resources available.
2. **Worksheet Section**: Includes the steps necessary to complete the lab, with progress questions.
3. **Answers Section**: Provides the answers to the questions in the lab worksheets.

Semester 3 Labs

Cisco Labs – Semester 3 – Routing and Switching
EXERCISE 1.1 – OSI MODEL REVIEW – OVERVIEW
(Estimated time: 20 minutes)

Objectives:

- Relate devices and terminology to the various layers of the OSI model
- Match OSI layers with those of the TCP/IP model
- Identify TCP/IP protocols and utilities that operate at each layer

Background:

This lab serves as a refresher to reinforce understanding of the seven layers of the OSI model as they relate to the TCP/IP model. Focus is on where terms and devices fit in the OSI model. This lab can be a fun, collaborative, knowledge-competition activity.

Tools/Preparation:

Create a group competition! Count off and divide into teams of two to four people each. Without looking at your notes or answers, see how accurately your team can fill in the OSI table in the worksheet. The team with the most correct entries (points) in the table at the end of the specified time (perhaps 10 minutes) wins. If another team questions a term or table entry, it may challenge and receive the points if agreed upon by the review committee (which is made up of one member from each team).

Before beginning this lab, you should read Chapter 1 of *Cisco Networking Academy Program: Second-Year Companion Guide*, and Chapters 1, 9, and 10 of *Cisco Networking Academy Program: First-Year Companion Guide*. You should also review Semester 3 online Lesson 1.

Required Resources:

- PC workstation with Windows installed
- NIC installed and Cat 5 patch cable with connection to the Internet
- Browser software installed (Netscape Navigator 3.0 or higher, or Internet Explorer 4.0 or higher)
- Sample networking items, such as Ethernet and Token Ring NICs with different connectors (Coax, AUI, RJ45)
- Sample hubs, switches, and routers

NOTES:

_____

_____

_____

_____

_____

_____

_____

_____

_____

_____

Cisco Labs – Semester 3 – Routing and Switching
EXERCISE 1.1 – OSI MODEL REVIEW – WORKSHEET

Step 1. The OSI model and associated TCP/IP protocol stack layers.
  Task: Fill out the following chart based on your knowledge of the OSI and TCP/IP models.
  Explanation: Your understanding of the OSI model as it relates to the TCP/IP model will greatly increase your ability to absorb and categorize networking information as you learn it.

1. Given the OSI layer number, fill in the chart below. Compete with other teams, if possible, and try to think of as many protocols, standards, utilities, terms, and devices as possible without looking at your notes. Note: TCP/IP layers will relate to more than one OSI layer.

OSI Model and TCP/IP Protocol Stack

OSI #	OSI Layer Name (and Function)	TCP/IP #	TCP/IP Layer Name	Protocols, Standards, and Utilities at Each TCP/IP Layer	Devices and Terms Associated with This Layer
7					
6					
5					
4					
3					
2					
1					

Cisco Labs – Semester 3 – Routing and Switching
EXERCISE 1.1 – OSI MODEL REVIEW – ANSWERS

Step 1: The OSI model and associated TCP/IP protocol stack layer.
   Task: Fill in the following chart based on your knowledge of the OSI and TCP/IP models.

OSI Model and TCP/IP Protocol Stack

OSI #	OSI Layer Name (and Function)	TCP/IP #	TCP/IP Layer Name	Protocols, Standards, and Utilities at Each TCP/IP Layer	Devices and Terms Associated with This Layer
7	Application (network processes to applications)	4	Application	FTP, HTTP, SMTP, DNS, TFTP, NFS, Telnet, Rlogin	Data, software, gateways
6	Presentation (data representation)	4	Application	ASCII, EBCDIC, MIDI, MPEG, PICT, TIFF, JPEG	Data coding, software, encryption, compression, redirectors
5	Session (interhost communication)	4	Application	NFS, SQL, RPC	Data, software, client-server
4	Transport (end-to-end connections)	3	Transport	TCP or UDP	Router, port numbers, flow control, windowing, connection-oriented, connectionless
3	Network (address and best path)	2	Internetwork	IP, ICMP, ARP, RARP, Ping, Traceroute	Router, brouter, Layer 3 switch, packet, datagram IP addressing, subnets, path determination, routed (IP, IPX) and routing (RIP, IGRP) protocols
2	Data Link (access to media)	1	Network (interface)	IEEE 802.2, 802.3, 802.5	Ethernet, NIC (LLC and MAC address), bridge, switch, frame, WAN link protocols (HDLC, and so on)
1	Physical (binary transmission)	1	Network (interface)	IEEE 802.3, 802.5	Ethernet, NIC (physical connectors – BNC, AUI, RJ45), media (cable – coax, UTP, fiber), repeater, hub, DCE and DTE, bits, encoding

Cisco Labs – Semester 3 – Routing and Switching
LAB 1.2 – ROUTER LAB SETUP REVIEW – OVERVIEW
(Estimated time: 30 minutes)

Router Name - LAB A
Router Type - 2514
E 0 = 192.5.5.1
E 1 = 205.7.5.1
S 0 = 201.100.11.1
SM = 255.255.255.0

Router Name - LAB C
Router Type - 2503
E 0 = 223.8.151.1
S 0 = 204.204.7.1
S 1 = 199.6.13.2
SM = 255.255.255.0

Router Name - LAB E
Router Type - 2501
E 0 = 210.93.105.2
SM = 255.255.255.0

Router Name - LAB B
Router Type - 2503
E 0 = 219.17.100.1
S 0 = 199.6.13.1
S 1 = 201.100.11.2
SM = 255.255.255.0

Router Name - LAB D
Router Type - 2501
E 0 = 210.93.105.1
S 1 = 204.204.7.2
SM = 255.255.255.0

LEGEND
= ROUTER   User Exec Password = cisco
= HUB   Enable Secret Exec Password = class
= LAN SWITCH   Terminal vty Password = cisco
= CONSOLE CABLE

Objectives:
- Set up the Cisco lab equipment according to the Semester 2 topology diagram shown above, or analyze the physical connections of an existing lab setup.
- Document the cabling and connections between devices
- Use ConfigMaker to draw a diagram of your lab equipment setup

Background:
This lab serves as a refresher for how the Cisco lab routers are set up and connected for the Semester 2 topology (see previous diagram). This is a review of the Semester 2 network topology. You will set up and document the physical connections between these routers and the other lab hardware components such as hubs, switches, and workstations. If it is not possible to start with the equipment disconnected, document an existing lab setup. This lab will utilize the standard setup consisting of five routers, four hubs, one switch and at least five workstations, plus all associated cabling and adapters.

It is a good idea to work on this lab and the next one (Lab 1.3) simultaneously, if possible. The next lab will give you an opportunity to develop an IP addressing scheme based on multiple Class B subnet addresses. You may work in teams of three to five; while one group is configuring the router lab physical setup, the other can be designing the Class B addressing scheme on the board.

Cisco Labs – Semester 3 – Routing and Switching
LAB 1.2 – ROUTER LAB SETUP REVIEW – OVERVIEW

Tools/Preparation:

Before starting this lab, you will need to have the equipment from the standard five-router lab available (routers, hubs, switch). The routers and hubs should be disconnected and stacked. Each cabling type (WAN, LAN, console, power) should be grouped together. If it is not possible to start with equipment disconnected, you should review the steps of the lab with the equipment already connected. This will reinforce your knowledge of the physical connections and the device interfaces.

Start with the routers, switches, hubs, and cabling disconnected, if possible. Your team will need to connect them according to the topology diagram in the overview at the beginning of this lab and then document your findings. This lab requires that you assemble the routers into the standard lab topology, or as close as possible, depending on the equipment you have. Lab 1.3 will provide instructions for configuring the routers and workstations using Class B network address with subnets. Work in teams of three or more. Before beginning this lab, you should review Chapter 1 in *Cisco Networking Academy Program: Second-Year Companion Guide* and Semester 3 online Chapter 1.

Required Resources:

- A minimum of five PC workstations, with a Windows operating system and HyperTerminal installed
- Five Cisco Routers (model 1600 series or 2500 series, with IOS 11.2 or later)
- Four Ethernet hubs (10Base-T with four to eight ports)
- One Ethernet switch (Cisco Catalyst 1900 or comparable)
- Five serial console cables to connect the workstation to the router console port (with RJ45 to DB9 converters)
- Three sets of V.35 WAN serial cables (DTE male and DCE female) to connect routers
- CAT5 Ethernet cables wired straight through to connect routers and workstations to both hubs and switches
- AUI (DB15) to RJ45 Ethernet transceivers (quantity depends on the number of routers with AUI ports) to convert router AUI interfaces to 10Base-T RJ45

Web Site Resources:

- **Routing basics** – http://www.cisco.com/univercd/cc/td/doc/cisintwk/ito_doc/routing.htm
- **General information on routers** – http://www.cisco.com/univercd/cc/td/doc/pcat/#2
- **2500 series routers** – http://www.cisco.com/warp/public/cc/cisco/mkt/access/2500/index.shtml
- **1600 series routers** – http://www.cisco.com/warp/public/cc/cisco/mkt/access/1600/index.shtml
- **Terms and acronyms** – http://www.cisco.com/univercd/cc/td/doc/cisintwk/ita/index.htm
- **IP routing protocol IOS command summary** –
  http://www.cisco.com/univercd/cc/td/doc/product/software/ios120/12cgcr/rbkixol.htm
- **Cisco ConfigMaker information and download** –
  http://www.cisco.com/warp/public/cc/cisco/mkt/enm/config/index.shtml

Notes: _____

_____

_____

_____

Cisco Labs – Semester 3 – Routing and Switching
LAB 1.2 – ROUTER LAB SETUP REVIEW – WORKSHEET

Step 1. Router lab LAN/WAN preliminary planning.
When setting up the lab equipment from scratch, you will need to give some thought to the questions listed below. Even if you are starting with an existing assembled lab setup, you should review all steps and answer all questions to become more familiar with how the routers are connected. Even though you may not be actually connecting the equipment, you should locate, examine, and document the cabling and physical connections between routers, hubs, and workstations.

- Where should the PCs be placed?
- Where should the routers be placed?
- Where should the switch and hubs be placed?
- How should the Ethernet, serial, and power cables be run?
- How many outlets and power strips will be needed?
- Which PC connects to which router?
- Which PC connects to which hub or switch?
- Which router connects to which hub or switch?
- How should devices and cabling be labeled?

Step 2. Arrange lab equipment.
Your arrangement of the routers and equipment will vary depending on space and the physical setup of your lab area. The goal is to group each combination of router/hub/workstation closely together because they can represent separate LANs and geographical locations in the real world. It is easier to see the relationships among equipment with this arrangement. Equipment should be positioned so that all interfaces are facing the same direction, and cabling and connections can be accessed easily.

Step 3. Connect serial WAN cabling.
Next, you will connect serial cables (DCE-DTE) between routers. With this lab setup, the router interface serial 0 (S0) is connected to the DCE cable. DCE refers to data circuit-terminating equipment (or data communications equipment) connections and represents the clocking end of the synchronous WAN link. The DCE cable has a large female V.35 (34-pin) connector on one end and a DB-60 connector on the other end that attaches to the router serial interface. Interface serial 1 (S1) is connected to the data terminal equipment (DTE) cable. The DTE cable has a large male V.35 connector on one end and a DB60 on the other end that attaches to the router serial interface. Cables are also labeled as DCE or DTE.

1. Examine the WAN cables and connections between the routers and document them in the table:

From Router Name	Interface	To Router Name	Interface

Cisco Labs – Semester 3 – Routing and Switching
LAB 1.2 – ROUTER LAB SETUP REVIEW – WORKSHEET

Step 4. Connect the router Ethernet cabling.

For routers that have an attachment unit interface (AUI) Ethernet 0 (E0) or E1 port, you will need an external transceiver that converts the DB15 AUI to an RJ45 10Base-T connector. The 2500 series routers usually have an AUI port. The 1600 series has both AUI and RJ45 ports, and you can use the RJ45 port without the need for the external transceiver. All Ethernet cabling from routers to hubs or switches must be Category 5 (Cat 5) and wired "straight-through" (pin 1 to pin 1, pin2 to pin 2). Connect the Ethernet cabling as indicated in the diagram, and then label the cabling at each end. Hubs should be numbered Hub 1, Hub 2, and so on.

2. Record the router Ethernet interfaces in use and which hub (or switch) they attach to in the table:

From Router Name	Router Interface	To Which Ethernet Device
Lab-A		
Lab-A		
Lab-B		
Lab-C		
Lab-D		
Lab-E		

Step 5. Connect the workstation Ethernet cabling.

Place the PCs at their planned locations, and label them (WS-1, WS-2, and so on from left to right according to the diagram. Run straight-through CAT 5 cables from each PC to where the switch and hubs are located. Connect the Ethernet cabling as indicated, and then label the cables at each end depending on what device and interface they connect to. The following table shows the connections for all 10 workstations. Connect at least one workstation to each hub or switch.

3. Indicate which Ethernet device each workstation connects to in the following table:

From Workstation	To Which Ethernet Device
WS-1	
WS-2	
WS-3	
WS-4	
WS-5	
WS-6	
WS-7	
WS-8	
WS-9	
WS-10	

Cisco Labs – Semester 3 – Routing and Switching
LAB 1.2 – ROUTER LAB SETUP REVIEW – WORKSHEET

Step 6. Connect the console workstations to routers.
Connect one end of the rollover cables from workstations 4, 6, 8, 9, and 10 to the console interface of routers Lab-A, B, C, D, and E. Connect the other end of each of the rollover cables to an RJ45-to-DB-9 serial connector. Connect the serial connector to the serial ports of the five workstations. Label the cables at each end.

4.   What type of cable is the console cable? _____

Step 7. Connect power cords to all devices.
Plug in and turn on all devices. Verify that all are activated by checking their indicator lights.

5.   Are the link lights for the switch, the hubs, and the network interface cards (NICs) in the workstations on? _____   Are the OK lights on the back of the routers on? _____

Step 8. Draw your lab diagram using ConfigMaker.

6.   Use ConfigMaker to redraw the router lab diagram to match your physical setup (routers, switches, hubs, workstations, and so on). This steps you though the process of hooking up all the lab equipment and specifying all IP addressing for all equipment and interfaces. ConfigMaker also generates the actual configuration files that you can use for reference or to configure the router. Be sure to label all equipment (such as Lab-A, Lab-B, and so on). A ConfigMaker introduction lab can be found in the Semester 2 labs, and you can also run the tutorial if you are not familiar with the product. When you finish your ConfigMaker diagram, keep a copy in your workbook or journal.

Note: If you do not have access to ConfigMaker, contact your instructor or download it from the Cisco web site listed in "Web Site Resources" in the "Overview" section of this lab.

You may use the space below to sketch your lab setup or for your notes.

Cisco Labs – Semester 3 – Routing and Switching
LAB 1.2 – ROUTER LAB SETUP REVIEW – ANSWERS

1. Examine the WAN cables and connections between the routers and document them in the table:

From Router Name	Interface	To Router Name	Interface
Lab-A	S0 (DCE)	Lab-B	S1 (DTE)
Lab-B	S0 (DCE)	Lab-C	S1 (DTE)
Lab-C	S0 (DCE)	Lab-D	S1 (DTE)

2. Record the router Ethernet interfaces in use and which hub (or switch) they attach to in the table:

From Router Name	Router Interface	To Which Ethernet Device
Lab-A	E0	Hub # 1
Lab-A	E1	Switch
Lab-B	E0	Hub # 2
Lab-C	E0	Hub # 3
Lab-D	E0	Hub # 4
Lab-E	E0	Hub # 4

3. Indicate which Ethernet device each workstation connects to in the table:

From Workstation	To Which Ethernet Device
WS-1	Switch
WS-2	Switch
WS-3	Hub # 1
WS-4	Hub # 1
WS-5	Hub # 2
WS-6	Hub # 2
WS-7	Hub # 3
WS-8	Hub # 3
WS-9	Hub # 4
WS-10	Hub # 4

4. What type of cable is the console cable? **Rollover (pin 1 to pin 8, pin 2 to pin 7)**

5. Are the link lights for the switch, the hubs, and the network interface cards (NICs) in the workstations on? **Yes**   Are the OK lights on the back of the routers on? **Yes**

6. Draw your lab diagram.
    The lab diagrams may vary depending on what type of equipment is present. Focus should be on the physical components and on the communications links between them, including LAN (Ethernet) and WAN (serial) connections.

Cisco Labs – Semester 3 – Routing and Switching
LAB 1.3 – ROUTER SUBNETS REVIEW – OVERVIEW
(Estimated time: 30 minutes)

Router Name - LAB A
Router Type - 2514
E 0 = 192.5.5.1
E 1 = 205.7.5.1
S 0 = 201.100.11.1
SM = 255.255.255.0

Router Name - LAB B
Router Type - 2503
E 0 = 219.17.100.1
S 0 = 199.6.13.1
S 1 = 201.100.11.2
SM = 255.255.255.0

Router Name - LAB C
Router Type - 2503
E 0 = 223.8.151.1
S 0 = 204.204.7.1
S 1 = 199.6.13.2
SM = 255.255.255.0

Router Name - LAB D
Router Type - 2501
E 0 = 210.93.105.1
S 1 = 204.204.7.2
SM = 255.255.255.0

Router Name - LAB E
Router Type - 2501
E 0 = 210.93.105.2
SM = 255.255.255.0

LEGEND
= ROUTER   User Exec Password = cisco
= HUB   Enable Secret Exec Password = class
= LAN SWITCH   Terminal vty Password = cisco
= CONSOLE CABLE

Objectives:
- Develop a Class B addressing scheme with subnets for the five-router lab setup
- Use IOS commands to configure routers to your Class B subnet scheme
- Assign IP network numbers, interfaces, IP addresses, and subnet mask information for the local-area networks (LANs) and wide-area networks (WANs) in use.
- Use the **Control Panel/Network icon** or **winipcfg.exe** utility at each workstation to verify IP address, subnet mask, and default gateway settings.
- Use the **Ping** command to test the router and workstation connections.

Background:
This is an important lab that will demonstrate your understanding of how the Cisco lab is set up (see the previous diagram) and how subnetting applies to multiple routers. You will develop an addressing scheme based on a Class B network address and then subnet it to accommodate your current physical network with room for growth. You should be able to configure the routers and workstations without looking at your notes and using only the IOS help facility.

Lab 1.2 provided an opportunity to set up the physical lab configuration. You may work in teams of three to five; while one group is configuring the router lab physical setup, the other can be designing the Class B addressing scheme and assigning IP addresses to devices.

Cisco Labs – Semester 3 – Routing and Switching
LAB 1.3 – ROUTER SUBNETS REVIEW – OVERVIEW

Tools/Preparation:

Before starting this lab, you will need to have the equipment for the standard five-router lab available (routers, hubs, switch, cables). This lab assumes that you have completed Lab 1.2 and that the lab equipment (routers, hub, workstations) is assembled and connected in the standard lab topology. Work in teams of three or more. Before beginning this lab, you should review Chapter 1 in *Cisco Networking Academy Program: Second-Year Companion Guide* and Semester 3 online Chapter 1.

Required Resources:

- A minimum of five PC workstations, with Windows operating system and HyperTerminal installed
- Five Cisco Routers (model 1600 series or 2500 series, with IOS 11.2 or later)
- Four Ethernet hubs (10Base-T with four to eight ports)
- One Ethernet switch (Cisco Catalyst 1900 or comparable)
- Five serial console cables to connect the workstation to the router console port (with RJ45-to-DB9 converters)
- Three sets of V.35 WAN serial cables (DTE male and DCE female) to connect routers
- CAT5 Ethernet cables wired straight through to connect both routers and workstations to hubs and switches
- AUI (DB15) to RJ45 Ethernet transceivers (quantity depends on the number of routers with AUI ports) to convert router AUI interfaces to 10Base-T RJ45

Web Site Resources:

- **Routing basics** – http://www.cisco.com/univercd/cc/td/doc/cisintwk/ito_doc/routing.htm
- **General information on routers** – http://www.cisco.com/univercd/cc/td/doc/pcat/#2
- **2500 series routers** – http://www.cisco.com/warp/public/cc/cisco/mkt/access/2500/index.shtml
- **1600 series routers** – http://www.cisco.com/warp/public/cc/cisco/mkt/access/1600/index.shtml
- **Terms and acronyms** – http://www.cisco.com/univercd/cc/td/doc/cisintwk/ita/index.htm
- **IP routing protocol IOS command summary** –
  http://www.cisco.com/univercd/cc/td/doc/product/software/ios120/12cgcr/rbkixol.htm

Notes: _____

_____

_____

_____

_____

_____

_____

Cisco Labs – Semester 3 – Routing and Switching
LAB 1.3 – ROUTER SUBNETS REVIEW – WORKSHEET

Step 1. Verify that all physical connections are correct.
Review the standard Semester 2 lab diagram in the "Overview" section of this lab, or review the diagram you created in the prior lab and check all physical devices, cables, and connections. Verify that the routers have been physically configured correctly.

Step 2. Develop a Class B addressing scheme.
You have received a Class B network address of 172.16.0.0 (actually a private Internet address) for the five-router network to accommodate the five LANs and three WANs that you must define. **You must borrow more or less than 8 bits from the host portion of the address, but you must allow for at least 100 hosts per subnet**. Answer the following questions about your subnet design:

1. Write the Class B address here: _____

2. How many bits did you borrow? _____

3. What is your subnet mask? _____

4. How many useable subnets does this allow you to create? _____

5. How many hosts can each subnet have? _____

6. Fill in the following table with information about the first 10 subnets (do not use the zero subnet when assigning subnets to the lab diagram).

Subnet #	Subnet Address	Subnet Broadcast Address	Host Address Range
0 (not used)			
1			
2			
3			
4			
5			
6			
7			
8			
9			

Cisco Labs – Semester 3 – Routing and Switching
LAB 1.3 – ROUTER SUBNETS REVIEW – WORKSHEET

Step 3. Configure the routers.

A. Log on to the first router Lab-A.
Verify that you have a good console connection from the workstation to the router, and start the HyperTerminal program (Start/Programs/Accessories/Communications). Enter the password **cisco** if prompted to enter user mode. The prompt should be **Lab-A>**.

B. Enter Privileged Exec mode.
Type **enable** at the router prompt. Enter the password of **class** if prompted. The prompt should now be **Lab-A#**.

C. Apply your IP subnet addressing scheme to the routers.
Decide which subnet you will use with each network and which IP address you will apply to each router interface (E0, S0, and so on); then configure the router accordingly. Use the RIP or IGRP routing protocol. Use the worksheet to assign interface information for each of the five routers based on your subnets defined in the prior table. You may use the setup configuration utility or enter commands directly in configuration mode. You may use the IOS help facility at any time. Work in teams, and try not to look at your notes. Sample configuration commands for router Lab-A can be found at the end of the answers section. Answers will vary.

7. Fill in the following table with IP interface information for each of the five routers.

Cisco Lab Class B Subnet Router IP Configuration

Router Name	Lab-A	Lab-B	Lab-C	Lab-D	Lab-E
Model Number					
Interface E0 IP Address					
Interface E0 Subnet Mask					
Interface E1 IP Address					
Interface E1 Subnet Mask					
Interface S0 IP Address					
Interface S0 Subnet Mask					
Interface S0 Clock Rate					
Interface S1 IP Address					
Interface S1 Subnet Mask					

Cisco Labs – Semester 3 – Routing and Switching
LAB 1.3 – ROUTER SUBNETS REVIEW – WORKSHEET

Step 4. Configure the workstations.

Use the following worksheet to assign interface information for each workstation based on your subnets defined earlier. Be sure that workstation IP addresses and default gateways are compatible with the same LAN the router Ethernet interface is on. Answers will vary.

8. Fill in the following table with the IP addressing information for the workstation. Number the workstations on the diagram from left to right, starting with the LAN attached to E1 on router Lab-A.

Workstation IP Address Configuration (Your Answers May Vary)

Workstation #	Workstation IP Address	Workstation Subnet Mask	Default Gateway IP Address
1 (Lab-A E1)			
2 (Lab-A E1)			
3 (Lab-A E0)			
4 (Lab-A E0)			
5 (Lab-B E0)			
6 (Lab-B E0)			
7 (Lab-C E0)			
8 (Lab-C E0)			
9 (Lab-D E0)			
10 (Lab-E E0)			

Step 5. Test the router lab connectivity.

A. Ping from router to router.
  Begin with router Lab-A and use the console workstation connection to it. Start the HyperTerminal program, and ping the S1 interface of router Lab-B. This verifies that the WAN link between Lab-A and Lab-B is okay. Ping the serial interfaces of the other routers.
  Lab-A> ping xxx.xxx.xxx.xxx (S1 interface of Lab-B)

9. Was the ping from router Lab-A to Lab-B successful? _____

B. Ping from workstation to router.
  Begin with a workstation connected to the first hub. Click Start/Programs/MS-DOS Prompt, and ping the S1 interface of router Lab-B. This verifies that the workstation's IP configuration and the WAN link between Lab-A and Lab-B is okay. Ping the serial interfaces of the other routers and the IP addresses of the other workstations to verify that the network is configured properly.
  C:\WINDOWS> ping xxx.xxx.xxx.xxx (S1 interface of lab-B)

10. Was the ping from router Workstation 1 to Lab-B successful? _____

Cisco Labs – Semester 3 – Routing and Switching
LAB 1.3 – ROUTER SUBNETS REVIEW – ANSWERS

Step 1. Answer the following questions about your subnet design (answers will vary):

1. What is your Class B address? **172.16.0.0**

2. How many bits did you borrow? **9**

3. What is your subnet mask? **255.255.255.128**

4. How many useable subnets does this create? $2^9 = 512-2 = 510$ **possible subnets**

5. How many hosts per subnet can you have? $2^7 = 128 - 2 = 126$ **hosts per subnet**

6. Fill in the following table with information about the first 10 subnets (do not use the zero subnet).

Subnet #	Subnet Address	Subnet Broadcast Address	Host Address Range
0 (don't use)	172.16.0.0	172.16.0.127	172.16.0.1 to 172.16.0.126
1	172.16.0.128	172.16.0.255	172.16.0.129 to 172.16.0.254
2	172.16.1.0	172.16.1.127	172.16.1.1 to 172.16.1.126
3	172.16.1.128	172.16.1.255	172.16.1.129 to 172.16.1.254
4	172.16.2.0	172.16.2.127	172.16.2.1 to 172.16.2.126
5	172.16.2.128	172.16.2.255	172.16.2.129 to 172.16.2.254
6	172.16.3.0	172.16.3.127	172.16.3.1 to 172.16.3.126
7	172.16.3.128	172.16.3.255	172.16.3.129 to 172.16.3.254
8	172.16.4.0	172.16.4.127	172.16.4.1 to 172.16.4.126
9	172.16.4.128	172.16.4.255	172.16.4.129 to 172.16.4.254

Cisco Labs – Semester 3 – Routing and Switching
LAB 1.3 – ROUTER SUBNETS REVIEW – ANSWERS

7. Fill in the following table with IP interface information for each of the five routers.

Cisco Lab Class B Subnet Router IP Configuration (Your Answers May Vary)

Router Name	Lab-A	Lab-B	Lab-C	Lab-D	Lab-E
Model Number	2514	2503	2503	2501	2501
Interface E0 IP Address	172.16.0.129	172.16.2.1	172.16.3.1	172.16.4.1	172.16.4.2
Interface E0 Subnet Mask	255.255.255.128	255.255.255.128	255.255.255.128	255.255.255.128	255.255.255.128
Interface E1 IP Address	172.16.1.1	Not Present	Not Present	Not Present	Not Present
Interface E1 Subnet Mask	255.255.255.128	Not Present	Not Present	Not Present	Not Present
Interface S0 IP Address	172.16.1.129	172.16.2.129	172.16.3.129	Not Used	Not Used
Interface S0 Subnet Mask	255.255.255.128	255.255.255.128	255.255.255.128	Not Used	Not Used
Interface S0 * Clock Rate	56000	56000	56000	Not Used	Not Used
Interface S1 IP Address	Not Used	172.16.1.130	172.16.2.130	172.16.3.130	Not Used
Interface S1 Subnet Mask	Not Used	255.255.255.128	255.255.255.128	255.255.255.128	Not Used
Other Interface(s)	Console, AUX	ISDN BRI0, Console, AUX	ISDN BRI0, Console, AUX	Console, AUX	Console, AUX

* Clock rate must be set on the DCE end (S0) of the WAN link between routers.

8. Fill in the following table with the IP addressing information obtained from each workstation.

Workstation IP Address Configuration (Your Answers May Vary)

Workstation #	Workstation IP Address	Workstation Subnet Mask	Default Gateway IP Address
1 (Lab-A E1)	172.16.1.2	255.255.255.128	172.16.1.1
2 (Lab-A E1)	172.16.1.3	255.255.255.128	172.16.1.1
3 (Lab-A E0)	172.16.0.130	255.255.255.128	172.16.0.129
4 (Lab-A E0)	172.16.0.131	255.255.255.128	172.16.0.129
5 (Lab-B E0)	172.16.2.2	255.255.255.128	172.16.2.1
6 (Lab-B E0)	172.16.2.3	255.255.255.128	172.16.2.1
7 (Lab-C E0)	172.16.3.2	255.255.255.128	172.16.3.1
8 (Lab-C E0)	172.16.3.3	255.255.255.128	172.16.3.1
9 (Lab-D E0)	172.16.4.3	255.255.255.128	172.16.4.1
10 (Lab-E E0)	172.16.4.4	255.255.255.128	172.16.4.1

Cisco Labs – Semester 3 – Routing and Switching
LAB 1.3 – ROUTER SUBNETS REVIEW – ANSWERS

9. Was the ping from router Lab-A to Lab-B successful? **Yes – If not, check connections and obtain assistance from instructor or lab assistant.**

10. Was the ping from router Lab-A to Lab-B successful? **Yes – If not, check connections and obtain assistance from instructor or lab assistant.**

Sample Router Lab-A (2514) Basic Configuration Commands

The following set of IOS commands can be used to configure route Lab-A. Explanations are provided for each command. Use these commands and the information that you entered earlier to configure each router. The exact commands required to configure the other routers will vary somewhat depending on which interfaces are in use and what IP addresses should be set on those interfaces. (Your answers may vary depending on the number of bits borrowed.)

Step Description/ Explanation	Router Command Prompt	IOS Command
Enable privileged mode	Router>	Enable
Configure (the router) from Terminal (keyboard)	Router#	Config T
Name Router Lab-A (the prompt will change)	Router(config)#	Hostname LAB-A
Set privileged mode encrypted (secret) password to class	Lab-A(config)#	Enable secret class
Set privileged mode text password (optional)	Lab-A(config)#	Enable password cisco
Disable DNS lookup	Lab-A(config)#	No ip domain-lookup
Select E0 interface	Lab-A(config)#	Interface Ethernet0
Provide description for E0 (optional on any interface)	Lab-A(config-if)#	Description connected to LAN A
Set E0 IP address and subnet mask	Lab-A(config-if)#	IP address 172.16.0.129 255.255.255.228
Bring interface E0 up	Lab-A(config-if)#	No shutdown
Select E1 interface	Lab-A(config)#	Interface Ethernet1
Set E1 IP addr. & subnet mask	Lab-A(config-if)#	IP address 172.16.1.1 255.255.255.128
Bring interface E0 up	Lab-A(config-if)#	No shutdown
Select S0 interface	Lab-A(config-if)#	Interface Serial0
Set S0 IP addr. & subnet mask	Lab-A(config-if)#	IP address 172.16.1.129 255.255.255.228
Set IGRP bandwidth metric	Lab-A(config-if)#	Bandwidth 56
Set DCE clock synch at 56000	Lab-A(config-if)#	Clock rate 56000
Bring interface S0 up	Lab-A(config-if)#	No shutdown

Cisco Labs – Semester 3 – Routing and Switching
LAB 1.3 – ROUTER SUBNETS REVIEW – ANSWERS

Select S1 interface (unused)	Lab-A(config-if)#	Interface Serial1
Set no IP address for S1	Lab-A(config-if)#	No IP address
Administratively shut down S1	Lab-A(config-if)#	Shutdown
Exit interface config mode	Lab-A(config-if)#	Exit
Start RIP routing protocol	Lab-A(config)#	Router rip
Specify directly connected network for routing updates	Lab-A(config-router)#	Network 172.16.0.0
Exit router config mode	Lab-A(config-router)#	Exit
Enable browser management	Lab-A(config)#	IP http server
Define router host name table	N/A	N/A
Specify host table entry for Lab-A (with interface IP addresses)	Lab-A(config)#	IP host Lab-A 172.16.0.129 172.16.1.1 172.16.1.129
Specify host table entry for Lab-B (with interface IP addresses)	Lab-A(config)#	IP host Lab-B 172.16.2.1 172.16.2.129 172.16.1.130
Specify host table entry for Lab-C (with interface IP addresses)	Lab-A(config)#	IP host Lab-C 172.16.3.1 172.16.3.129 172.16.2.130
Specify host table entry for Lab-D (with interface IP addresses)	Lab-A(config)#	IP host LAB-D 172.16.4.1 172.16.3.130
Specify host table entry Lab-E with interface IP addresses	Lab-A(config)#	IP host LAB-E 172.16.4.2
Disable classless IP routing	Lab-A(config)#	No IP classless
Configure console line (direct attach to console port)	Lab-A(config)#	Line con 0
Enable console login password checking	Lab-A(config-line)#	Login
Set user mode password for console connection login	Lab-A(config-line)#	Password cisco
Configure telnet line (virtual terminal or VTY)	Lab-A(config-line)#	Line vty 0 4
Enable telnet login password checking	Lab-A(config-line)#	Login
Set user mode password for telnet connection login	Lab-A(config-line)#	Password cisco
Save the current running configuration to the startup configuration	Lab-A#	Copy running-config startup-config

Cisco Labs – Semester 3 – Routing and Switching
LAB 1.4 – IOS UPDATE/TFTP– OVERVIEW
(Estimated time: 30 minutes)

Router Name - LAB A
Router Type - 2514
E 0 = 192.5.5.1
E 1 = 205.7.5.1
S 0 = 201.100.11.1
SM = 255.255.255.0

Router Name - LAB B
Router Type - 2503
E 0 = 219.17.100.1
S 0 = 199.6.13.1
S 1 = 201.100.11.2
SM = 255.255.255.0

Router Name - LAB C
Router Type - 2503
E 0 = 223.8.151.1
S 0 = 204.204.7.1
S 1 = 199.6.13.2
SM = 255.255.255.0

Router Name - LAB D
Router Type - 2501
E 0 = 210.93.105.1
S 1 = 204.204.7.2
SM = 255.255.255.0

Router Name - LAB E
Router Type - 2501
E 0 = 210.93.105.2
SM = 255.255.255.0

LEGEND

= ROUTER   User Exec Password = cisco

= HUB   Enable Secret Exec Password = class

= LAN SWITCH   Terminal vty Password = cisco

= CONSOLE CABLE

Objectives:
- Display information about current IOS software and router memory
- Review IOS 12.0 memory requirements and update options
- Use a TFTP server to back up a router's existing IOS image from Flash memory
- Use a TFTP server to update a router to a new version of the IOS software

Background:
As new versions of the Cisco IOS software become available, it is necessary to periodically update the existing IOS image to support the latest features and improvements. In this lab, you will determine what version and IOS your router is currently running and become familiar with the requirements for updating to a newer version. You will check to see how much Flash memory the router has and how much of it is currently used by IOS image and how much is free. You will always want to back up your current IOS before upgrading to a newer version. It is a good idea to keep a backup copy of the IOS image file for each router. The process of downloading a new IOS image from Cisco Connection Online (CCO) will also be reviewed. The TFTP server method of updating your IOS will be covered in this lab as well. The primary goal of this lab is to get your router updated to IOS 12.0.

Cisco Labs – Semester 3 – Routing and Switching
LAB 1.4 – IOS UPDATE/TFTP – OVERVIEW

Tools/Preparation:

Before starting the lab, you will need to connect a PC workstation with HyperTerminal to a router using the router's console interface with a rollover cable. You will also need an Ethernet connection to the router. The instructor or lab assistant should have a Windows 9x PC with a TFTP server installed and should have the latest downloaded IOS 12.0 image on the PC hard drive. Verify that the TFTP server is accessible by the router. The Cisco TFTP server and latest IOS updates can be downloaded from the web sites listed below. Although the instructions in this lab for downloading the IOS image software can be done only by someone with a CCO account, you should read through them to become familiar with the process.

You should review Chapter 16 in the Cisco *Networking Academy Program: First-Year Companion Guide* and review Semester 3 online curriculum Lesson 1 before starting this lab. You may work individually or in teams.

Required Resources:
- PC with monitor, keyboard, mouse, power cords, and other essentials
- Windows operating system (Windows 95, 98, NT, or 2000) installed on the PC
- HyperTerminal program configured for router console connection
- PC connected to the router console port with a rollover cable
- PC connected to a hub that the router is connected to, or a crossover cable directly to the router
- PC on a network that the router can send and receive to running a TFTP daemon (server)

Web Site Resources:
- **Routing basics** – http://www.cisco.com/univercd/cc/td/doc/cisintwk/ito_doc/routing.htm
- **General information on routers** – http://www.cisco.com/univercd/cc/td/doc/pcat/#2
- **2500 series routers** – http://www.cisco.com/warp/public/cc/cisco/mkt/access/2500/index.shtml
- **1600 series routers** – http://www.cisco.com/warp/public/cc/cisco/mkt/access/1600/index.shtml
- **Terms and acronyms** – http://www.cisco.com/univercd/cc/td/doc/cisintwk/ita/index.htm
- **IP routing protocol IOS command summary** –
  http://www.cisco.com/univercd/cc/td/doc/product/software/ios120/12cgcr/rbkixol.htm
- **Cisco TFTP Server** (Windows 9x version) – ftp://ftp.cisco.com/pub/netmgmt/utilities/tftp.zip
- **TFTP command syntax** –
  http://www.cisco.com/univercd/cc/td/doc/product/10_100hb/1538m_mh/cli/1538_cli.htm
- **Cisco IOS images** – http://www.cisco.com

Notes:

_____
_____
_____
_____
_____
_____

Cisco Labs – Semester 3 – Routing and Switching
LAB 1.4 – IOS UPDATE/TFTP – WORKSHEET

Step 1. Log in to the router.
Connect to the router with the console connection, and log in. Enter the password **cisco** if prompted. Enter privileged mode with the **enable** command. Use the password of **class**.

Step 2. Check the current IOS version.
Use the **show version** command to check the IOS version

1. What version of the IOS is the router currently running? _____

Step 3. Check the IOS image file and Flash memory.
Use the **show flash** command to obtain information about Flash memory and the IOS image.

2. Document the following information from the **show flash** command.
   a. How much Flash memory is used and available? _____
   _____
   b. What is the file that is stored in Flash memory? _____
   c. What is the size in bytes of the Flash memory? _____
   _____

Step 4. Review IOS image memory requirements.
Your options for updating the router IOS will vary depending on the router model number, the version of IOS you are currently running, and the amount of Flash memory and the amount of DRAM memory the router has. The following table shows various IOS images updates available and their memory requirements. (Note: All images shown here run from Flash memory.)

Cisco Router Series	IOS Version/ Feature Set	*Image Name	Image Size	Required Flash Memory	Required DRAM Memory
1600	11.2(21) – **IP/IPX	C1600-ny-l.112-21.P.bin	3729 KB	4 MB	2 MB
1600	12.0(10) – **IP/IPX	C1600-ny-l.120-10.bin	5031 KB	6 MB	4 MB
2500	11.2(21) – **IP/IPX/AT/DEC	C2500-d-l.112-21.bin	5292 KB	8 MB	4 MB
2500	12.0(9) **IP/IPX/AT/DEC	C2500-d-l.120-9.bin	6728 KB	8 MB	4 MB

* The last character of the feature portion of the IOS image name (such as C1600-ny-l) is a
lowercase letter L not a number 1.
** Feature sets: IP = TCP/IP protocol, IPX = Novell IPX protocol, AT = AppleTalk protocol,
DEC = DECnet protocol

There may be newer releases available, but these have the desired feature sets and require the least DRAM and flash memory. All images shown above run from Flash memory

Cisco Labs – Semester 3 – Routing and Switching
LAB 1.4 – IOS UPDATE/TFTP – WORKSHEET

Step 5. Review options for obtaining the IOS image file.
You may obtain an IOS image by purchasing an IOS Software Feature Pack (SFP) or by downloading the IOS from the Cisco web site. You may also be able to use a backup image from another router if it has a newer version. All options must be in accordance with the IOS software licensing agreement.

A.   Software Feature Pack (SFP)
The SFP typically comes in a package for a specific router series such as a 2500 and includes instructions, release notes, and a CD with several IOS versions: the Cisco TFTP server for Windows 9x and the Router Software Loader (RSL). RSL is a Windows 9x software application utility that helps with loading new IOS images; it will be covered later in this lab. SFPs can be obtained from Cisco or an authorized reseller. If you do not have an SFP with RSL, you will need to download the IOS image from the Cisco web site (www.cisco.com) and use the TFTP method. The RSL method of router IOS update will be covered in the next lab using the Software Feature Pack.

B. Cisco web site
The latest IOS versions can be downloaded from the Cisco web site (www.cisco.com), and you can choose from several different feature sets for different router series (1600, 2500, and so on). There is also an abundance of information on IOS versions, feature sets, capabilities, and requirements. After you download the image, you can use it to update the router using TFTP. The TFTP procedure will be covered in this lab. You will need a Cisco SmartNet Service agreement and a Cisco Connection Online (CCO) login account to download IOS files.

C. IOS Backup from another router
If you have a router of the same series and model number with a newer IOS, you can sometimes copy the existing IOS from the Flash memory of that router to a TFTP server. You can then load this image into the new router from the TFTP server. The TFTP procedure is covered in this lab.

Step 6. Download the IOS image file.

A. Log in at the www.cisco.com web site.
Start your browser, go to the www.cisco.com web site, and log in. You must have a CCO account. If you do not log in with a CCO account, you will not get download rights. All Cisco academies should have SmartNet Service Agreements for their router lab equipment. If you have a SmartNet agreement, you or your academy representative (instructor or main contact) should also have a CCO login account.

B. Navigate to download location.
Click on **Software Center** under **Service and Support**. At the **Software Center**, click **IOS Upgrade Planner**, and then click **IOS 12.0**. Note: You may want to download version 11.2 as well to practice upgrading an older IOS.

Cisco Labs – Semester 3 – Routing and Switching
LAB 1.4 – IOS UPDATE/TFTP – WORKSHEET

C. Select platform and release.

Select the platform (router series) for the IOS you will be downloading (as in 1601-1604 or 2501-2525). Select a **Major Release Update (for example, IOS 12.0 release 9 or 10)**. You should generally use the latest major release available depending on memory required and available. If possible, avoid the early deployment releases, which end with the letter T (as in 12.0.5T).

D. Select software features.

Select the software feature set you want. Note: The more features, the more memory that version of the IOS usually takes. Select the IP/IPX feature set. The next screen confirms the platform, the IOS version, the release, and the feature set you have chosen. It also lets you know the minimum recommended Flash memory and DRAM memory that this version requires. Verify that the router you will be updating has enough memory to support this version. **(Note: Most 1600 series router have only 6 MB of Flash memory and 4 MB RAM; most 2500 routers series have 8 MB of Flash memory and 4 to 8 MB of RAM.)** This information is displayed:

1601-1604   12.0.10   IP/IPX
Minimum recommended memory to download image — 6 MB Flash and 4 MB RAM

Click the button that reads "I have read the above requirements and agree with them."

E. Start IOS image download.

Confirm the IOS image information displayed (see below), and click the filename to start the download. Read the Software License Agreement, and then click Yes that you agree. Select the HTTP (or FTP) download site. Click the Save to Disk button, and then select the local directory where you want the IOS image file to be downloaded.

Software Download

Filename	Description	Size 'Bytes'	Date Published	More Info
c1600-ny-l.120-10.bin	IP/IPX	5151224	03/27/2000 05:46:22	?

When the download is complete, you can load the IOS image into the router using TFTP.

Step 7. Verify connection between the router and the TFTP server.

From the router you are going to update, enter **ping xxx.xxx.xxx.xxx** (the IP address of the workstation running the TFTP server.)

3. What was the result of the **ping** command? _____

Step 8. Verify TFTP server file location.

Check the TFTP server root directory location; this is where the backup copy of the existing IOS and the new IOS image file should be stored. Be sure to copy the new downloaded IOS image to this directory on the PC before starting the IOS update. Click View/Options, and either note the location or browse and change the location to another directory.

4. What is the default location for the TFTP server root directory?

_____

Cisco Labs – Semester 3 – Routing and Switching
LAB 1.4 – IOS UPDATE/TFTP – WORKSHEET

Step 9. Back up the existing IOS software image.
Enter **copy flash tftp** at the router prompt. The router will ask for either the IP address or the host name of the TFTP host. Enter the IP address of the TFTP server.

5.   What was the IP address of the TFTP server? _____

6.   What was the file that was written to the TFTP server? _____

7.   How did the router respond when copying the file?
_____

Step 10. Verify that the backup IOS file was copied to the TFTP server.
Check the TFTP server using Windows Explorer, the **DIR** command, or the **ls UNIX** command for the file you just wrote.

8.   What is the size of the file that was written in bytes? _____

Step 11. Load the new downloaded IOS image from the TFTP server.
Enter **copy tftp flash** at the router prompt. The router will ask for the IP address or the host name of the TFTP host. Enter the IP address of the TFTP server. Then enter the name of the new IOS image that was previously downloaded when you are prompted to do so. You will also be prompted to erase Flash memory before starting. This process will copy the new IOS software from a TFTP host to the router's Flash memory.

9.   Write down some of the prompts and responses you saw on the router screen. **Note: You can use HyperTerminal or Windows copy/paste to capture the copy process as it progresses.**
_____
_____
_____
_____

Step 12. Check the IOS version after the update.
Use the **show version** command to check the IOS version.

10. What version of the IOS is the router now running after the update? _____

Step 13. Check the IOS image file and Flash memory after the update.
Use the **show flash** command to obtain information about Flash memory and the IOS image.

11. Document the following information from the **show flash** command after the IOS update.
    a.   How much Flash memory is used and available? _____
    _____
    b.   What is the file that is stored in Flash memory? _____
    c.   What is the size in bytes of the Flash memory? _____
    _____

Cisco Labs – Semester 3 – Routing and Switching
LAB 1.4 – IOS UPDATE/TFTP – ANSWERS

Step 2. Check the current IOS version.
Use the **show version** command to check the IOS version.

1. What version of the IOS is the router currently running? <u>**Version 11.1(5)**</u>

Step 3. Check the IOS image file and Flash memory.
Use the **show flash** command to obtain information about Flash memory and the IOS image.

2. Document the following information from the **show flash** command.
   a. How much Flash memory is used and available? <u>**6881812 bytes used, 1506796 available, 8388608 total**</u>
   b. What is the file that is stored in Flash memory? <u>**igs-j-l.111-5**</u>
   c. What is the size in bytes of the Flash memory? <u>**8192K bytes of processor board system flash (read only)**</u>

Step 7. Verify the connection between the router and the TFTP server.
From the router you are going to update, enter **ping xxx.xxx.xxx.xxx** (the IP address of the workstation running the TFTP server).

3. What was the result of the ping command? <u>**The ping was successful.**</u>

Step 8. Verify TFTP server file location.
Check the TFTP server root directory location; this is where the backup copy of the existing IOS and the new IOS image file should be stored. **Be sure to copy the new downloaded IOS image to this directory on the PC before starting the IOS update**. Click View/Options and note the location, or browse and change the location to another directory.

4. What is the default location for the TFTP server root directory?
   <u>**C:\PROGRAM FILES\CISCO SYSTEMS\CISCO TFTP SERVER**</u>

Step 9. Back up the existing IOS software image.
Enter **copy flash tftp** at the router prompt. The router will ask for the IP address or the host name of the TFTP host. Enter the IP address of the TFTP server.

5. What was the IP address of the TFTP server? <u>**192.5.5.2 (workstation IP - will vary)**</u>

6. What was the name of the file that was written to the TFTP server? <u>**igs-j-l.111-5**</u>

7. How did the router respond when copying the file? <u>**Exclamation marks !!!!!!!!!!!!!!!!!!!!!!**</u>

Cisco Labs – Semester 3 – Routing and Switching
LAB 1.4 – IOS UPDATE/TFTP – ANSWERS

Step 10. Verify that the backup IOS file was copied to the TFTP server.
Check the TFTP server using Windows Explorer, the **DIR** command or the **ls UNIX** command for the file you just wrote.

8.   What is the size of the file that was written in bytes? **6721 KB.**

Step 11. Load the new IOS image from the TFTP server.
Enter **copy tftp flash** at the router prompt (in privileged mode). The router will ask for the IP address or the host name of the TFTP host. Enter the IP address of the TFTP server. Enter the name of the new IOS image when you are prompted to do so. You will also be prompted to erase Flash memory before starting. This will copy the IOS software from a TFTP host to router Flash memory.

9.   Write down some of the prompts and responses you saw on the router screen. You can use HyperTerminal or Windows copy/paste to capture the copy process as it progresses.

The following is the router output from the update of IOS 11.1-5 to IOS 12.0-10. It was captured on a Cisco 2514 with HyperTerminal using the Transfer/Capture Text option.

```
Lab-A# copy tftp flash


                **** NOTICE ****
Flash load helper v1.0
This process will accept the copy options and then terminate
The current system image to use the ROM based image for the copy.
Routing functionality will not be available during that time.
If you are logged in via telnet, this connection will terminate.
Users with console access can see the results of the copy operation.
        ---- ******** ----
Proceed? [confirm]

System flash directory:
File  Length  Name/status
  1   6881748  /igs-j-l.111-5
[6881812 bytes used, 1506796 available, 8388608 total]
Address or name of remote host [255.255.255.255]? 192.5.5.2
Source file name? c2500-d-l.120-10.bin
Destination file name [c2500-d-l.120-10.bin]?
Accessing file 'c2500-d-l.120-10.bin' on 192.5.5.2...
Loading c2500-d-l.120-10.bin .from 192.5.5.2 (via Ethernet0): ! [OK]

Erase flash device before writing? [confirm]
Flash contains files. Are you sure you want to erase? [confirm]

Copy 'c2500-d-l.120-10.bin' from server
  as 'c2500-d-l.120-10.bin' into Flash WITH erase? [yes/no]yes
```

Cisco Labs – Semester 3 – Routing and Switching
LAB 1.4 – IOS UPDATE/TFTP – ANSWERS

%SYS-4-CONFIG_NEWER: Configurations from version 11.1 may not be correctly understood.
%FLH: c2500-d-l.120-10.bin from 192.5.5.2 to flash ...

System flash directory:
File Length   Name/status
  1   6881748 /igs-j-l.111-5
[6881812 bytes used, 1506796 available, 8388608 total]
Accessing file 'c2500-d-l.120-10.bin' on 192.5.5.2...
Loading c2500-d-l.120-10.bin from 192.5.5.2 (via Ethernet0): ! [OK]

Erasing device... eeeeeeeeeeeeeeeeeeeeeeeeeeeeeeee ...erased
Loading c2500-d-l.120-10.bin from 192.5.5.2 (via Ethernet0):
!!!
!!!
!!!
!!! **(Note: output truncated to save space)**
[OK - 6891520/8388608 bytes]

Verifying checksum... OK (0x1A62)
Flash copy took 0:03:26 [hh:mm:ss]
%FLH: Re-booting system after download
F3: 6799388+89240+456028 at 0x3000060
         Restricted Rights Legend
Use, duplication, or disclosure by the Government is
subject to restrictions as set forth in subparagraph
(c) of the Commercial Computer Software - Restricted
Rights clause at FAR sec. 52.227-19 and subparagraph
(c) (1) (ii) of the Rights in Technical Data and Computer
Software clause at DFARS sec. 252.227-7013.
         cisco Systems, Inc.
         170 West Tasman Drive
         San Jose, California 95134-1706
Cisco Internetwork Operating System Software
IOS (tm) 2500 Software (C2500-D-L), Version 12.0(9), RELEASE SOFTWARE (fc1)
Copyright (c) 1986-2000 by cisco Systems, Inc.
Compiled Mon 24-Jan-00 22:06 by bettyl
Image text-base: 0x030387D0, data-base: 0x00001000
cisco 2500 (68030) processor (revision L) with 6144K/2048K bytes of memory.
Processor board ID 03853220, with hardware revision 00000000
Bridging software.
X.25 software, Version 3.0.0.
2 Ethernet/IEEE 802.3 interface(s)
2 Serial network interface(s)
32K bytes of non-volatile configuration memory.
8192K bytes of processor board System flash (Read ONLY)

Cisco Labs – Semester 3 – Routing and Switching
LAB 1.4 – IOS UPDATE/TFTP – ANSWERS

Step 12. Check the IOS version after the update,
Use the **show version** command to check the IOS version.

10. What version of the IOS is the router now running after the update? **Version 12.0(10)**

Step 13. Check the IOS image file and Flash memory after the update.
Use the **show flash** command to obtain information about Flash memory and the IOS image.

11. Document the following information from the **show flash** command after the IOS update.
   a. How much Flash memory is used and available? **6891520 bytes used, 1497008 available, 8388608 total**
   b. What is the file that is stored in flash memory? **C2500-d-l.120-10 (Note the lowercase letter L after the lowercase letter D.)**
   c. What is the size in bytes of the Flash memory? **8192K bytes of processor board system flash (read only)**

Output from show flash command on router Lab-A - Cisco 2514

```
Press RETURN to get started!

User Access Verification
Password:

LAB-A>enable
Password:

LAB-A#show flash

System flash directory:
File  Length  Name/status
  1   6891520  c2500-d-l.120-10.bin

[6891520 bytes used, 1497008 available, 8388608 total]
8192K bytes of processor board System flash (Read ONLY)

LAB-A#
```

Cisco Labs – Semester 3 – Routing and Switching
LAB 1.5 – IOS UPDATE/RSL – OVERVIEW
(Estimated time: 30 minutes)

Router Name - LAB A
Router Type - 2514
E 0 = 192.5.5.1
E 1 = 205.7.5.1
S 0 = 201.100.11.1
SM = 255.255.255.0

Router Name - LAB B
Router Type - 2503
E 0 = 219.17.100.1
S 0 = 199.6.13.1
S 1 = 201.100.11.2
SM = 255.255.255.0

Router Name - LAB C
Router Type - 2503
E 0 = 223.8.151.1
S 0 = 204.204.7.1
S 1 = 199.6.13.2
SM = 255.255.255.0

Router Name - LAB D
Router Type - 2501
E 0 = 210.93.105.1
S 1 = 204.204.7.2
SM = 255.255.255.0

Router Name - LAB E
Router Type - 2501
E 0 = 210.93.105.2
SM = 255.255.255.0

LEGEND
= ROUTER   User Exec Password = cisco
= HUB   Enable Secret Exec Password = class
= LAN SWITCH Terminal vty Password = cisco
= CONSOLE CABLE

Objectives:
- Display information about IOS software and router memory
- Use a Software Feature Pack to update a router IOS
- Use Router Software Loader (RSL) to back up both the startup configuration and the existing IOS image
- Use RSL to download the newer IOS image to the router and to restore the startup configuration file

Background:
As new versions of the Cisco IOS software become available, it is necessary to periodically update the existing IOS image to support the latest features and improvements. In this lab, you will determine what version and IOS your router is currently running. You will check to see how much Flash memory the router has and also how much of it is currently used by IOS image and how much is free. You will then use the Router Software Loader (RSL) from the Software Feature Pack (SFP) to back up your existing IOS and load the new version. You will always want to back up your current IOS before upgrading to a newer version. It is a good idea to keep a backup copy of the IOS image file for each router. IOS images can be backed up and loaded with a TFTP server. RSL is an optional graphical user interface (GUI) that comes with the SFP and can help with IOS updates.

Cisco Labs – Semester 3 – Routing and Switching
LAB 1.5 – IOS UPDATE/RSL – OVERVIEW

Tools/Preparation:

Before starting the lab, you will need to connect a PC workstation with HyperTerminal to a router using the router's console interface with a rollover cable. You will also need an Ethernet connection to the router. The instructor or lab assistant should have an IOS 12.0 Software Feature Pack CD that includes RSL. RSL should be installed on a Windows 9x PC.

You should review Chapter 16 in the *Cisco Networking Academy Program: First-Year Companion Guide*, and review Semester 3 online curriculum Lesson 1 before starting this lab. You may work individually or in teams.

Required Resources:

- PC with monitor, keyboard, mouse, power cords, and other essentials
- Windows operating system (Windows 95, 98, NT, or 2000) installed on the PC
- HyperTerminal program configured for router console connection
- Software Feature Pack CD with Router Software Loader (RSL) program
- Router Software Loader (RSL) installed on PC (CPSWinst.exe)
- PC connected to the router console port with a rollover cable
- PC connected to a hub that the router is connected to, or a crossover cable directly to the router

Web Site Resources:

- **Routing basics** – http://www.cisco.com/univercd/cc/td/doc/cisintwk/ito_doc/routing.htm
- **General information on routers** – http://www.cisco.com/univercd/cc/td/doc/pcat/#2
- **2500 series routers** – http://www.cisco.com/warp/public/cc/cisco/mkt/access/2500/index.shtml
- **1600 series routers** – http://www.cisco.com/warp/public/cc/cisco/mkt/access/1600/index.shtml
- **Terms and acronyms** – http://www.cisco.com/univercd/cc/td/doc/cisintwk/ita/index.htm
- **IP routing protocol IOS command summary** –
  http://www.cisco.com/univercd/cc/td/doc/product/software/ios120/12cgcr/rbkixol.htm

Notes:

_____
_____
_____
_____
_____
_____
_____
_____
_____
_____

Cisco Labs – Semester 3 – Routing and Switching
LAB 1.5 – IOS UPDATE/RSL – WORKSHEET

Step 1. Log in to the router.
Connect to the router with the console connection and log in. Enter the password **cisco** if prompted. Enter privileged mode with the **enable** command. Use the password of **class**.

Step 2. Check the current IOS version before update.
Use the **show version** command to check the IOS version.

1. What version of the IOS is the router currently running? _____

Step 3. Check the IOS image file and Flash memory before the update.
Use the **show flash** command to obtain information about Flash memory and the IOS image.

2. Document the following information from the **show flash** command.
    a. How much Flash memory is used and available? _____
    b. What is the file that is stored in Flash memory? _____
    c. What is the size in bytes of the Flash memory? _____

Step 4. Review IOS image memory requirements.
Your options for updating the router IOS will vary depending on the router model number, the version of IOS you are currently running, and the amount of Flash memory and DRAM memory the router has. The following table shows various IOS image updates available and their memory requirements:

Cisco Router Series	IOS Version/ Feature Set	*Image Name	Image Size	Required Flash Memory	Required DRAM Memory
1600	11.2(21) – **IP/IPX	C1600-ny-l.112-21.P.bin	3729 KB	4 MB	2 MB
1600	12.0(10) – **IP/IPX	C1600-ny-l.120-10.bin	5031 KB	6 MB	4 MB
2500	11.2(21) – **IP/IPX/AT/DEC	C2500-d-l.112-21.bin	5292 KB	8 MB	4 MB
2500	12.0(9) **IP/IPX/AT/DEC	C2500-d-l.120-9.bin	6728 KB	8 MB	4 MB

  * The last character of the feature portion of the IOS image name (as in C1600-ny-l) is a lowercase letter L not a number 1.
** Feature sets: IP = TCP/IP protocol, IPX = Novell IPX protocol, AT = AppleTalk protocol, DEC = DECnet protocol

There may be newer releases available, but these have the desired feature sets and require the least DRAM and flash memory. All images shown above run from Flash memory

Cisco Labs – Semester 3 – Routing and Switching
LAB 1.5 – IOS UPDATE/RSL – WORKSHEET

Step 5. Use Software Feature Pack (SFP) and RSL to update the router IOS.

A. Obtain the Software Feature Pack and RSL.
The SFP typically comes in a package for a specific router series, such as a 2500, and includes instructions, release notes, and a CD with several IOS versions. The Cisco TFTP server for Windows 9x and the Router Software Loader (RSL) are also included. SFPs can be obtained from Cisco or an authorized reseller. With RSL, you can load a Cisco IOS image from the CD to a Cisco router through a direct physical cable connection. RSL automatically backs up your existing startup configuration and IOS files. You can also display device information, such as the platform name, Flash memory and RAM configurations, and the current Cisco software image status. In addition, RSL works with routers that have no configuration as well as routers that are already configured.

B. Connect the PC to the router and prepare for the IOS update.
Connect the PC serial port to the router with a rollover serial console cable. Connect the PC to the router with an Ethernet cable. This can be a direct connection using a crossover cable from the PC NIC to the router Ethernet interface, or the PC and the router can both be connected to an Ethernet hub or switch. Make sure that all devices are powered on. Also make sure that the IP addressing for the PC is compatible with the router (on the same subnet). If you have made any changes to the running configuration, be sure to copy them to the startup configuration with the **copy run start** command before starting the RSL program.

C. Start the RSL program and connect wizard.
RSL can be run from the Software Feature Pack CD or from the hard drive, if it has been downloaded. Open Windows Explorer and navigate to the software location where the cpswinst.exe file is located; then double-click the executable (cpswinst.exe). The Connect Wizard dialog box should open to establish a connection to the target router. Select the interface type (Ethernet or Fast Ethernet), and click Next.

Cisco Labs – Semester 3 – Routing and Switching
LAB 1.5 – IOS UPDATE/RSL – WORKSHEET

D. Select router configuration type.
Select either "New router that has no configuration" or "Preconfigured router." If you choose "Preconfigured router," the startup configuration will be saved to the PC's hard drive and then will be restored after the IOS is updated. You will be prompted for a console password and an enable password. Click Finish.

E. Select the desired IOS image and begin the download.

If there is more than one image available, select one from the list. Click Load Image. The "Flash Copy Options" screen will default to "Erase Flash before downloading" and "Back up all Flash files." You will need to erase Flash because you do not have enough Flash memory for both images. The file you are downloading will appear at the top of the screen. Select the "Do not restore any Flash files" option, and then click OK. Select the backup directory next, and click OK to proceed with the download. The router configuration file should be restored automatically when you exit RSL.

Cisco Labs – Semester 3 – Routing and Switching
LAB 1.5 – IOS UPDATE/RSL – WORKSHEET

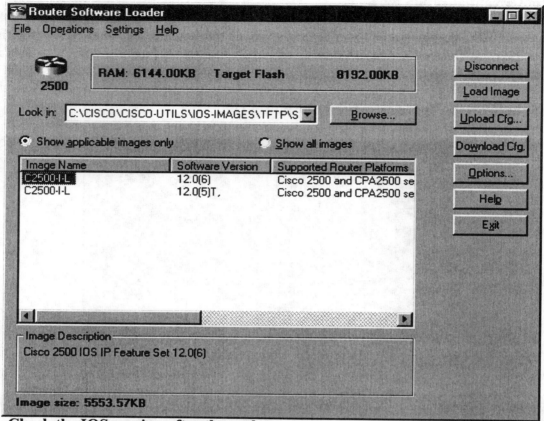

Step 6. Check the IOS version after the update.
Use the **show version** command to check the IOS version.

3.   What version of the IOS is the router now running after the update? _____

Step 7. Check the IOS image file and Flash memory after the update.
   Use the **show flash** command to obtain information about Flash memory and the IOS image.

4.   Document the following information from the **show flash** command after the IOS update.
   a.   How much Flash memory is used and available? _____
   b.   What is the file that is stored in Flash memory? _____
   c.   What is the size in bytes of the Flash memory? _____

Cisco Labs – Semester 3 – Routing and Switching
LAB 1.5 – IOS UPDATE/RSL – ANSWERS

Step 2. Check the current IOS version.
Use the **show version** command to check the IOS version.

1. What version of the IOS is the router currently running? <u>**Version 11.1(5)**</u>

Step 3. Check the IOS image file and Flash memory before the update.
Use the **show flash** command to obtain information about Flash memory and the IOS image.

2. Document the following information from the **show flash** command.
    a. How much Flash memory is used and available? <u>**6881812 bytes used, 1506796 available, 8388608 total**</u>
    b. What is the file that is stored in Flash memory? <u>**igs-j-l.111-5**</u>
    c. What is the size in bytes of the Flash memory? <u>**8192K bytes of processor board system flash (read only)**</u>

Step 6. Check the IOS version after the update.
Use the **show version** command to check the IOS version.

3. What version of the IOS is the router now running after the update? <u>**Version 12.0(6)**</u>
    <u>**(Note that this image is smaller than the 11.1 IOS because it includes only the IP feature set and does not have support IPX or AppleTalk.)**</u>

Step 7. Check the IOS image file and Flash memory after the update.
Use the **show flash** command to obtain information about Flash memory and the IOS image.

4. Document the following information from the **show flash** command after the IOS update.
    a. How much Flash memory is used and available? <u>**5686294 bytes used, 2701684 available, 8388608 total**</u>
    b. What is the file that is stored in Flash memory? <u>**Aaa0850.bin**</u>
    c. What is the size in bytes of the Flash memory? <u>**8192K bytes of processor board system flash (read only)**</u>

Cisco Labs – Semester 3 – Routing and Switching
LAB 1.6 – ROUTER MEMORY UPGRADE – OVERVIEW
(Estimated time: 30 minutes)

Router Name - LAB A
Router Type - 2514
E 0 = 192.5.5.1
E 1 = 205.7.5.1
S 0 = 201.100.11.1
SM = 255.255.255.0

Router Name - LAB B
Router Type - 2503
E 0 = 219.17.100.1
S 0 = 199.6.13.1
S 1 = 201.100.11.2
SM = 255.255.255.0

Router Name - LAB C
Router Type - 2503
E 0 = 223.8.151.1
S 0 = 204.204.7.1
S 1 = 199.6.13.2
SM = 255.255.255.0

Router Name - LAB D
Router Type - 2501
E 0 = 210.93.105.1
S 1 = 204.204.7.2
SM = 255.255.255.0

Router Name - LAB E
Router Type - 2501
E 0 = 210.93.105.2
SM = 255.255.255.0

LEGEND

	= ROUTER	User Exec Password = cisco
	= HUB	Enable Secret Exec Password = class
	= LAN SWITCH	Terminal vty Password = cisco
	= CONSOLE CABLE	

Objectives:
- Display information about current IOS software and router memory
- Review the steps for upgrading router DRAM memory
- Review the steps for upgrading router Flash memory

Background:
In this lab, you will determine what version and IOS your router is currently running and will become familiar with the requirements for updating to a newer version. You will check to see how much Flash memory the router has, as well as how much of it is currently used by the IOS image (system code) and how much is free. You will also check the amount of dynamic random-access memory (DRAM).

With Cisco 1600 and 2500 routers and most IOS images, the IOS usually runs from Flash memory. If you determine that you do not have enough Flash memory to update to a newer, larger IOS image, you will need to perform a Flash memory upgrade. You also might need to upgrade the DRAM SIMM (Simple In-line Memory Module) if you upgrade the Cisco IOS feature set or release, or if your router maintains large routing tables or other memory-intensive features, such as spoofing or protocol translations. If a 2500 series router does not have 8 MB Flash memory *and* 4 MB RAM, you might need to obtain and install additional memory modules. The procedure for upgrading the DRAM and Flash SIMMs for a Cisco 2500 is outlined in this lab.

Cisco Labs – Semester 3 – Routing and Switching
LAB 1.6 – ROUTER MEMORY UPGRADE – OVERVIEW

Tools/Preparation:
Before starting the lab, you will need to connect a PC workstation with HyperTerminal to a router using the router's console Interface with a roll-over cable. You will also need an Ethernet connection to the router. A TFTP server should be available to back up the IOS before you replace the Flash SIMMs. Although the instructions in this lab for upgrading router Flash memory may not be required for your lab setup, you should read through them to become familiar with the process.

Review Chapter 16 in the *Cisco Networking Academy Program: First-Year Companion Guide*, and review Semester 3 online curriculum Lesson 1 before starting this lab. You may work in teams. Note that detailed instructions can be found at the web sites listed below. A PDF file can be downloaded.

Resources Required:
- PC with monitor, keyboard, mouse, power cords, and other essentials
- Windows operating system (Windows 95, 98, NT or 2000) installed on the PC
- HyperTerminal program configured for router console connection
- PC connected to the router console port with a rollover cable
- PC connected to a hub that the router is connected to, or a crossover cable directly to the router
- PC on a network that the router can send and receive to running a TFTP daemon (server)
- Medium-size flat-blade screwdriver (1/4 inch [0.625 cm])
- ESD-preventive wrist strap
- The DRAM SIMM required for your planned upgrade
- System-code SIMM(s)

Web Site Resources:
- **Routing basics** – http://www.cisco.com/univercd/cc/td/doc/cisintwk/ito_doc/routing.htm
- **General information on routers** – http://www.cisco.com/univercd/cc/td/doc/pcat/#2
- **2500 series routers** – http://www.cisco.com/warp/public/cc/cisco/mkt/access/2500/index.shtml
- **1600 series routers** – http://www.cisco.com/warp/public/cc/cisco/mkt/access/1600/index.shtml
- **Terms and acronyms** – http://www.cisco.com/univercd/cc/td/doc/cisintwk/ita/index.htm
- **IP routing protocol IOS command summary** – http://www.cisco.com/univercd/cc/td/doc/product/software/ios120/12cgcr/rbkixol.htm
- **Cisco TFTP Server** (Win 9x version) – ftp://ftp.cisco.com/pub/netmgmt/utilities/tftp.zip
- **TFTP command syntax** – http://www.cisco.com/univercd/cc/td/doc/product/10_100hb/1538m_mh/cli/1538_cli.htm
- **Maintaining and upgrading the 2500 router** – http://www.cisco.com/univercd/cc/td/doc/product/access/acs_fix/cis2500/2501/2500ug/maint.htm#xtocid207584

Notes:
_____
_____
_____
_____
_____

Cisco Labs – Semester 3 – Routing and Switching
LAB 1.6 – ROUTER MEMORY UPGRADE – WORKSHEET

Section 1 – Checking IOS and Installed Memory

Step 1. Log in to the router.
Connect to the router with the console connection, and log in. Enter the password **cisco** if prompted. Enter privileged mode with the **enable** command. Use the password of **class**.

Step 2. Check the current IOS version and amount of DRAM.
Use the **show version** command to check the IOS version and amount of DRAM.

1. What version of the IOS is the router currently running? _____

2. How much DRAM is installed? _____

Step 3. Check the IOS image file and Flash memory.
Use the **show flash** command to obtain information about Flash memory and the IOS image.

3. Document the following information from the **show flash** command.
    a. How much Flash memory is used and available? _____
        _____
    b. What is the file that is stored in Flash memory? _____
        _____
    c. What is the size in bytes of the Flash memory? _____

Step 4. Review IOS image memory requirements.
Your options for updating the router IOS will vary depending on the router model number, the version of IOS you are currently running, and the amount of Flash memory and DRAM memory the router has. This table shows various IOS image updates available and their memory requirements:

Cisco Router Series	IOS Version/ Feature Set	*Image Name	Image Size	Required Flash Memory	Required DRAM Memory
1600	11.2(21) – **IP/IPX	C1600-ny-l.112-21.P.bin	3729 KB	4 MB	2 MB
1600	12.0(10) – **IP/IPX	C1600-ny-l.120-10.bin	5031 KB	6 MB	4 MB
2500	11.2(21) – **IP/IPX/AT/DEC	C2500-d-l.112-21.bin	5292 KB	8 MB	4 MB
2500	12.0(9) **IP/IPX/AT/DEC	C2500-d-l.120-9.bin	6728 KB	8 MB	4 MB

 * **The last character of the feature portion of the IOS image name (as in C1600-ny-l) is a lowercase letter L, not a number 1.**

** **Feature sets: IP = TCP/IP protocol, IPX = Novell IPX protocol, AT = AppleTalk protocol, DEC = DECnet protocol.**

There may be newer releases available, but these have the desired feature sets and require the least DRAM and flash memory. All images shown above run from Flash memory

Cisco Labs – Semester 3 – Routing and Switching
LAB 1.6 – ROUTER MEMORY UPGRADE – WORKSHEET

Section 2 - Cisco 2500 Series Router System Card Layouts

Cisco Model 2501, 2501, 2502, 2503, and 2504 System Board (SIMMs in place)

Cisco Model 2514 System Board (SIMMs removed)

Cisco Labs – Semester 3 – Routing and Switching
LAB 1.6 – ROUTER MEMORY UPGRADE – WORKSHEET

Section 3 - Upgrading the DRAM SIMM

This section describes how to upgrade the DRAM SIMM on the system card. Take the following steps to install the DRAM SIMMs.

Step 1. Power off the router.

Step 2. Attach an ESD-preventive wrist strap.

Step 3. Open the cover.
Follow the instructions in the section "Opening the Chassis" of the web document.

Step 4. Remove the existing DRAM SIMM.
Pull outward on the connectors to unlatch them, as shown. Be careful not to break the holders on the SIMM connector.

Step 5. Install the new SIMM.
Position the new SIMM so that the polarization notch is located at the left end of the SIMM socket. (See figure below.)

Step 6. Insert the new DRAM SIMM.
Slide the end with the metal fingers into the SIMM connector socket at approximately a 45-degree angle to the system card. Gently rock the SIMM back into place until the latch on either side snaps into place. Do not use excessive force because the connector may break.

Step 7. Replace the router cover.

Cisco Labs – Semester 3 – Routing and Switching
LAB 1.6 – ROUTER MEMORY UPGRADE – WORKSHEET

Section 4 - Upgrading the System Code Flash SIMM

Step 1. Power off the router.

Step 2. Attach an ESD-preventive wrist strap.

Step 3. Open the cover.
Follow the instructions in the section "Opening the Chassis" of the web document.

Step 4. Prepare to install the system-code SIMM.
Two system-code (Flash memory) SIMM sockets exist on the system board. If you want to install system-code SIMMs in both sockets, the SIMMs must be the same size. For example, if a 4 MB system-code SIMM is already installed in your router, the new SIMM must also be 4 MB. This upgrade would give you a total of 8 MB.

Caution: The system code is stored on the Flash memory SIMMs, but new system-code SIMMs are shipped without preinstalled software. Before proceeding with this procedure, use the <u>copy flash tftp</u> command to back up the system code to a TFTP server. The TFTP server backup/ restore process is described in Lab 1.4.

Step 5. Replace Flash SIMM(s).
If you are replacing a 4 MB SIMM with an 8 MB SIMM, that 8 MB SIMM must be placed in SIMM socket 0. If you are adding SIMMs that are to be placed side by side on the system card, the SIMMs must be of equal size (two 4MB SIMMs, not one 4 MB and one 8 MB together).

Locate the SIMM sockets, labeled CODE 0 and CODE 1, on the system card. If necessary, remove the existing system-code SIMM by pulling outward on the connector holders to unlatch them. If you are installing system-code SIMMs in both sockets (CODE0 and CODE1), both SIMMs must be the same size. Populate the SIMM socket labeled CODE0 first; and then populate CODE1.

Step 6. Reconfigure the Flash memory partition (if necessary).
After adding the Flash SIMM, if the router **show flash** command indicates that Flash memory has two partitions, you will need to reconfigure that partition from the router. The repartition process involves erasing Flash memory, so you will first have to reboot the router to run in ROM mode.

A. Reconfigure the router to boot to ROM.
Change the config-register to 0x2101 and reload, using the following commands:

Router#configure terminal
Enter configuration commands, one per line. End with CNTL/Z.
Router(config)#config-register 0x2101
Router(config)#exit
Router#reload

Cisco Labs – Semester 3 – Routing and Switching
LAB 1.6 – ROUTER MEMORY UPGRADE – WORKSHEET

Note: This brings the router up in boot mode, and Flash memory will be idle. You cannot change the partition when the router is running under a full IOS from Flash memory. You will see a different router prompt, but enable passwords and most commands will remain the same.

Router(boot)>enable
Password:
Router(boot)#

B. Erase Flash memory, including both partitions.
Caution: You will need to have a backup IOS image already stored on your tftp server because this will erase all Flash files (and Flash memory is where a 2500 stores IOS, by default!).

Router(boot)#erase flash

The router will prompt you through erasing both partitions (you will need to confirm overwrite and erasure of Flash memory).

C. Repartition Flash memory.
Now you must repartition the Flash memory into one partition with a size of 8 MB (if you have installed two 4 MB SIMMs).

Router(boot)#configure t
Router(boot)(config)#partition flash 1 8

D. Copy the stored IOS image back into Flash memory.
Use the command **copy tftp flash** to retrieve the backed up IOS image back into Flash memory. The TFTP server backup/restore procedure is described in Lab 1.4, "IOS Update/TFTP (IOS 12.0)."

E. Change the config-register to boot from Flash memory.
Change the configuration register to cause the router to examine NVRAM for boot system commands ("config-register 0x2102"), which will load the IOS image from Flash memory. Exit and reload; the router should now read "8192k bytes of processor board System flash."

Router(boot)(config)#config-register 0x2102
Router(boot)(config)#exit
Router(boot)#reload

Cisco Labs – Semester 3 – Routing and Switching
LAB 1.6 – ROUTER MEMORY UPGRADE – ANSWERS

Step 1. Log in to the router.
Connect to the router with the console connection, and log in. Enter the password **cisco** if prompted. Enter privileged mode with the **enable** command. Use the password of **class**.

Step 2. Check the current IOS version and amount of DRAM.
Use the **show version** command to check the IOS version and amount of DRAM.

1. What version of the IOS is the router currently running? **Version 11.1(5)**

2. How much DRAM is installed? **4092K/2048K (or 6MB DRAM)**
   Cisco 2500 (68030) processor (revision X) with 4092 K/2048 K bytes of memory
   (This line shows how much memory is installed (in this example, 4092 K/2048 K). The first number represents primary memory, and the second number represents shared memory.)

Step 3. Check the IOS image file and Flash memory.
Use the **show flash** command to obtain information about Flash memory and the IOS image.

3. Document the following information from the **show flash** command. **(Answers will vary.)**
   a. How much Flash memory is used and available? **6881812 bytes used, 1506796 available, 8388608 total (Note that this router already had 8 MB of Flash memory.)**
   b. What is the file that is stored in Flash memory? **igs-j-l.111-5**
   c. What is the size in bytes of the Flash memory? **8192K bytes of processor board system Flash (read only)**

Cisco Labs – Semester 3 – Routing and Switching
LAB 2.1 – SWITCH CHARACTERISTICS – OVERVIEW
(Estimated time: 30 minutes)

Objectives:

- Determine the model number of an Ethernet switch and what physical interfaces (ports) it has
- Identify the cables, connections, and devices that can attach to a switch
- Check and/or modify HyperTerminal configuration parameters
- Connect to the switch as its console using the PC and HyperTerminal

Background:

In this lab, you will examine an Ethernet Switch to gather information about its physical characteristics, and you will begin to appreciate the function of switches in a network. You will determine the model number and features of a specific switch, including which interfaces are present and to which cabling and devices they are connected.

A switch is a Layer 2 (data link layer) network device that acts as the concentration point for the attachment of workstations, servers, routers, hubs, and other switches. A hub is an earlier type of concentration device that provides multiple ports similar to a switch, except that with a hub, all workstations share the bandwidth (10 Mbps with Standard Ethernet) and collisions will occur. Hubs operate at half-duplex (can only send or receive) because they must be able to detect the collisions. A switch provides a dedicated point-to-point connection (virtual circuit) between two networking devices (such as workstations, servers, and routers), so there are no collisions. They do not have to detect collisions, so they can operate in full-duplex mode (simultaneously send and receive), which effectively doubles throughput. Ethernet switches are available in several speeds, including 10 Mbps (standard Ethernet), 100 Mbps (Fast Ethernet), and 1000 Mbps (Gigabit Ethernet).

Cisco Labs – Semester 3 – Routing and Switching
LAB 2.1 – SWITCH CHARACTERISTICS – OVERVIEW

Switches are sometimes referred to as multiport bridges and are the newest technology for today's Ethernet star-wired local-area networks (LANs). Like routers, switches are dedicated PCs that contain a CPU, RAM, and an operating system (IOS). As with a router, a switch can be managed by connecting to the console port to allow you to view and make changes to the configuration. Many of the newer switches have a web (HTTP) server built in and can also be managed via their IP address using a PC and a browser interface such as Netscape or Internet Explorer. The ability to understand and configure switches is essential for network support.

Tools/Preparation:

A switch should be available with a PC workstation connected as a console with HyperTerminal installed and properly configured to access the switch. The switch should be exposed with all sides clearly visible so that all physical connections and cables can be inspected. Because there may be only one switch available, the instructor should demonstrate this lab at a minimum, and students should work in larger teams to get hands-on experience. While one team is doing switch labs, the others could be doing web-based research on switches at the Cisco web site URLs listed below. Before beginning this lab, you should read Chapter 2, on LAN switching, in *Cisco Networking Academy Program: Second-Year Companion Guide*. You should also review Semester 3 online Lesson 2.

Required Resources:
- Windows PC with HyperTerminal installed
- Cisco switch (19xx or 28xx model) with manuals
- Console cable (rollover)
- CAT5 Ethernet cable from the workstation to the switch

Web Site Resources:
- **LAN switching basics** – http://www.cisco.com/univercd/cc/td/doc/cisintwk/ito_doc/lanswtch.htm
- **General information on all Cisco products (scroll down to Chapter 15, "Switches")** – http://www.cisco.com/univercd/cc/td/doc/pcat/#2
- **1900/2820 series Ethernet switches** – http://www.cisco.com/warp/public/cc/cisco/mkt/switch/cat/c1928/prodlit/s1928_ov.htm
- **2900 series Fast Ethernet switches** – http://www.cisco.com/warp/public/cc/cisco/mkt/switch/cat/2900xl/prodlit/290xl_ov.htm
- **3500 series Gigabit Ethernet switches** – http://www.cisco.com/warp/public/cc/cisco/mkt/switch/cat/3500xl/prodlit/3500x_ov.htm
- **Cisco switch clustering technology** – http://www.cisco.com/warp/public/cc/cisco/mkt/switch/cat/3500xl/prodlit/clust_ov.htm

Notes:
_____
_____
_____
_____
_____

Cisco Labs – Semester 3 – Routing and Switching
LAB 2.1 – SWITCH CHARACTERISTICS – WORKSHEET

Step 1. Examine the Ethernet LAN switch, both front and back.
Answer the following questions. (Note: Answers will vary depending on the switch model.) You may want to refer to the Installation and Configuration Guide for the switch you are working with.

1. What is the model number of the switch? _____

2. What is the system serial number of the switch? _____

3. Do you see a console port? (Y/N) _____   What port is it connected to on the console terminal (PC workstation)? _____

4. What type of cable is the console cable (rollover, cross-connect, or straight-through)?
_____

5. Do you see an AUI port? (Y/N) _____   What does the abbreviation AUI mean, and what could this port be used for? _____
_____

6. What type of cable or adapter could be used with the AUI port? _____
_____

7. Is there a power ON/OFF switch? (Y/N) _____   How do you turn on the switch? _____
_____

8. What is the total number of ports on the front of the switch for connection of workstations, servers, routers, hubs, or other switches? _____

9. How many ports are 10 Mbps Ethernet? _____

10. Are these crossover ports? _____   How can you tell? _____

11. What kind of connector(s) are used? _____

12. How many ports are 100 Mbps Fast Ethernet? _____

13. Are these crossover ports? _____   How can you tell? _____

14. What kind of connector(s) are used? _____

15. What indicator lights (LEDs) are on the front of the switch? _____

16. What button is on the front of the switch? _____   What is it used for? _____
_____

Cisco Labs – Semester 3 – Routing and Switching
LAB 2.1 – SWITCH CHARACTERISTICS – WORKSHEET

Step 2. Review your answers to Step 1, and record interface information.
Use the following table to list and summarize the characteristics of all interfaces (or port connectors) on the switch. If there is no cable attached to a port, identify the cable type or connector that would normally be used.

Switch Interface/ Port Identifier	Cable Type/Connector	Device and Port to Which Cable Is Connected/Number of Ports

Step 3. Review the workstation's HyperTerminal configuration.

1. Click Start/Programs/Accessories/Communications and then HyperTerminal. Right-click the icon that is defined for console access to the switch, and then click Properties. The icon may be named cisco.ht or something similar. If one does not exist, you can create it using the settings shown in the answers to the worksheet. On the Properties screen, click the Phone Number tab and then click the Configure button. Fill in the following table with the information indicated.

Configuration Option	Current Setting(s)
COM Port	
Bits per second	
Data bits	
Parity	
Stop bits	
Flow control	

Cisco Labs – Semester 3 – Routing and Switching
LAB 2.1 – SWITCH CHARACTERISTICS – ANSWERS

Step 1. Examine the LAN switch, both front and back.
Answer the following questions. (Note: Answers will vary depending on the switch model.)

1. What is the model number of the switch? **Catalyst 1900 Series – WS-C1924-A**

2. What is the system serial number of the switch? **FAA0246W0XT**

3. Do you see a console port? (Y/N) **Yes**   What port is it connected to on the console terminal (PC workstation)? **9-pin serial COM1 port with a DB9/RJ45 converter**

4. What type of cable is the console cable (rollover, cross-connect, or straight-through)? **The cable is rollover (pin 1 to pin 8, pin 2 to pin 7, and so on).**

5. Do you see an AUI port? (Y/N) **Yes**   What does AUI mean, and what could this port be used for? **Attachment unit interface, used for interconnecting switches on a backbone**

6. What type of cable or adapter could be used with the AUI port? **AUI connector (also called DB15 or DIX) with a drop cable to an external transceiver, as with 10Base-5 Ethernet. Could also have a converter from AUI to RJ45 (for unshielded twisted-pair) or to BNC (for thinnet coaxial cable).**

7. Is there a power on/off switch? (Y/N) **No**   How do you turn on the switch? **Plug the power cord into an AC power receptacle or use the remote DC input power supply.**

8. What is the total number of ports on the front of the switch for connection of workstations, servers, routers, hubs, or other switches? **26**

9. How many ports are 10 Mbps Ethernet? **24 (numbered 1 through 24)**

10. Are these crossover ports? **Yes**   How can you tell? **"X" is next to the port number.**

11. What kind of connector(s) are used? **RJ45 (10BaseT style)**

12. How many ports are 100 Mbps Fast Ethernet? **2 (lettered A and B)**

13. Are these crossover ports? **Yes**   How can you tell? **"X" is next to the port letter.**

14. What kind of connector(s) are used? **One RJ45 copper or two SC fiber connectors**

15. What indicator lights (LEDs) are on the front of the switch? **System (to indicate that the switch is on), RPS (to indicate that a remote power supply is in use), and an activity light for each Ethernet port**

16. What button is on the front of the switch? **Mode**   What is it used for? **To indicate how the port lights are to be interpreted. Modes are: STAT = Status (default), UTL = Utilization (traffic), FDUP = Full-Duplex (refer to manual for details)**

Cisco Labs – Semester 3 – Routing and Switching
LAB 2.1 – SWITCH CHARACTERISTICS – ANSWERS

Step 2. Review your answers to Step 1, and record all interfaces.

Use the following table to list and summarize the characteristics of all interfaces (or port connectors) on the switch. If there is no cable attached to a port, identify the cable type or connector that would normally be used.

Switch Interface/ Port Identifier	Cable Type/Connector	Device and Port to Which Cable Is Connected/Number of Ports
Console	Rollover (asynchronous)	PC serial port COM1 (9-pin)
AUI	Coax, DB15 drop cable (for 10Base5 thicknet)	Can be used to connect switches using a linear bus topology
10 Mbps crossover ports (10BaseT)	CAT 5 unshielded twisted pair (UTP) and 8-pin RJ45	Workstations, servers, routers, and so on (usually 12 to 24 10BaseT ports)
100 Mbps crossover ports (100BaseTX)	CAT 5 unshielded twisted pair (UTP) and 8-pin RJ45	Servers and connection to other switches (usually two 100BaseTX – copper)
100 Mbps fiber ports (100BaseFX)	62.5/125 micron multimode fiber – dual SC connector	Backbone connection to switches in wiring closets in other buildings. (usually one or two 100Base-FX – fiber ports)
DC input port	18-pin power cable	For remote (external) power source)

Step 3. Review the workstation's HyperTerminal configuration.

1. Click on Start/Programs/Accessories/Communications and then HyperTerminal. Right-click the icon that is defined for console access to the switch, and then click Properties. The icon may be named cisco.ht or something similar. If one does not exist, you can create it using the settings shown in the answers to the worksheet. On the Properties screen, click the Phone Number tab and then click the Configure button. Fill in the following table.

Configuration Option	Current Setting(s)
COM port	Direct to COM1 (or COM2, depending on your PC)
Bits per second	9600
Data bits	8
Parity	None
Stop bits	1 or 2
Flow control	Hardware

Cisco Labs – Semester 3 – Routing and Switching
LAB 2.1 – SWITCH CHARACTERISTICS – ANSWERS

The following screen capture from Windows HyperTerminal on a PC workstation shows what the Com Port settings should be for most switches.

Cisco Labs – Semester 3 – Routing and Switching
LAB 2.2 – SWITCH MANAGEMENT CONSOLE – OVERVIEW
(Estimated time: 60 minutes)

Router Name - LAB A
Router Type - 2514
E 0 = 192.5.5.1
E 1 = 205.7.5.1
S 0 = 201.100.11.1
SM = 255.255.255.0

Router Name - LAB C
Router Type - 2503
E 0 = 223.8.151.1
S 0 = 204.204.7.1
S 1 = 199.6.13.2
SM = 255.255.255.0

Router Name - LAB E
Router Type - 2501
E 0 = 210.93.105.2
SM = 255.255.255.0

Router Name - LAB B
Router Type - 2503
E 0 = 219.17.100.1
S 0 = 199.6.13.1
S 1 = 201.100.11.2
SM = 255.255.255.0

Router Name - LAB D
Router Type - 2501
E 0 = 210.93.105.1
S 1 = 204.204.7.2
SM = 255.255.255.0

LEGEND

= ROUTER	User Exec Password = cisco
= HUB	Enable Secret Exec Password = class
= LAN SWITCH	Terminal vty Password = cisco
= CONSOLE CABLE	

Objectives:

- Explore the Switch Management Console user interface menus
- Determine the switch model number and MAC address
- Document the primary user interface menu options
- Use the Management Console menus to view and configure basic IP address settings
- Document the IP address configuration menu options
- Check workstation network settings to verify compatibility with switch and router settings

Background:

This lab will help you develop a basic understanding of Ethernet switch management and will help prepare you for more advanced switching lessons such as VLANs. You will work with the Switch Management Console user interface menus to configure some basic switch options. Switch management can be done through a menu-driven interface such as the Management Console or through a command-line interface (CLI), as with most routers.

In this lab, you will console into the switch and view the menu options available with the user interface menus to become familiar with the types of settings and actions that can be performed when configuring a switch. You will also set the IP address of the switch using the Management Console and will use the Control Panel/Networks utility on the workstation to verify that its IP address settings are compatible with the switch IP address. Familiarity with switches and their management is critical to the successful support of today's Ethernet networks.

Cisco Labs – Semester 3 – Routing and Switching
LAB 2.2 – SWITCH MANAGEMENT CONSOLE – OVERVIEW

Tools/Preparation:

Before you start the lab, the teacher or lab assistant should have a switch available with the default VLAN settings. A workstation with HyperTerminal should be available to console into the switch, and an Ethernet connection should be available to Telnet into the switch. Because there may be only one switch available, the instructor should demonstrate this lab at a minimum, and students should work in larger teams to get hands-on experience. While one team is doing switch labs, the others could be doing web-based research on switches at the Cisco web site URLs listed below. Before you begin this lab, you should read Chapter 2, "LAN Switching," of *Cisco Networking Academy Program: Second-Year Companion Guide*. You should also review Semester 3 online Lesson 2.

Required Resources:

- Windows PC with HyperTerminal installed (configured for console connection to switch)
- Cisco switch (19xx, 28xx, or 29xx model)
- Console cable (rollover)
- CAT 5 Ethernet cable from the workstation to a switch Ethernet port

Web Site Resources:

- **LAN switching basics** – http://www.cisco.com/univercd/cc/td/doc/cisintwk/ito_doc/lanswtch.htm
- **General information on all Cisco products (scroll down to Chapter 15, "Switches")** – http://www.cisco.com/univercd/cc/td/doc/pcat/#2
- **1900/2820 series Ethernet switches** – http://www.cisco.com/warp/public/cc/cisco/mkt/switch/cat/c1928/prodlit/s1928_ov.htm
- **2900 series Fast Ethernet switches** – http://www.cisco.com/warp/public/cc/cisco/mkt/switch/cat/2900xl/prodlit/290xl_ov.htm
- **3500 series Gigabit Ethernet switches** – http://www.cisco.com/warp/public/cc/cisco/mkt/switch/cat/3500xl/prodlit/3500x_ov.htm
- **Cisco switch clustering technology** – http://www.cisco.com/warp/public/cc/cisco/mkt/switch/cat/3500xl/prodlit/clust_ov.htm

Notes:

_____
_____
_____
_____
_____
_____
_____
_____

Cisco Labs – Semester 3 – Routing and Switching
LAB 2.2 – SWITCH MANAGEMENT CONSOLE – WORKSHEET

Step 1. Connect the workstation to the switch console port and turn on the switch.
Wait a few minutes for the switch to boot up; it will display a menu of options known as the
Management Console (1900 version). This exercise will help you become familiar with the various
menu options available.

1. What is the model number of the switch? _____

2. What is the Ethernet address (Layer 2 MAC address) of the switch? _____

3. Fill in the following table with the Main Menu options available. (Answers will vary depending
   on the switch model and firmware.)

Menu Options from a Cisco Catalyst 1924 (10 Mbps) Ethernet Switch

Menu Option	Menu Option Description	Submenu Options (List Two or More)

Cisco Labs – Semester 3 – Routing and Switching
LAB 2.2 – SWITCH MANAGEMENT CONSOLE – WORKSHEET

Step 2. Use the Management Console menu options to configure IP access.
The IP address of the switch can be used to ping or Telnet to the switch. It is not required to assign an IP address to a switch, but it can be useful for remote switch management. On some newer switches, the IP address can be used to access the switch using a web-based browser management interface. When managing a switch, the management domain is always VLAN 1. All ports are assigned to VLAN 1 by default.

4. Select IP Configuration from the menus. Using the table below, list the first five settings on the IP configuration menu and their values. What is the first action available? _____

Menu Options from a Cisco Catalyst 1912 (10 Mbps) Ethernet Switch

Setting	Setting/Action Description	Setting Value
I	IP address	
S	Subnet mask	
D	Default gateway	
V	Management VLAN	
M	IP address of DNS server 1	
P	Ping	

5. Assign an IP address and subnet mask to the switch. Be sure to use an IP address and subnet mask that are compatible with the network or subnet that the switch is currently on. If the switch is connected to Router Lab-A, Interface E1 (205.7.5.1), as shown in the standard lab setup diagram, then assign a compatible IP address and subnet mask to the switch.

   IP address: _____   **Subnet mask:** _____

6. Verify that all ports are assigned to VLAN 1. List the ports that are currently assigned to default VLAN 1: _____

7. Configure a workstation with TCP/IP network settings to be compatible with the switch IP address and the router interface (E1) address. Be sure to set the workstation IP address, the subnet mask, and the default gateway (nearside router interface).

   IP address: _____   **Subnet mask:** _____

   Default gateway: _____

Cisco Labs – Semester 3 – Routing and Switching
LAB 2.2 – SWITCH MANAGEMENT CONSOLE – ANSWERS

Step 1. Connect the workstation to the switch console port and turn on the switch.
Wait a few minutes for the switch to boot up; it will display a menu of options known as the
Management Console (1900 version).

1. What is the model number for the switch? **Catalyst 1900 series – WS-C1924-A**

2. What is the Ethernet address (Layer 2 MAC address) of the switch? **00-90-92-31-C5-8D**

3. Fill in the following table with the Main Menu options available. (Answers will vary depending
    on the switch model and firmware.)

Main Menu Options from a Cisco Catalyst (10 Mbps) Ethernet Switch

Menu Option	Menu Option Description	Submenu Options (List Two or More)
C	Console settings	Password intrusion threshold, Default mode of status LED, Modify password
S	System	Name of system, Location, Switching mode, Address aging time, Network port
N	Network management	IP configuration (address, subnet mask, ping), SNMP management, Cisco Discovery Protocol (CDP), HTTP server configuration
P	Port configuration	Select port (1 to 24, AUI, ports A and B), Description/ name of port, Status of port, Full duplex
A	Port addressing	Select port (1 to 24, AUI, ports A and B), Address table size, Addressing security, Add a static address
D	Port statistics detail	Select port (1 to 24, AUI, ports A and B), Transmit statistics (good frames, runt frames), Receive statistics (broadcasts, collisions, errors)
M	Monitoring	Capture frames to the monitor, Monitor port assignment
V	VLANs	List VLANs; Modify VLANs; VLAN membership; Add, Delete VLANs
R	Multicast registration	Register a multicast address, List all multicast addresses, Unregister a multicast address
F	Firmware	Flash memory size: 1024 K bytes (1 MB), Firmware (IOS) version: V8.01.02 : Standard Edition, TFTP server name or IP address and firmware upgrade options
I	RS-232 interface	Baud rate: 9600, Data bits: 8, Stop bits: 1, Parity setting: None, Auto answer
U	Usage summaries	Port status report, Port addressing report, Exception status report, Utilization status report, Bandwidth usage report
H	Help	Provides general help for menus
K	Command line	Enter command-line interface (CLI) mode
X	Exit	Exits Management Console

Cisco Labs – Semester 3 – Routing and Switching
LAB 2.2 – SWITCH MANAGEMENT CONSOLE – ANSWERS

Step 2. Use the Management Console menu options to configure IP access.
The IP address of the switch can be used to ping or Telnet to the switch. It is not required to assign an IP address to a switch, but it is recommended for switch management. On some newer switches, the IP address can be used to access the switch using a web-based browser management interface. When managing a switch, the management domain is always VLAN 1. All ports are assigned to VLAN 1 by default.

4. Select IP Configuration from the menus. Using the table below, list the first five settings on the IP configuration menu and their values. What is the first action available? **Ping**

IP Menu Options from a Cisco Catalyst 1912 (10 Mbps) Ethernet Switch

Setting	Setting/Action Description	Setting Value
I	IP address	0.0.0.0
S	Subnet mask	255.255.255.0
D	Default gateway	0.0.0.0
V	Management VLAN	1
M	IP address of DNS server 1	0.0.0.0
P	Ping	Command (action)

5. Assign an IP address and subnet mask to the switch. Be sure to use an IP address and subnet mask that are compatible with the network or subnet that the switch is currently on. If the switch is connected to Router Lab-A, Interface E1 (205.7.5.1), as shown in the standard lab setup diagram, then assign a compatible IP address and subnet mask to the switch.

   IP address: 205.7.5.2   **Subnet mask: 255.255.255.0**

6. Verify that all ports are assigned to VLAN 1. List the ports that are currently assigned to VLAN 1: **Ports 1-12, AUI, A, B (assuming that this is 12-port switch)**

7. Configure a workstation with TCP/IP network settings to be compatible with the switch IP address and the router interface (E1) address. Be sure to set the workstation IP address, the subnet mask, and the default gateway (nearside router interface).

   IP address: 205.7.5.3   **Subnet mask: 255.255.255.0**   **Default gateway: 205.7.5.1**

Cisco Labs – Semester 3 – Routing and Switching
LAB 2.3 – SWITCH PORT OPTIONS – OVERVIEW
(Estimated time: 20 minutes)

Router Name - LAB A
Router Type - 2514
E 0 = 192.5.5.1
E 1 = 205.7.5.1
S 0 = 201.100.11.1
SM = 255.255.255.0

Router Name - LAB B
Router Type - 2503
E 0 = 219.17.100.1
S 0 = 199.6.13.1
S 1 = 201.100.11.2
SM = 255.255.255.0

Router Name - LAB C
Router Type - 2503
E 0 = 223.8.151.1
S 0 = 204.204.7.1
S 1 = 199.6.13.2
SM = 255.255.255.0

Router Name - LAB D
Router Type - 2501
E 0 = 210.93.105.1
S 1 = 204.204.7.2
SM = 255.255.255.0

Router Name - LAB E
Router Type - 2501
E 0 = 210.93.105.2
SM = 255.255.255.0

LEGEND
= ROUTER   User Exec Password = cisco
= HUB   Enable Secret Exec Password = class
= LAN SWITCH   Terminal vty Password = cisco
= CONSOLE CABLE

Objectives:
- Work with the Management Console user interface menus to determine the switch model number, MAC address, and firmware revision
- Use the System Configuration menu to configure FragmentFree operation
- Use the Port Configuration menu to enable full-duplex operation
- Use the Port Configuration menu to enable Port Fast operation

Background:
In this lab, you will work with the Management Console interface menus to configure a switch to operate in FragmentFree switching mode. You will also configure a port to enable full-duplex and Port Fast operation. Most switches can be configured with these options.

FragmentFree Operation
Switches can operate in three modes: 1) Cut-through or Fast-Forward, 2) Store-and-Forward, and 3) FragmentFree. In Fast-Forward mode, the switch only reads the destination MAC address of the frame header and then immediately forwards the frame. This mode is the fastest but can also forward collision fragments of less than 64 bytes (a runt). Store-and-Forward waits for the entire frame to be received (up to 1,518 bytes) before forwarding the frame. It is the slowest switching mode but results in the fewest errors. FragmentFree mode reduces delay by making the forwarding decision after the first 64 bytes have been received. This means that no runts will be forwarded, which is the most common type of bad Ethernet frame. FragmentFree is the best compromise between speed and errors. Cisco switches can be set to operate in Store-and-Forward, FragmentFree, or Fast-Forward modes, depending on the model.

Cisco Labs – Semester 3 – Routing and Switching
LAB 2.3 – SWITCH PORT OPTIONS – OVERVIEW

Full-Duplex Operation
When full-duplex operation is enabled on a port, it can double the bandwidth by allowing it to simultaneously transmit and receive. This means that a 10 Mbps Ethernet port can operate at 20 Mbps as long as the network interface of the attached device (NIC or router interface) can also support full-duplex operation. Because a switch provides virtual circuit to the device with no collisions, this is dedicated bandwidth to the device. A 100 Mbps Fast Ethernet port can operate at 200 Mbps dedicated bandwidth. Full-duplex operation must be set for each port.

Port Fast Operation
When a switch port comes up, it normally goes through the normal 802.1d spanning tree states of blocking, listening, learning, and forwarding. This process can take from up to 45 seconds to occur. When Port Fast mode (spanning tree) is enabled, the Spanning Tree Protocol (STP) can transition the port's state from blocking to forwarding without going through the intermediate states of listening and learning. This can be beneficial especially in Novell Network IPX environments, where the client request can sometimes time out because of the time it takes for a switch port to respond.

Tools/Preparation:
Before you start the lab, the teacher or lab assistant should have a switch available with the default VLAN settings. A workstation with HyperTerminal should be available to console into the switch, and an Ethernet connection should be available to Telnet into the switch. Because there may be only one switch available, the instructor should demonstrate this lab at a minimum, and students should work in larger teams to get hands-on experience. While one team is doing switch labs, the others could be doing web-based research on switches at the Cisco web site URLs listed below. Before you begin this lab, you should read Chapter 2, "LAN Switching," in *Cisco Networking Academy Program: Second-Year Companion Guide*. You should also review Semester 3 online Lesson 2.

Required Resources:
- Windows PC with HyperTerminal installed (configured for console connection to switch)
- Cisco switch (19xx or 28xx model)
- Console cable (rollover)
- Straight-through CAT 5 Ethernet cable from the workstation to a switch Ethernet port

Web Site Resources:
- **LAN switching basics** – http://www.cisco.com/univercd/cc/td/doc/cisintwk/ito_doc/lanswtch.htm
- **General information on all Cisco products (scroll down to Chapter 15, "Switches")** – http://www.cisco.com/univercd/cc/td/doc/pcat/#2
- **1900/2820 series Ethernet switches** – http://www.cisco.com/warp/public/cc/cisco/mkt/switch/cat/c1928/prodlit/s1928_ov.htm
- **2900 series Fast Ethernet switches** – http://www.cisco.com/warp/public/cc/cisco/mkt/switch/cat/2900xl/prodlit/290xl_ov.htm
- **3500 series Gigabit Ethernet switches** – http://www.cisco.com/warp/public/cc/cisco/mkt/switch/cat/3500xl/prodlit/3500x_ov.htm
- **Cisco switch clustering technology** – http://www.cisco.com/warp/public/cc/cisco/mkt/switch/cat/3500xl/prodlit/clust_ov.htm

Cisco Labs – Semester 3 – Routing and Switching
LAB 2.3 – SWITCH PORT OPTIONS – WORKSHEET

Step 1. Connect the workstation to the switch console port and turn on the switch.
Wait a few minutes for the switch to boot up; it will display a menu of options known as the Management Console (1900 version).

1. What is the model number for the switch? _____

2. What is the Ethernet address (Layer 2 MAC address) of the switch? _____

3. What is the switch firmware revision and type? _____

Step 2. Configure the switch for FragmentFree operation.
Select the [S] System option from the main menu, and review the menu options under Settings.

4. What is the current switch mode set to? _____

5. What menu option will allow you to change the mode? _____

6. What options are available? _____

Step 3. Configure a port for full-duplex operation.
Exit to the main menu and select the [P] Port Configuration option from the menu.

7. List the ports that are available to select from: Identify Port: _____
   _____
   Specify the port you wish to work with (such as port 5). _____

8. Is full-duplex mode enabled? _____ What option is used to enable it? _____

Step 4. Configure a port for Port Fast mode.
From the Port Configuration menu, select the Port Fast configuration option from the menu.

9. What option selects Port Fast? _____

Step 5. Check the switch IP configuration.
From the [N] Network Management option on the main menu, select [I] for IP configuration.

10. Does the switch have an IP address? _____ If so, what is it? _____

Cisco Labs – Semester 3 – Routing and Switching
LAB 2.3 – SWITCH PORT OPTIONS – ANSWERS

Step 1. Connect the workstation to the switch console port and turn on the switch.
Wait a few minutes for the switch to boot up; it will display a menu of options known as the Management Console (1900 version). Answers will vary.

1. What is the model number for the switch? **Catalyst 1900 -WS-C1924-A**

2. What is the Ethernet address (Layer 2 MAC address) of the switch? **00-90-BF-75-83-00 (Exit the management console, and it can be seen on the first screen or under IP Configuration.)**

3. What is the switch firmware revision and type? **V8.01.02: Standard Edition**

Step 2. Configure the switch for FragmentFree operation.
Select the [S] System option from the main menu and review the menu options under Settings.

4. What is the current switch mode set to? **Fast-Forward (the default)**

5. What menu option will allow you to change the mode? **[S] Switching Mode**

6. What options are available? **Store-and-Forward, FragmentFree, or Fast-Forward**

Step 3. Configure a port for full-duplex operation.
Exit to the main menu and select the [P] Port Configuration option from the menu.

7. List the ports that are available to select from: Identify Port: **1 to 24[1-24], [AUI], [A], [B]: Select [1 - 24, AUI, A, B]:**
    Specify the port you wish to work with (as in port 5). _____

8. Is full duplex enabled? **No**   What option is used to enable it? **[F] Full Duplex/Enabled**

Step 4. Configure a port for Port Fast mode.
From the Port Configuration menu, select the Port Fast configuration option from the menu.

9. What option selects Port Fast? **Option [H] Port Fast mode (spanning tree)**

Step 5. Check the switch IP configuration.
From the [N] Network Management option on the main menu, select [I] for IP configuration.

10. Does the switch have an IP address? **No**   If so, what is it? **The switch does not have an IP address by default. If there is one, then someone has assigned it to be able to ping, Telnet, or browse to the switch.**

Cisco Labs – Semester 3 – Routing and Switching
LAB 2.4 – SWITCH CONFIGURATION USING A BROWSER – OVERVIEW
(Estimated time: 30 minutes)

Router Name - LAB A
Router Type - 2514
E 0 = 192.5.5.1
E 1 = 205.7.5.1
S 0 = 201.100.11.1
SM = 255.255.255.0

Router Name - LAB C
Router Type - 2503
E 0 = 223.8.151.1
S 0 = 204.204.7.1
S 1 = 199.6.13.2
SM = 255.255.255.0

Router Name - LAB E
Router Type - 2501
E 0 = 210.93.105.2
SM = 255.255.255.0

Router Name - LAB B
Router Type - 2503
E 0 = 219.17.100.1
S 0 = 199.6.13.1
S 1 = 201.100.11.2
SM = 255.255.255.0

Router Name - LAB D
Router Type - 2501
E 0 = 210.93.105.1
S 1 = 204.204.7.2
SM = 255.255.255.0

LEGEND

= ROUTER — User Exec Password = cisco

= HUB — Enable Secret Exec Password = class

= LAN SWITCH — Terminal vty Password = cisco

= CONSOLE CABLE

Objectives:

- Use the Management Console menus to view and configure switch IP address settings
- Check workstation network settings to verify compatibility with switch and router settings
- Test cabling and IP connectivity from workstation to switch with the **ping** and **telnet** commands
- Use a workstation with browser software to connect to the switch and check port status

Background:

This lab provides an opportunity to configure a switch for IP and Hypertext Transfer Protocol (HTTP) access. By assigning an IP address to the switch, you will be able to ping it and Telnet to it. You will also be able to use your workstation browser (Netscape or Internet Explorer) to connect to the switch and check switch settings and port statistics. The browser will provide a graphical interface showing a frontal view of the switch and will allow you to select any port to check out its statistics and characteristics. Many newer switches have HTTP web server software built in to support browser-based switch management. With Cisco switch clustering technology, you can manage up to 16 switches with one IP address. It is very important to assign a password to the switch if you will assign an IP address.

Cisco Labs – Semester 3 – Routing and Switching
LAB 2.4 – SWITCH CONFIGURATION USING A BROWSER – OVERVIEW

Tools/Preparation:
Before you start the lab, the teacher or lab assistant should have a switch available with the default VLAN settings. A workstation with HyperTerminal should be available to console into the switch and an Ethernet connection to Telnet and browser into the switch. Because there may be only one switch available, the instructor should demonstrate this lab at a minimum, and students should work in larger teams to get hands-on experience. While one team is doing switch labs, the others could be doing web-based research on switches at the Cisco web site URLs listed below. Before you begin this lab, you should read Chapter 2, "LAN Switching," in *Cisco Networking Academy Program: Second-Year Companion Guide*. You should also review Semester 3 online Lesson 2.

Required Resources:
- Windows PC with HyperTerminal installed (configured for console connection to switch)
- Cisco switch (19xx or 28xx model)
- Console cable (rollover)
- CAT 5 Ethernet cable from the workstation to a switch Ethernet port

Web Site Resources:
- **LAN switching basics** – http://www.cisco.com/univercd/cc/td/doc/cisintwk/ito_doc/lanswtch.htm
- **General information on all Cisco products (scroll down to Chapter 15, "Switches")** – http://www.cisco.com/univercd/cc/td/doc/pcat/#2
- **1900/2820 series Ethernet switches** – http://www.cisco.com/warp/public/cc/cisco/mkt/switch/cat/c1928/prodlit/s1928_ov.htm
- **2900 series Fast Ethernet switches** – http://www.cisco.com/warp/public/cc/cisco/mkt/switch/cat/2900xl/prodlit/290xl_ov.htm
- **3500 series Gigabit Ethernet switches** – http://www.cisco.com/warp/public/cc/cisco/mkt/switch/cat/3500xl/prodlit/3500x_ov.htm
- **Cisco switch clustering technology** – http://www.cisco.com/warp/public/cc/cisco/mkt/switch/cat/3500xl/prodlit/clust_ov.htm

Notes:
_____
_____
_____
_____
_____
_____
_____
_____
_____
_____
_____
_____

Cisco Labs – Semester 3 – Routing and Switching
LAB 2.4 – SWITCH CONFIGURATION USING A BROWSER – WORKSHEET

Step 1. Connect the workstation to the switch console port and turn on the switch.
Depending on the switch, you will need either a rollover RJ45 cable with a DB9 adapter (on the PC end), or a DB9-to-DB9 null modem (modem eliminator) cable. Wait a few minutes for the switch to boot up; it will display a menu of options known as the Management Console.

1. What is the model number for the switch? _____

2. What is the Ethernet address (Layer 2 MAC address) of the switch? _____

Step 2. Use the Management Console to configure IP access to the switch.
The IP address of the switch can be used to ping or Telnet to the switch and browse into it. It is not required to assign an IP address to a switch, but it is recommended for switch management. When managing a switch, the management domain is always VLAN 1. All ports are assigned to VLAN 1 by default.

3. Select [N] Network Management and then [I] IP Configuration from the menus. Assign an IP address and subnet mask to the switch. Be sure to use an IP address and subnet mask that are compatible with the network or subnet that the switch is currently on. If the switch is connected to Router Lab-A, Interface E1 (205.7.5.1), as shown in the standard lab setup diagram, then assign a compatible IP address and subnet mask to the switch.

   IP address: _____ **Subnet mask:** _____

4. Select [V] Virtual LAN from the menu, and verify that all ports are assigned to VLAN 1. List the ports that are currently assigned to default VLAN 1: _____

Step 3. Use the Management Console to configure HTTP access.

5. Select the [N] Network Management menu, and verify that the switch will accept HTTP requests. What option is used to configure the switch to be an HTTP server? _____ What TCP port number is used by HTTP (by default)? _____
   (Note: This option may not be available on all switches.)

Step 4. Configure the workstation for Ethernet access to the switch.
Configure the workstation with TCP/IP network settings to be compatible with the switch IP address and the router interface (E1) address. Be sure to set the workstation IP address, subnet mask, and default gateway (nearside router interface).

6. Write down the workstation IP address information here:

   IP address: _____ **Subnet mask:** _____
   Default gateway: _____

Cisco Labs – Semester 3 – Routing and Switching
LAB 2.4 – SWITCH CONFIGURATION USING A BROWSER – WORKSHEET

Step 5. Ping the IP address of the switch
Connect the workstation Ethernet cable (straight-through) to port 1 on the switch, and use the **ping** command from the workstation DOS prompt to test connectivity and IP configuration between the workstation and switch.

    C:\WINDOWS> ping 205.7.5.4

7. Was the **ping** command successful? _____

Step 6. Telnet to the switch IP address.
Telnet to the switch from the workstation DOS prompt to test upper-layer connectivity and IP configuration between the workstation and the switch. You should see the same menu as when you are connected via the console.

    C:\WINDOWS> telnet 205.7.5.4

8. Was the Telnet successful? _____

Step 7. Use your browser to access the switch.
Start your browser software (Netscape or Internet Explorer). Type in the IP address you just assigned to the switch in the browser address area where you would normally type in the URL of a web site. The Switch Management graphical user interface (GUI) should be displayed by the HTTP server in the switch. Remember that you can always use the Forward and Back buttons with the browser. The browser GUI is somewhat limited in what you can configure.

9. Did the Switch Management browser interface come up? _____

Step 8. Make some configuration changes to the switch using the browser interface.

10. Enter a name for the switch. _____

11. Enter a password for the switch, and confirm it. _____

12. What color will the port be if the link is faulty or the port is disabled? _____

13. Select the port where your workstation is connected (port 1), and click it with the mouse. Scroll down the port table until you get to port 0/1. What is the current actual duplex mode? _____ Change the mode from half-duplex to full-duplex operation. (The NIC in your workstation may not support full-duplex operation.)

14. Check the port statistics for frames received and transmitted by clicking the Stats button. Enter the number of packets below:
    Good frames received: _____   Packets transmitted: _____

Cisco Labs – Semester 3 – Routing and Switching
LAB 2.4 – SWITCH CONFIGURATION USING A BROWSER – ANSWERS

1. What is the model number for the switch? **Catalyst 1900 Series – WS-C1924-A**

2. What is the Ethernet address (Layer 2 MAC address) of the switch? **00-90-92-31-C5-8D**

3. Select [N] Network Management and then [I] IP Configuration from the menus. Assign an IP address and subnet mask to the switch. Be sure to use an IP address and subnet mask that are compatible with the network or subnet that the switch is currently on. If the switch is connected to Router Lab-A, Interface E1 (205.7.5.1), as shown in the standard lab setup diagram, then assign a compatible IP address and subnet mask to the switch.

    IP address: 205.7.5.4   **Subnet mask: 255.255.255.0**

4. Select [V] Virtual LAN from the menu, and verify that all ports are assigned to VLAN 1. List the ports that are currently assigned to default VLAN 1: **Ports 1-12, AUI, A, B (assuming that this is 12-port switch)**

5. Select the [N] Network Management menu, and verify that the switch will accept HTTP requests. What option is used to configure the switch to be an HTTP server? **[H] HTTP server configuration** What TCP port number is used by HTTP (by default)? **Port 80** **(Note: This option may not be available on all switches.)**

6. Write down the workstation IP address information here:

    IP address: 205.7.5.3   **Subnet mask: 255.255.255.0**

    Default gateway: 205.7.5.1

7. Was the **ping** command successful? **Yes. If not, check connections and IP settings.**

8. Was the Telnet successful? **Yes. If not, check connections and IP settings.**

Cisco Labs – Semester 3 – Routing and Switching
LAB 2.4 – SWITCH CONFIGURATION USING A BROWSER – ANSWERS

9. Did the Switch Manager browser interface come up? **Yes. If not, recheck prior steps. It is possible that the switch you are working with does not support http/browser.**

Step 8. Make some configuration changes to the switch using the browser interface.

10. Enter a name for the switch. **Ethernet LAN 1**

11. Enter a password for the switch, and confirm it. **Enter the password of cisco or class.**

12. What color will the port be if the link is faulty or the port is disabled? **Orange/red**

Cisco Labs – Semester 3 – Routing and Switching
LAB 2.4 – SWITCH CONFIGURATION USING A BROWSER – ANSWERS

13. Select the port where your workstation is connected (port 1), and click it with the mouse. Scroll down the port table until you get to port 0/1. What is the current actual duplex mode? **Half-duplex** Change the mode from half-duplex to full-duplex operation. (The NIC in your workstation may not support full-duplex operation.)

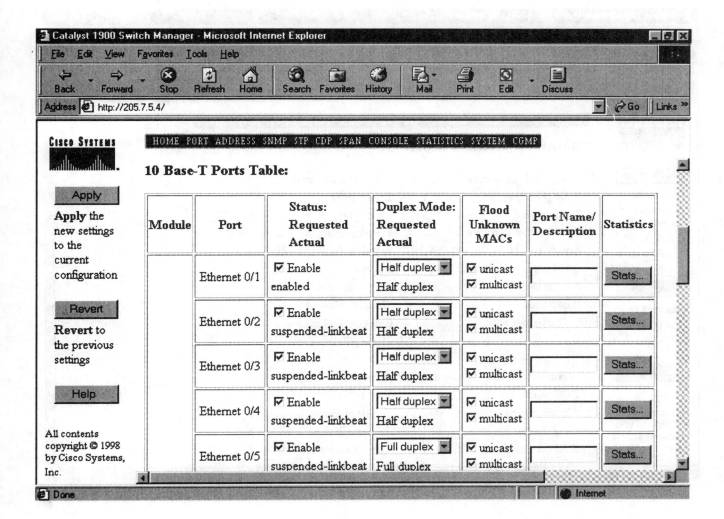

Cisco Labs – Semester 3 – Routing and Switching
LAB 2.4 – SWITCH CONFIGURATION USING A BROWSER – ANSWERS

14. Check the port statistics for frames received and transmitted by clicking the Stats button. Enter the number of packets below:

Good Frames Received: <u>621</u>   Packets Transmitted: <u>1096</u>

Cisco Labs – Semester 3 – Routing and Switching
LAB 3.1 – CREATING VLANS – OVERVIEW
(Estimated time: 45 minutes)

Router Name - LAB A
Router Type - 2514
E 0 = 192.5.5.1
E 1 = 205.7.5.1
S 0 = 201.100.11.1
SM = 255.255.255.0

Router Name - LAB C
Router Type - 2503
E 0 = 223.8.151.1
S 0 = 204.204.7.1
S 1 = 199.6.13.2
SM = 255.255.255.0

Router Name - LAB E
Router Type - 2501
E 0 = 210.93.105.2
SM = 255.255.255.0

Router Name - LAB B
Router Type - 2503
E 0 = 219.17.100.1
S 0 = 199.6.13.1
S 1 = 201.100.11.2
SM = 255.255.255.0

Router Name - LAB D
Router Type - 2501
E 0 = 210.93.105.1
S 1 = 204.204.7.2
SM =255.255.255.0

LEGEND

= ROUTER	User Exec Password = cisco
= HUB	Enable Secret Exec Password = class
= LAN SWITCH	Terminal vty Password = cisco
= CONSOLE CABLE	

Objectives:
- Console into the switch to determine the firmware version
- Check the IP address and subnet mask for the switch
- Use the Management Console to check VLAN-related menu options
- Check workstation network settings to verify compatibility with switch and router settings
- Create a new VLAN, name it, and move member ports to it
- Test VLAN functionality by moving a workstation from one VLAN to another

Background:
In this lab, you will work with Ethernet virtual local-area networks (VLANs). VLANs can be used to separate groups of users based on function rather than physical location. Normally, all the ports on a switch are in the same default VLAN 1. A network administrator can create additional VLANs and move some ports into those VLANs to create isolated groups of users regardless of where they are physically located. This creates smaller broadcast domains, which helps to reduce and localize network traffic. If a switch with 24 ports is divided into two VLANs of 12 ports each, the users on one VLAN will not be able to access resources (such as servers or printers) on the other VLAN. VLANs can also be created using ports from multiple switches that are "trunked" together on a backbone. For two VLANs to communicate, they must be connected by a router. Security can be controlled using router access control lists (ACLs), which will be covered in Lab 6.3.

Cisco Labs – Semester 3 – Routing and Switching
LAB 3.1 – CREATING VLANS – OVERVIEW

You will console into the switch and use the Management Console user interface menus to view options available to manage VLANs and to check current VLAN configuration. You will also use Telnet to access the switch and check settings, as well as move your connection from one VLAN to another to determine the effects of the management domain. When managing a switch, the management domain is always VLAN 1. The network administrator's workstation must have access to a port in the VLAN 1 management domain. All ports are assigned to VLAN 1 by default. This lab also demonstrates how VLANs can be used to separate traffic and reduce broadcast domains.

Tools/Preparation:

Before you start the lab, the teacher or lab assistant should have a switch available with the default VLAN settings. A workstation with HyperTerminal should be available to console into the switch, and an Ethernet connection should be available to Telnet into the switch. Because there may be only one switch available, the instructor should demonstrate this lab at a minimum, and students should work in larger teams to get hands-on experience. While one team is doing switch labs, the others could be doing web-based research on switches at the Cisco web site URLs listed below. Before you begin this lab, you should read Chapter 3, "VLANs," in *Cisco Networking Academy Program: Second-Year Companion Guide*. You should also review Semester 3 online Lesson 3.

Required Resources:

- Two Windows PC workstations with HyperTerminal installed (configured for console connection to switch and compatible IP addresses)
- Cisco switch (19xx or 28xx model)
- Console cable (rollover)
- CAT 5 Ethernet cable from each workstation to a switch Ethernet port

Web Site Resources:

- **LAN switching basics** – http://www.cisco.com/univercd/cc/td/doc/cisintwk/ito_doc/lanswtch.htm
- **General information on all Cisco products (scroll down to Chapter 15, "Switches")** – http://www.cisco.com/univercd/cc/td/doc/pcat/#2
- **1900/2820 series Ethernet switches** – http://www.cisco.com/warp/public/cc/cisco/mkt/switch/cat/c1928/prodlit/s1928_ov.htm
- **2900 series Fast Ethernet switches** – http://www.cisco.com/warp/public/cc/cisco/mkt/switch/cat/2900xl/prodlit/290xl_ov.htm
- **3500 series Gigabit Ethernet switches** – http://www.cisco.com/warp/public/cc/cisco/mkt/switch/cat/3500xl/prodlit/3500x_ov.htm
- **Virtual LANs for 1900/2820 switches** – http://www.cisco.com/univercd/cc/td/doc/product/lan/28201900/1928v8x/eescg8x/02vlans.htm

Notes:

_____

_____

_____

_____

_____

Cisco Labs – Semester 3 – Routing and Switching
LAB 3.1 – CREATING VLANS – WORKSHEET

Step 1. Console into the LAN switch.
Console into the switch by attaching the workstation serial port to the switch console port with the rollover cable. Answer the following questions. Use the switch attached to Router Lab-A or another one. (Note: Answers will vary depending on the switch model number.)

1. What is the model number of the switch? _____

2. Does this switch have Standard Edition or Enterprise Edition software? _____

3. What is the firmware version of the switch? _____

4. What option on the switch menu is used to create or modify VLANs? _____

Step 2. Check the IP address of the router, the switch, and the attached workstations.

5. Check the IP address and subnet mask of the router, switch, and workstations to verify that they are compatible and on the same network. If the switch is connected to router Lab-A, interface E1, as shown in the standard lab setup diagram, then assign IP addresses, subnet masks, and default gateways as appropriate. Record your settings below:

Router IP: _____   Subnet mask: _____
Switch IP: _____   Subnet mask: _____
Workstation 1 IP: _____   Subnet mask: _____   Default gateway: _____
Workstation 2 IP: _____   Subnet mask: _____   Default gateway: _____

Step 3. Enter VLAN configuration mode.

6. What is the maximum number of VLANs you can create? _____

7. Select the [L] List VLANs option from the submenu, and then enter the word All. What VLANs are currently listed? _____

8. List the options on the VLAN configuration menu and submenus in the following table:

VLAN Menu Options from a Cisco Catalyst 1912 (10 Mbps) Ethernet Switch

Menu Option	VLAN Menu Option Description	Submenu Options (List Two or More)

Cisco Labs – Semester 3 – Routing and Switching
LAB 3.1 – CREATING VLANS – WORKSHEET

Step 4. Using the VLAN menu options, configure the VLANs.
Note: The following steps were performed on a Catalyst 1912 WS-C1912C-EN (12-port) switch with Enterprise Edition firmware version V8.01.02. Your answers may vary.

9. Check the configuration of the default VLAN by selecting [M] Modify VLANs option, and then select VLAN 1. What are the current member ports in VLAN 1? _____

10. Create a new Ethernet VLAN and name it. Give it a name (such as your last name plus a number: smith1). What name did you give it? _____

11. What is the VLAN number for your new VLAN? _____

12. List the steps required to create and name the new VLAN: _____

13. Assign ports 7 through 12 and port B to your new VLAN. List the steps required to do this:
    _____
    _____

14. Check VLAN 1 again. What changes do you see? _____
    _____

    Exit out to the main menu and then to the Management Console.

Step 5. Test the functionality of the two VLANs.

    To see your VLAN in action, set up two workstations and verify that the IP addresses are on the same subnetwork. (See Step 2.) Restart computers as needed.

    From workstation 1, plug the Ethernet cable from the NIC card into a port from 1-6 on the switch. From workstation 2, plug the Ethernet cable from the NIC card into a port from 1-6 on the switch.

15. Issue a ping to each workstation. Was the ping successful? _____

16. Now take workstation 2's Ethernet port from the switch and plug it into one of the ports on VLAN 2 (ports 7-12). Ping each workstation again. Was the ping successful? _____
    _____
    _____

Cisco Labs – Semester 3 – Routing and Switching
LAB 3.1 – CREATING VLANS – ANSWERS

Step 1. Console into the LAN switch.

Console into the switch by attaching the workstation serial port to the switch console port using a rollover cable. Answer the following questions. Use the switch attached to router Lab-A or another one. (Note: Answers will vary depending on switch model number.)

1. What is the model number of the switch? **Cisco Catalyst 1900 series WS-C1912C-EN**

2. Does this switch have Standard Edition or Enterprise Edition software? **Enterprise Edition**

3. Use the menu option [F] to determine the firmware version in this switch: **V8.01.02**

4. What option on the switch menu is used to create or modify VLANs? **[V] Virtual LAN**

Step 2. Check the IP address of the router, the switch, and the attached workstations.

5. Check the IP address and subnet mask of the router, switch, and workstations to verify that they are compatible and on the same network. If the switch is connected to router Lab-A, interface E1, as shown in the standard lab setup diagram, then assign IP addresses, subnet masks, and default gateways as appropriate. Record your settings below:

Router IP: **205.7.5.1**   Subnet mask: **255.255.255.0**
Switch IP: **205.7.5.2**   Subnet mask: **255.255.255.0**
Workstation 1 IP: **205.7.5.3** Subnet mask: **255.255.255.0**   Default gateway: **205.7.5.1**
Workstation 2 IP: **205.7.5.4** Subnet mask: **255.255.255.0**   Default gateway: **205.7.5.1**

Step 3. Enter VLAN configuration mode.

6. What is the maximum number of VLANs you can create? **4 or 1005 (Firmware Edition)**

7. Select the [L] List VLANs option from the submenu, and then enter the word **All**. What VLANs are currently listed? **VLAN 1 (default Ethernet), and possibly others**

8. List the options on the VLAN configuration menu and submenus in the following table:

VLAN Menu Options from a Cisco Catalyst 1912 (10 Mbps) Ethernet Switch

Menu Option	VLAN Menu Option Description	Submenu Options (List Two or More)
L	List VLAN	Enter VLAN number or "All"
M	Modify VLAN	Select VLAN
E	VLAN membership	Membership type, VLAN assignment
T	Trunk configuration	Select trunk port (A or B)
P	VTP statistics	Virtual Trunking Protocol (VTP) statistics
A	Add VLAN	Ethernet, FDDI, Token Ring
D	Delete a VLAN	Select VLAN to delete (1-1005)
S	VLAN membership servers	VLAN membership policy server
W	VTP password	Set and confirm VTP password
X	Exit	Exit to main menu

Cisco Labs – Semester 3 – Routing and Switching
LAB 3.1 – CREATING VLANS – ANSWERS

Step 4. Using the VLAN menu options, configure the VLANs.
Note: The following steps were performed on a Catalyst 1912 WS-C1912C-EN (12-port) switch with Enterprise Edition firmware version V8.01.02. Your answers may vary.

9. Check the configuration of the default VLAN by selecting [M] Modify VLANs option, and then select VLAN 1. What are the current member ports in VLAN 1? **Ports 1-12, AUI, A and B**

10. Create a new Ethernet VLAN, and name it. Give it a name (such as your last name plus a number: smith1). What name did you give it? **Smith1**

11. What is the VLAN number for your new VLAN? **2 (Default VLAN 1 already exists)**

12. List the steps required to create and name the new VLAN: **Select [A] to add VLAN, select VLAN type of 1 (Ethernet), select [V] for VLAN name and enter the new name, select [S] for save and exit.**

13. Assign ports 7 through 12 and port B to your new VLAN. List the steps required to do this: **Select [E] for VLAN membership, select [V] for VLAN assignment, enter port numbers 7-12 and port B, select VLAN number 2 (your new one), select X for exit.**

14. Check VLAN 1 again. What changes do you see? **Ports 7 through 12 and port B are no longer in VLAN 1.**

    Exit out to the main menu and then to the Management Console.

Step 5. Test the functioning of the two VLANs.
To see your VLAN in action, set up two workstations and verify that the IP addresses are on the same subnetwork. Restart computers as needed.

From workstation 1, plug the Ethernet cable from the NIC card into a port from 1-6 on the switch.
From workstation 2, plug the Ethernet cable from the NIC card into a port from 1-6 on the switch.

15. Issue a ping to each workstation. Was the ping successful? **Yes; if done properly, it should be a success.**

16. Now take workstation 2's Ethernet port from the switch and plug it into one of the ports on VLAN 2 (ports 7-12). Ping each workstation again. Was the ping successful? **No; the two workstations are on different VLANs and there should be no communication between them.**

Cisco Labs – Semester 3 – Routing and Switching
LAB 3.2 – SWITCH MANAGEMENT VLANS – OVERVIEW
(Estimated time: 45 minutes)

Router Name - LAB A
Router Type - 2514
E 0 = 192.5.5.1
E 1 = 205.7.5.1
S 0 = 201.100.11.1
SM = 255.255.255.0

Router Name - LAB B
Router Type - 2503
E 0 = 219.17.100.1
S 0 = 199.6.13.1
S 1 = 201.100.11.2
SM = 255.255.255.0

Router Name - LAB C
Router Type - 2503
E 0 = 223.8.151.1
S 0 = 204.204.7.1
S 1 = 199.6.13.2
SM = 255.255.255.0

Router Name - LAB D
Router Type - 2501
E 0 = 210.93.105.1
S 1 = 204.204.7.2
SM = 255.255.255.0

Router Name - LAB E
Router Type - 2501
E 0 = 210.93.105.2
SM = 255.255.255.0

LEGEND
= ROUTER   User Exec Password = cisco
= HUB   Enable Secret Exec Password = class
= LAN SWITCH   Terminal vty Password = cisco
= CONSOLE CABLE

Objectives:
- Console into the switch and check switch characteristics and configuration parameters
- View/configure the IP address and subnet mask for the switch
- Check workstation network settings to verify compatibility with switch and router settings
- Use the Management Console to check and change VLAN configuration for the switch
- Telnet to the switch based on VLAN and port location
- Work with the switch management domain

Background:
In this lab, you will work with virtual local-area networks (VLANs). You will console into the switch and view the menu options available to manage VLANs, and you will check the current VLAN configuration. You will also use Telnet to access the switch and check some settings, as well as move your connection from one VLAN to another to determine the effects of the management domain. When managing a switch, the management domain is always VLAN 1. The network administrator's workstation must have access to a port in the VLAN 1 management domain. All ports are assigned to VLAN 1 by default.

Cisco Labs – Semester 3 – Routing and Switching
LAB 3.2 – SWITCH MANAGEMENT VLANS – OVERVIEW

Tools/Preparation:
Before you start the lab, the teacher or lab assistant should have a switch available with the default VLAN settings. A workstation with HyperTerminal should be available to console into the switch, and an Ethernet connection should be available to Telnet into the switch. Because there may be only one switch available, the instructor should demonstrate this lab at a minimum, and students should work in larger teams to get hands-on experience. While one team is doing switch labs, the others could be doing web-based research on switches at the Cisco web site URLs listed below. Before you begin this lab, you should read Chapter 3, "VLANs," in *Cisco Networking Academy Program: Second-Year Companion Guide*. You should also review Semester 3 online Lesson 3.

Required Resources:
- Two Windows PC workstations with HyperTerminal installed (configured for console connection to switch)
- Cisco switch (19xx or 28xx model)
- Console cable (rollover)
- CAT 5 Ethernet cable from the workstation to a switch Ethernet port

Web Site Resources:
- **LAN switching basics** – http://www.cisco.com/univercd/cc/td/doc/cisintwk/ito_doc/lanswtch.htm
- **General information on all Cisco products (scroll down to Chapter 15, "Switches")** – http://www.cisco.com/univercd/cc/td/doc/pcat/#2
- **1900/2820 series Ethernet switches** – http://www.cisco.com/warp/public/cc/cisco/mkt/switch/cat/c1928/prodlit/s1928_ov.htm
- **2900 series Fast Ethernet switches** – http://www.cisco.com/warp/public/cc/cisco/mkt/switch/cat/2900xl/prodlit/290xl_ov.htm
- **3500 series Gigabit Ethernet switches** – http://www.cisco.com/warp/public/cc/cisco/mkt/switch/cat/3500xl/prodlit/3500x_ov.htm
- **Cisco switch clustering technology** – http://www.cisco.com/warp/public/cc/cisco/mkt/switch/cat/3500xl/prodlit/clust_ov.htm
- **Virtual LANs for 1900/2820 switches** – http://www.cisco.com/univercd/cc/td/doc/product/lan/28201900/1928v8x/eescg8x/02vlans.htm

Notes:
_____
_____
_____
_____
_____
_____
_____

Cisco Labs – Semester 3 – Routing and Switching
LAB 3.2 – SWITCH MANAGEMENT VLANS – WORKSHEET

Step 1. Console into the LAN switch.

Console into the switch by attaching the workstation serial port to the switch console port with a rollover cable. Answer the following questions. Use the switch attached to router Lab-A or another one. (Note: Answers will vary depending on switch model number.)

1. What is the model number of the switch? _____

2. Does this switch have Standard Edition or Enterprise Edition software? _____

3. What is the firmware version of the switch? _____

4. What option on the menu is used to set the IP address of the switch? _____

5. What option on the switch menu is used to create or modify VLANs? _____

Step 2. Assign an IP address to the switch.

6. Assign an IP address and subnet mask to the switch. Be sure to use an IP address and subnet mask that are compatible with the network or subnet that the switch is currently on. If the switch is connected to router Lab-A, interface E1, as shown in the standard lab setup diagram, then assign a compatible IP address and subnet mask to the switch.

    IP address: _____   Subnet mask: _____

Step 3. Check VLAN configuration options.

7. Select the VLAN option from the menu. How many VLANs can be configured with this switch? _____

8. Verify that all ports are assigned to VLAN 1. List the ports that are currently assigned to VLAN 1. _____

9. List the first three actions that are available on the VLAN submenu. Which menu option is used to move a port to a different VLAN? _____

Menu Option	VLAN Menu Option Description	Submenu Options (List Two or More)

Cisco Labs – Semester 3 – Routing and Switching
LAB 3.2 – SWITCH MANAGEMENT VLANS – WORKSHEET

Step 4. Attach a workstation and Telnet to the switch.

Connect the workstation to the switch with a straight-through CAT5 Ethernet cable using port 12 on the switch. Verify that the workstation has IP address, subnet mask, and default gateway settings that are compatible with the switch and router. Telnet to the switch from the workstation DOS prompt.

10. What command did you use? _____

11. Were you able to Telnet to the switch? _____

12. Move port 12 to VLAN 2. What happened to the Telnet session?

    _____

13. With the workstation attached to port 12 on VLAN 2, can you still manage the switch? _____

14. Why or why not? _____

15. Move your workstation connection to port 11 on the switch. Can you Telnet to the switch now?

    _____

16. Why or why not? _____

17. Explain why your Telnet session failed when you moved your workstation from port 11 (VLAN 1) to port 12 (VLAN 2) on the switch.

    _____

    _____

    _____

    _____

Cisco Labs – Semester 3 – Routing and Switching
LAB 3.2 – SWITCH MANAGEMENT VLANS – ANSWERS

Step 1. Console into the LAN switch.
Console into the switch by attaching the workstation serial port to the switch console port. Answer the following questions. Use the switch attached to router Lab-A or another one. (Note: Answers will vary depending on switch model number.)

1. What is the model number of the switch? **Catalyst 1900 series – WS-C1912C-EN**

2. Does this switch have Standard Edition or Enterprise Edition software? **Enterprise Edition**

3. What is the Firmware version of the switch? **V8.01.02**

4. What option on the menu is used to set the IP address of the switch? **N (Network Management)**

5. What option on the switch menu is used to create or modify VLANS? **V (VLAN)**

Step 2. Assign an IP address to the switch.

6. Assign an IP address and subnet mask to the switch. Be sure to use an IP address and subnet mask that are compatible with the network or subnet the switch is currently on. If the switch is connected to router Lab-A, interface E1, as shown in the standard lab setup diagram, then assign a compatible IP address and subnet mask to the switch.

   IP address: 205.7.5.2   Subnet mask: 255.255.255.0

Step 3. Check VLAN configuration options.
(Note: Answers will vary depending on the switch model, firmware version and whether it is Standard or Enterprise Edition.)

7. Select the VLAN option from the menu. How many VLANS can be configured with this switch? **Either 4 or 1005, depending on whether it is Standard or Enterprise Edition**

8. Verify that all ports are assigned to VLAN 1. List the ports that are currently assigned to VLAN 1: **1 to 24, AUI, A, B**

9. List the first three actions that are available on the VLAN submenu. Which menu option is used to move a port to a different VLAN? **[E] VLAN Membership**

Menu Option	VLAN Menu Option Description	Submenu Options (List Two or More)
L	List VLAN	Enter VLAN number or "All"
M	Modify VLAN	Select VLAN
E	VLAN membership	Membership type, VLAN assignment

Cisco Labs – Semester 3 – Routing and Switching
LAB 3.2 – SWITCH MANAGEMENT VLANS – ANSWERS

Step 4. Attach a workstation and Telnet to the switch.
Connect the workstation to the switch with a straight-through CAT5 Ethernet cable using port 12 on the switch. Verify that the workstation has IP address, subnet mask, and default gateway settings that are compatible with the switch and router. Telnet to the switch from the workstation DOS prompt.

10. What command did you use? **Telnet 205.7.5.2**

11. Were you able to Telnet to the switch? **Yes**

12. Move port 12 to VLAN 2. What happened to the Telnet session?
    The Telnet connection failed.

13. With the workstation attached to port 12 on VLAN 2, can you still manage the switch? **No**

14. Why or why not? **Port 12 is not in the management domain VLAN 1.**

15. Move your workstation connection to port 11 on the switch. Can you Telnet to the switch now?
    Yes

16. Why or why not? **Port 11 is in VLAN 1, which is the management domain.**

17. Explain why your Telnet session failed when you moved your workstation from port 11 (VLAN 1) to port 12 (VLAN 2) on the switch. **The management domain for a switch is VLAN 1. All Ethernet ports on the switch are assigned to VLAN 1 by default. When port 12 was assigned to VLAN 2, it was no longer in the management domain of the switch. When the workstation attached is moved to port 11, it is now back in VLAN 1, which is the management domain.**

Cisco Labs – Semester 3 – Routing and Switching
LAB 3.3 – MULTISWITCH VLANS – OVERVIEW
(Estimated time: 60 minutes)

Objectives:
- Console into the switch to determine the firmware version
- Check the IP address and subnet mask for the switch
- Use the Management Console to check VLAN-related menu options
- Check workstation network settings to verify compatibility with the switch
- Create two VLANs that span multiple switches, name them, and then move member ports to them on each switch
- Test VLAN functionality by moving a workstation from one VLAN to another
- Enable Inter-Switch Link (ISL) trunking on trunk ports for the two switches

Background:
In this lab, you will work with Ethernet virtual local-area networks (VLANs). VLANs can be used to separate groups of users based on function rather than physical location. Normally, all the ports on a switch are in the same default VLAN 1. A network administrator can create additional VLANs and move some ports into those VLANs to create isolated groups of users, regardless of where they are physically located. This creates smaller broadcast domains, which helps to reduce and localize network traffic. If a switch with 24 ports is divided into two VLANs of 12 ports each, the users on one VLAN will not be able to access resources (such as servers or printers) on the other VLAN. VLANs can also be created using ports from multiple switches that are "trunked" together on a backbone. For two VLANs to communicate, they must be connected by a router; security can be controlled with router access control lists (ACLs), which will be covered in Lab 6.3.

Cisco Labs – Semester 3 – Routing and Switching
LAB 3.3 – MULTISWITCH VLANS – OVERVIEW

You will console into the switch and use the Management Console user interface menus to view the options available to manage VLANs and to check the current VLAN configuration. You will also use Telnet to access the switch and check some settings, as well as move your connection from one VLAN to another to determine the effects of the management domain. When managing a switch, the management domain is always VLAN 1. The network administrator's workstation must have access to a port in the VLAN 1 management domain. All ports are assigned to VLAN 1 by default. This lab also helps demonstrate how VLANs can be used to separate traffic and reduce broadcast domains.

Tools/Preparation:

Before you start the lab, the teacher or lab assistant should have two switches available with the default VLAN settings, and each switch must be running the Enterprise Edition firmware. If your switches are not, then the Enterprise Edition firmware must be downloaded from the Cisco web site by a person with a CCO login account (your academy contact or instructor). The procedure for upgrading switch firmware will be covered in a subsequent lab. A workstation with HyperTerminal should be available as a console and for Telnetting into the switch. Because there may be only a couple switches available, the instructor should demonstrate this lab at a minimum, and students should work in larger teams to get hands-on experience. While one team is doing switch labs, the others could be doing web-based research on switches at the Cisco web site URLs listed below. Before you begin this lab, you should read Chapter 3, "VLANs," of *Cisco Networking Academy Program: Second-Year Companion Guide*. You should also review Semester 3 online Lesson 3.

Required Resources:
- Two Windows PC workstations with HyperTerminal installed (configured for console connection to switch and compatible IP addresses)
- Two Cisco switches (19xx or 28xx model) with Enterprise Edition software, with at least one 100Base-TX (CAT 5 copper) trunk port (A or B)
- Console cable (rollover)
- CAT 5 Ethernet cable from each workstation to a switch Ethernet port
- CAT 5 crossover cable to connect the switch trunk ports (100Base-TX)

Web Site Resources:
- **LAN switching basics** – http://www.cisco.com/univercd/cc/td/doc/cisintwk/ito_doc/lanswtch.htm
- **General information on all Cisco products (scroll down to Chapter 15, "Switches")** – http://www.cisco.com/univercd/cc/td/doc/pcat/#2
- **1900/2820 series Ethernet switches** – http://www.cisco.com/warp/public/cc/cisco/mkt/switch/cat/c1928/prodlit/s1928_ov.htm
- **2900 series Fast Ethernet switches** – http://www.cisco.com/warp/public/cc/cisco/mkt/switch/cat/2900xl/prodlit/290xl_ov.htm
- **3500 series Gigabit Ethernet switches** – http://www.cisco.com/warp/public/cc/cisco/mkt/switch/cat/3500xl/prodlit/3500x_ov.htm
- **Cisco switch clustering technology** – http://www.cisco.com/warp/public/cc/cisco/mkt/switch/cat/3500xl/prodlit/clust_ov.htm
- **Virtual LANs for 1900/2820 switches** – http://www.cisco.com/univercd/cc/td/doc/product/lan/28201900/1928v8x/eescg8x/02vlans.htm

Cisco Labs – Semester 3 – Routing and Switching
LAB 3.3 – MULTISWITCH VLANS – WORKSHEET

Step 1. Console into the LAN switch.

Console into the switch by attaching the workstation serial port to the switch console port. Answer the following questions. (Note: Answers will vary depending on switch model number). **For this lab, you must have Enterprise Edition software to create VLANs that span multiple switches**. If the switch needs to be upgraded to Enterprise Edition software, refer to Lab 3.4, "Switch Firmware Upgrade." You may need to use the [F] Firmware option from the switch main menu to determine the answers to the following:

1. What is the model number of the switch?
    Switch A: _____
    Switch B: _____

2. Does this switch have Standard Edition or Enterprise Edition software?
    Switch A: _____
    Switch B: _____

3. What is the firmware version of the switch?
    Switch A: _____
    Switch B: _____

4. What option on the switch menu is used to create or modify VLANs?
    Switch A: _____
    Switch B: _____

Step 2. Check the IP address of the switch and the attached workstations.

5. Check the IP address and subnet mask of the switch and workstations to verify that they are compatible and on the same network. Record your settings below:

    Switch A IP: _____   Subnet mask: _____
    Switch B IP: _____   Subnet mask: _____
    Workstation 1 IP: _____   Subnet mask: _____
    Workstation 2 IP: _____   Subnet mask: _____

Step 3. Enter VLAN configuration mode.

6. What is the maximum number of VLANs that can be created? _____

7. Select the [L] List VLANs option from the submenu, and then enter the word **All**. What VLANS are currently listed? _____

Cisco Labs – Semester 3 – Routing and Switching
LAB 3.3 – MULTISWITCH VLANS – WORKSHEET

8. List the options on the VLAN configuration menu and submenus in the following table:

VLAN Menu Options from a Cisco Catalyst 1912 (10 Mbps) Ethernet Switch

Menu Option	VLAN Menu Option Description	Submenu Options (List Two or More)

Step 4. Using the VLAN menu options, configure the VLANs.
Note: The following steps were performed on a Catalyst 1912 WS-C1912C-EN (12-port) switch with Enterprise Edition firmware version V8.01.02 (Switch-A) and Catalyst 1924 WS-C1924C-EN (24-port) switch with Enterprise Edition firmware version V8.01.02 (Switch-B). Your answers may vary.

9. Check the configuration of the default VLAN by selecting [M] Modify VLANs option, and then select VLAN 1. What are the current member ports in VLAN 1?

   _____

10. Create two new Ethernet VLANs, and name them. Give each one a name (such as your last name, plus the number of the VLAN: smith10 or smith20). What names did you give them?

   _____

   For the two VLANs you create, use numbers 10 and 20. Assign an SAID to each VLAN using the [I] 802.10 SAID VLANs option. Use SAID 10 and 20 for VLAN 10 and 20. Assign the first half of the ports to VLAN 10 and the second half to VLAN 20. Repeat this on Switch B using the same names, the same VLAN number, and the same SAID.

Step 5. Enable "trunking" on port B of both Switch A and Switch B.
Under VLAN configuration, select [T] Trunk Configuration and select port B. In the Trunk B Configuration menu, select [T] Trunking and then select 1 to turn on trunking. Repeat for Switch A and Switch B. By default, 1 to 1005 VLANs are allowed to use the trunk port.

Note: You need to use a CAT 5 crossover cable to connect Switch A port B to Switch B port B. This assumes that each of your switches has at least one 100BaseTX (CAT 5 copper) trunk or backbone port (port A or B). Some switches have one 100BaseTX and one 100BaseFX (fiber) trunk port; some have two 100BaseFX ports, depending on the model.

Cisco Labs – Semester 3 – Routing and Switching
LAB 3.3 – MULTISWITCH VLANS – WORKSHEET

Step 6. Test the functionality of the two VLANs.

To see your VLAN in action, set up two workstations and verify that the IP addresses are on the same subnetwork. Restart computers as needed. From workstation 1, plug the Ethernet cable from the NIC card into a port on Switch A VLAN 10. From workstation 2, plug the Ethernet cable from the NIC card into a port on Switch B VLAN 10.

11. Issue a ping to each workstation. Was the ping successful? _____

12. Now take workstation 2's Ethernet port from the switch, and plug it into Switch B VLAN 20. Ping each workstation again. Was the ping successful? _____

Cisco Labs - Semester 3 – Routing and Switching
LAB 3.3 – MULTISWITCH VLANS – ANSWERS

Step 1. Console into the LAN switch.
Console into the switch by attaching the workstation serial port to the switch console port. Answer the following questions. (Note: Answers will vary depending on switch model number.)

1. What is the model number of the switch?
    Switch A: **Cisco Catalyst 1900 series WS-C1912C-EN**
    Switch B: **Cisco Catalyst 1900 series WS-C1924C-EN**

2. Does this switch have Standard Edition or Enterprise Edition software?
    Switch A: **Enterprise Edition**
    Switch B: **Enterprise Edition**

3. Use the menu option [F] to determine the Firmware version in this switch:
    Switch-A: **V8.01.02**
    Switch-B: **V8.01.02**

4. What option on the switch menu is used to create or modify VLANS?
    Switch-A: **[V] Virtual LAN**
    Switch-B: **[V] Virtual LAN**

Step 2. Check the IP address of the router, the switch, and the attached workstations.

5. Check the IP address and subnet mask of the router, switch, and workstations to verify that they are compatible and on the same network. If the switch is connected to router Lab-A, interface E1, as shown in the standard lab setup diagram, then assign IP addresses, subnet masks, and default gateways as appropriate. Record your settings below:

    Switch A IP: **205.7.5.1**   Subnet mask: **255.255.255.0**
    Switch B IP: **205.7.5.2**   Subnet mask: **255.255.255.0**
    Workstation 1 IP: **205.7.5.3** Subnet mask: **255.255.255.0**
    Workstation 2 IP: **205.7.5.4** Subnet mask: **255.255.255.0**

Step 3. Enter VLAN configuration mode.

6. What is the maximum number of VLANS that can be created? **4 to 1005**

7. Select the [L] List VLANs option from the submenu and then enter the word "**All**." What VLANS are currently listed? **VLAN 1 (default Ethernet), and possibly others**

Cisco Labs - Semester 3 – Routing and Switching
LAB 3.3 – MULTISWITCH VLANS – ANSWERS

8. List the options on the VLAN configuration menu and submenus in the following table:

VLAN Menu Options from a Cisco Catalyst 1912 (10 Mbps) Ethernet Switch

Menu Option	VLAN Menu Option Description	Submenu Options (List Two or More)
L	List VLAN	Enter VLAN number or "All"
M	Modify VLAN	Select VLAN
E	VLAN membership	Membership type, VLAN assignment
T	Trunk configuration	Selects trunk port (A or B)
P	VTP statistics	Virtual Trunking Protocol (VTP) statistics
A	Add VLAN	Ethernet, FDDI, Token Ring
D	Delete a VLAN	Select VLAN to delete (1 to 1005)
S	VLAN membership servers	VLAN membership policy server
W	VTP password	Set and confirm VTP password
X	Exit	Exit to main menu

Step 4. Using the VLAN menu options, configure the VLANs.
Note: The following steps were performed on a Catalyst 1912 WS-C1912C-EN (12-port) switch with Enterprise Edition firmware version V8.01.02. Your answers may vary.

9. Check the configuration of the default VLAN by selecting [M] Modify VLANs option, and then select VLAN 1. What are the current member ports in VLAN 1? **Ports 1-12, AUI, A and B**

10. Create a new Ethernet VLAN and name it. Give it a name (such as your last name plus a number: smith1). What name did you give it? **Smith1**

Step 6. Test the functioning of the two VLANs.

11. Issue a ping to each workstation. Was the ping successful? **Yes; if done properly, it should be a success.**

12. Now take workstation 2's Ethernet port from the switch and plug it into one of the ports on VLAN 2 (ports 7-12). Ping each workstation again. Was the ping successful? **No; the two workstations are on different VLANs, so there should be no communication.**

Cisco Labs – Semester 3 – Routing and Switching
LAB 3.4 – SWITCH FIRMWARE UPDATE/TFTP – OVERVIEW
(Estimated time: 20 minutes)

Router Name - LAB A
Router Type - 2514
E 0 = 192.5.5.1
E 1 = 205.7.5.1
S 0 = 201.100.11.1
SM = 255.255.255.0

Router Name - LAB B
Router Type - 2503
E 0 = 219.17.100.1
S 0 = 199.6.13.1
S 1 = 201.100.11.2
SM = 255.255.255.0

Router Name - LAB C
Router Type - 2503
E 0 = 223.8.151.1
S 0 = 204.204.7.1
S 1 = 199.6.13.2
SM = 255.255.255.0

Router Name - LAB D
Router Type - 2501
E 0 = 210.93.105.1
S 1 = 204.204.7.2
SM = 255.255.255.0

Router Name - LAB E
Router Type - 2501
E 0 = 210.93.105.2
SM = 255.255.255.0

LEGEND
= ROUTER   User Exec Password = cisco
= HUB   Enable Secret Exec Password = class
= LAN SWITCH   Terminal vty Password = cisco
= CONSOLE CABLE

Objectives:
- Display information about current switch firmware
- Review switch memory and update options
- Use a TFTP server to update a switch to a new version of the firmware software

Background:
As new versions of the Cisco switch firmware software become available, it is necessary to periodically update the existing firmware image to support the latest features and improvements. In this lab, you will determine what version of firmware your switch is currently running and will become familiar with the requirements for updating to a newer version. The process of downloading a new switch firmware image from Cisco Connection Online (CCO) will also be reviewed. In addition, the TFTP server method of updating your firmware will be covered. The primary goal of this lab is to get your switch updated to Enterprise Edition.

Note: If your switch currently has an older version of the standard edition firmware, you must update to the newest version of Standard Edition first; then you can update to Enterprise Edition.

Cisco Labs – Semester 3 – Routing and Switching
LAB 3.4 – SWITCH FIRMWARE UPDATE/TFTP – OVERVIEW

Tools/Preparation:
Before you start the lab, you will need to connect a PC workstation with HyperTerminal to a switch using the switch's console interface with a rollover cable. You will also need an Ethernet connection to the switch. The instructor or lab assistant should have a Windows 9x PC with a TFTP server installed and should have the latest downloaded firmware image on the PC hard drive. Verify that the TFTP server is accessible by the switch. The Cisco TFTP server and latest firmware updates can be downloaded from the web sites listed below. Because there may be only one switch available, the instructor should demonstrate this lab at a minimum, and students should work in larger teams to get hands-on experience. While one team is doing switch labs, the others could be doing web-based research on switches at the Cisco web site URLs listed below.

You should review Chapters 2 and 3 in *Cisco Networking Academy Program: Second-Year Companion Guide,* and review Semester 3 online Lesson 3 before starting this lab. Although the instructions in this lab for downloading the firmware image software can be done only by someone with a CCO account, you should read through them to become familiar with the process.

Required Resources:
- PC with monitor, keyboard, mouse, power cords, and other essentials
- Windows operating system (Windows 95, 98, NT, or 2000) installed on the PC
- HyperTerminal program configured for router console connection
- PC connected to the switch console port with a rollover cable
- PC connected to a hub that the router is connected to, or a crossover cable directly to the router
- PC on a network that the router can send and receive to while running a TFTP daemon (server)

Web Site Resources:
- **LAN switching basics** – http://www.cisco.com/univercd/cc/td/doc/cisintwk/ito_doc/lanswtch.htm
- **General information on all Cisco products (scroll down to Chapter 15, "Switches")** – http://www.cisco.com/univercd/cc/td/doc/pcat/#2
- **1900/2820 series Ethernet switches** – http://www.cisco.com/warp/public/cc/cisco/mkt/switch/cat/c1928/prodlit/s1928_ov.htm
- **2900 series Fast Ethernet switches** – http://www.cisco.com/warp/public/cc/cisco/mkt/switch/cat/2900xl/prodlit/290xl_ov.htm
- **3500 series Gigabit Ethernet switches** – http://www.cisco.com/warp/public/cc/cisco/mkt/switch/cat/3500xl/prodlit/3500x_ov.htm
- **Cisco switch clustering technology** – http://www.cisco.com/warp/public/cc/cisco/mkt/switch/cat/3500xl/prodlit/clust_ov.htm
- **Virtual LANs for 1900/2820 switches** – http://www.cisco.com/univercd/cc/td/doc/product/lan/28201900/1928v8x/eescg8x/02vlans.htm

Notes:
_____

_____

_____

_____

Cisco Labs – Semester 3 – Routing and Switching
LAB 3.4 – SWITCH FIRMWARE UPDATE/TFTP – WORKSHEET

Step 1. Download the new switch firmware version.
Go to **www.cisco.com** and log in with your CCO account (your instructor or academy contact should be able to do this). Click Software Center under Services and Support. Click LAN Switching Software, and then click Catalyst 1900. Click Download Cisco Catalyst 1900 Software Image.

Note: If you have Standard Edition firmware, you must upgrade to the newest version and then upgrade to Enterprise Edition. Depending on the version of the switch firmware, you may not be able to upgrade to Enterprise Edition firmware.

Step 2. Log in to the switch.
Select option [M] for menu and then [F] for firmware.

Step 3. Check the current firmware version.
If your switch does not have Enterprise Edition software, you will need to upgrade to the Standard Edition version of the current firmware; then you can upgrade to the same version of Enterprise Edition.

1. What version of firmware is the switch currently running? _____

Step 4. Set the IP address of the switch.
Under the main menu, select [I] IP configuration. Then select [I] for IP address and [S] for subnet mask. Make sure that the IP address and subnet mask are on the same network as the TFTP server.

Step 5. Prepare for the firmware update.
A. Set the IP address of the TFTP server using option [S] TFTP server name or IP address.

B. Set the filename of the upgrade using [F] Filename for firmware upgrades

Step 6. Install the firmware update.
In the firmware configuration, select [T] for system TFTP upgrade. The switch asks you to confirm the upgrade. After you confirm that you want to proceed with firmware upgrade, the switch will become unresponsive for approximately 1 minute. This is normal.

Step 7. Confirm the firmware upgrade.
From main menu select **[M] for Menu** then **[F] for Firmware**.

2. What version of firmware is the switch running? _____

Cisco Labs – Semester 3 – Routing and Switching
LAB 3.4 – SWITCH FIRMWARE UPDATE/TFTP – ANSWERS

1. What version of firmware is the switch currently running? **Versions 8.xx.xx Standard Edition.** **(Your answers will vary.)**

2. What version of firmware is the switch currently running? **Version 9.00.02 Enterprise Edition** **(Your answers will vary.)**

Cisco Labs – Semester 3 – Routing and Switching
LAB 4.1 – SWITCHED LAN DESIGN – OVERVIEW
(Estimated time: 60 minutes)

Objectives:
- Analyze requirements for a simple local-area network with Internet access.
- Design a Layer 1 and 2 topology based on switched Ethernet and given requirements
- Determine the type, number, and location of Ethernet switches and cabling required based on wiring closet locations for MDF and multiple IDFs, and a simple floor plan
- Research the Cisco web site and those of Cisco vendors for models and costs

Background:
This lab helps prepare you for the Threaded Case Study. In this lab, you will be given some basic requirements for a small LAN that spans multiple buildings. Your focus is on the physical topology and data link layer components. The goal is to replace an aging 10Base2 thinnet Ethernet network with current technology Ethernet switches and cabling based on structured cabling standards and the extended star topology. You will decide which type of Ethernet switches to use and where to place them. You will also determine which type of cabling to use based on the requirements given. Your users will need access to several servers, and they will need to be placed in the most effective locations. You will use vendor catalogs and web-based research to find out the model numbers and costs of various switched Ethernet solutions.

Tools/Preparation:
This is a research lab and will not require a physical lab setup. You will need access to data communications equipment catalogs and to the web for research. Use the Cisco web site URLs listed below. Work in teams of three or more. Before you begin this lab, you should read Chapter 4, "LAN Design," in *Cisco Networking Academy Program: Second-Year Companion Guide*. You should also review Semester 3 online Lesson 4.

Required Resources:
- PC with Internet access for product research
- Data communication vendors catalogs

Web Site Resources:
- **LAN switching basics** – http://www.cisco.com/univercd/cc/td/doc/cisintwk/ito_doc/lanswtch.htm
- **General information on all Cisco products (scroll down to Chapter 15, "Switches")** – http://www.cisco.com/univercd/cc/td/doc/pcat/#2
- **1900/2820 series Ethernet switches** – http://www.cisco.com/warp/public/cc/cisco/mkt/switch/cat/c1928/prodlit/s1928_ov.htm
- **2900 series Fast Ethernet switches** – http://www.cisco.com/warp/public/cc/cisco/mkt/switch/cat/2900xl/prodlit/290xl_ov.htm
- **3500 series Gigabit Ethernet switches** – http://www.cisco.com/warp/public/cc/cisco/mkt/switch/cat/3500xl/prodlit/3500x_ov.htm
- **Cisco switch clustering technology** – http://www.cisco.com/warp/public/cc/cisco/mkt/switch/cat/3500xl/prodlit/clust_ov.htm

Cisco Labs – Semester 3 – Routing and Switching
LAB 4.1 – SWITCHED LAN DESIGN – WORKSHEET

Step 1. Review the requirements.

You are designing a LAN for a small company with one location and several buildings that need to be interconnected. Use the building diagram and requirements listed to decide what type of switches and cabling should be run where.

1. There are three buildings in a campus arrangement – the Administration, Engineering, and Manufacturing buildings.
2. Administration is building A, Engineering is building B, and Manufacturing is building C.
3. The Administration building is between Engineering and Manufacturing.
4. The distances between the buildings are shown in the diagram.
5. Each of the buildings has a wiring closet.
6. The wiring closet for the POP is in the Administration building.
7. 35 PCs and 5 printers need network access in the Administration building.
8. 27 PCs and 3 printers need network access in the Engineering building.
9. 18 PCs and 2 printers need network access in the Manufacturing building.
10. The customer wants the fastest Ethernet switching technology available for the backbone.
11. The customer wants to keep cost down for the workstation connections.
12. All users need access to the Internet and two centralized file and print servers.
13. Engineering users need local access to a high-performance departmental server.

XYZ Company Data Network

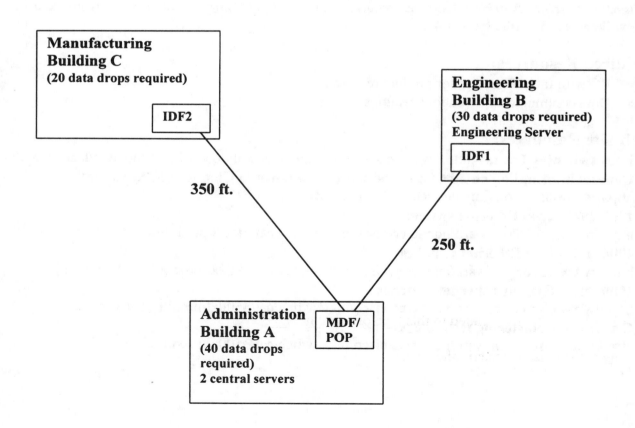

Cisco Labs – Semester 3 – Routing and Switching
LAB 4.1 – SWITCHED LAN DESIGN – WORKSHEET

Fill in the table and answer the following questions based on your knowledge of Ethernet switching equipment, routers, and structured cabling standards.

1. Administration Building A – MDF/POP Equipment (40 Data)

Equipment Type	Model No.	Qty.	No./Type Ports	Description/Function	Cost

2. Engineering Building B – IDF 1 Equipment (30 Data)

Equipment Type	Model No.	Qty.	No./Type Ports	Description/Function	Cost

3. Manufacturing Building C – IDF 2 Equipment (20 Data)

Equipment Type	Model No.	Qty.	No./Type Ports	Description/Function	Cost

4. What type of cabling will you run from the switches in the wiring closets to the users' desktop workstations, and why? _____

5. What will be the speed of these links? _____

6. What are some terms related to this type of cabling? _____

7. What type of cabling will you run from the MDF/POP in building A to buildings B and C, and why? _____

8. What will be the speed of these links? _____

9. What are some terms related to this type of cabling? _____

10. Why is the wiring closet in the Administration building the best place for the MDF?

_____

Cisco Labs – Semester 3 – Routing and Switching
LAB 4.1 – SWITCHED LAN DESIGN – ANSWERS

Answer the following questions based on your knowledge of Ethernet switching equipment and structured cabling standards.

1. Administration Building A – MDF/POP Equipment (40 Data)

Equipment Type	Model No.	Qty.	No./Type Ports	Description/Function	Cost (Varies)
Ethernet switch	3508G-XL	1	(4) 1000SX fiber (4) 1000TX copper	Gigabit backbone switch aggregation point (center of star)	
Ethernet switch	3548-XL	1	(48) 10/100TX copper (2) 1000TX copper	Fast Ethernet (10/100) switch for servers and desktops with 2 Gb copper uplink to 3508	
Router	2620	1	(1) 10/100TX (2) WAN serial	Internet router with Fast Ethernet interface to LAN	

2. Engineering Building B – IDF 1 Equipment (30 Data)

Equipment Type	Model No.	Qty.	No./Type Ports	Description/Function	Cost
Ethernet Switch	3524-XL	1	(24) 10/100TX copper (1) 1000TX cop (1) 1000SX fiber	Fast Ethernet (10/100) switch for servers and desktops with gigabit fiber uplink to 3508 in MDF	
Ethernet Switch	3512-XL	1	(12) 10/100TX copper (2) 1000TX copper	Fast Ethernet (10/100) switch for server and desktops with gigabit copper uplink to 3524	

3. Manufacturing Building C – IDF 2 Equipment (20 data)

Equipment Type	Model No.	Qty.	No./Type Ports	Description/Function	Cost
Ethernet Switch	3524-XL	1	(24) 10/100TX copper (1) 1000SX fiber	Fast Ethernet (10/100) switch for desktops with gigabit fiber uplink to 3508 in MDF	

4. What type of cabling will you run from the switches in the wiring closets to the users' desktop workstations, and why? **CAT5E UTP; distance is less than 100 ft., and cost is a concern**
5. What will be the speed of these links? **Fast Ethernet (100 Mbps) full-duplex = 200 Mbps**
6. What are some terms related to this type of cabling? **Horizontal, copper, 100BaseTX**
7. What type of cabling will you run from the MDF/POP in building A to buildings B and C, and why? **Multimode fiber due to distance, resistance to electrical problems, and security**
8. What will be the speed of these links? **Gigabit Ethernet (1000 Mbps) full-duplex = 2000 Mbps**
9. What are some terms related to this type of cabling? **Vertical, backbone, fiber, 1000BaseSX**
10. Why is the wiring closet in the Administration building the best place for the MDF? **It is centrally located, and the point of presence (POP) for the telco is there.**

Cisco Labs – Semester 3 – Routing and Switching
LAB 5.1 – ROUTED VS. ROUTING PROTOCOLS – OVERVIEW
(Estimated time: 30 minutes)

Router Name - LAB A
Router Type - 2514
E 0 = 192.5.5 1
E 1 = 205.7.5 1
S 0 = 201.100.11 1
SM = 255.255.255.0

Router Name - LAB C
Router Type - 2503
E 0 = 223.8.151 1
S 0 = 204.204.7 1
S 1 = 199.6.13 2
SM = 255.255.255.0

Router Name - LAB E
Router Type - 2501
E 0 = 210.93.105.2
SM = 255.255.255.0

Router Name - LAB B
Router Type - 2503
E 0 = 219.17.100.1
S 0 = 199.6.13 1
S 1 = 201.100.11 2
SM = 255.255.255.0

Router Name - LAB D
Router Type - 2501
E 0 = 210.93.105.1
S 1 = 204.204.7 2
SM = 255.255.255.0

LEGEND

= ROUTER	User Exec Password = cisco
= HUB	Enable Secret Exec Password = class
= LAN SWITCH	Terminal vty Password = cisco
= CONSOLE CABLE	

Objectives:
- Compare the characteristics of routed and routing protocols, and cite examples of each
- Examine a router to determine which routed and routing protocols are active
- Practice commands to determine which routed and routing protocols are supported
  (**show IP route**, **show protocols**, **show running config**, **setup command router ?**)
- Match terms for routed and routing protocols
- Diagram the relationship between routed, routing, dynamic, static, Layer 3 protocol, interior vs. exterior, distance vector, link state, and hybrid

Background:
This lab will reinforce your knowledge and understanding of routed and routing protocols, the primary protocols that enable a router to function. You will review examples of each type of protocol and use various IOS commands at the router to discover which routed and routing protocols are currently running or active on the router. You will also use the Help facility to explore what protocols the router could support that may not be currently running. Understanding the distinction between routed and routing protocols is critical to mastering the concepts of internetworking.

Cisco Labs – Semester 3 – Routing and Switching
LAB 5.1 – ROUTED VS. ROUTING PROTOCOLS – OVERVIEW

Routed Protocols

Protocols are the language or rules of communication between devices on a network. Routed protocols are those protocols that can be routed. Layer 3 (network) addressing information is put in the header of the data packet, which enables the packets to get from one network to another. These protocols are also called **routable** protocols, meaning that they are able to be routed. For a protocol to be routable, the addressing method must have at least two parts: a network number and a node number. The network portion of the address allows a packet to be routed from one network to another. All devices in a network normally run the same routed protocol-like common language to communicate. Most LAN protocols are routed protocols.

The most common routed protocol is the Internet Protocol (IP), which is an international standard. IP is sometimes referred to as TCP/IP, but TCP is actually a transport (Layer 4) protocol and is not involved directly with the routable IP protocol at Layer 3. For a device (workstation, server, router) to communicate on the Internet, it must be running the Internet protocol IP. IP addresses are 32 bits and have a network number and a node number assigned by a network administrator. Other routed LAN protocols are Novell's IPX, AppleTalk, and DECnet.

Routing Protocols

Routing protocols are used by routers to communicate between themselves to dynamically exchange information about the networks they can reach and the desirability of the routes available. Typically called dynamic routing protocols, these protocols facilitate the process of routing. They are not needed in a small network if only static routes are used. Routing protocol packets operate independently of the routed data packets that pass through the network and take up bandwidth. No information in an IP packet is related to the routing protocol being used. Routers periodically send information about routes (routing tables) to each other so that when they receive a routed protocol packet (such as IP), they know where to send it. If we think of the routed protocol address like an address on a letter, the routing protocol is like a messenger running between the routers to tell them which routes are open and which ones are the fastest. Routing protocols can be broadly categorized based on whether they are interior or exterior; they also are subdivided by type: distance vector or link state.

Interior Routing Protocols

Interior routing protocols are used within a private network. As an example, a company might have a number of LANs in different geographical locations that are connected by routers and dedicated WAN links (such as T1 or Frame Relay). If all these routers are under a common administration or autonomous system (not connected through the Internet), then they would use an interior routing protocol. Interior routing protocols can be subdivided by type: distance vector, link state, and hybrid. The distinction is in what metrics they use to select routes and in how they store and exchange routing table updates.

Exterior Routing Protocols

Exterior routing protocols are used to communicate between autonomous systems and over the Internet. Examples of exterior protocols include Border Gateway Protocol (BGP) and Exterior Gateway Protocol (EGP). BGP is the most common; the latest version is BGP4.

Cisco Labs – Semester 3 – Routing and Switching
LAB 5.1 – ROUTED VS. ROUTING PROTOCOLS – OVERVIEW

Tools/Preparation:

Before you start the lab, the teacher or lab assistant should have the standard router lab with all five routers set up with a routing protocol enabled (RIP or IGRP). Workstations with HyperTerminal should be available to console into the routers. You may work individually or in teams. Before beginning this lab, you should read Chapter 5, "Routing Protocols: IGRP," of *Cisco Networking Academy Program: Second-Year Companion Guide*. You should also review Semester 3 online Lesson 5.

Required Resources:

- Standard Cisco five-router lab setup with hubs and switches
- Workstations to connect to the routers
- Console cable (rollover)
- CAT 5 Ethernet cable from the workstation to the hub or switch

Web Site Resources:

- **Routing basics** – http://www.cisco.com/univercd/cc/td/doc/cisintwk/ito_doc/routing.htm
- **RIP routing protocol** – http://www.cisco.com/univercd/cc/td/doc/cisintwk/ito_doc/rip.htm
- **IGRP routing protocol** – http://www.cisco.com/univercd/cc/td/doc/cisintwk/ito_doc/igrp.htm
- **EIGRP routing protocol** – http://www.cisco.com/warp/public/103/1.html
- **OSPF routing protocol** – http://www.cisco.com/univercd/cc/td/doc/cisintwk/ito_doc/ospf.htm
- **BGP routing protocol** – http://www.cisco.com/univercd/cc/td/doc/cisintwk/ito_doc/bgp.htm
- **EGP routing protocol** – http://www.whatis.com/egp.htm
- **Tech tips for IGRP and EIGRP routing protocol** – http://www.cisco.com/warp/public/103/index.shtml
- **Configuring IP routing protocols** – http://www.cisco.com/univercd/cc/td/doc/product/software/ios100/rpcg/66010.htm
- **Basic IP addressing and troubleshooting guide** – http://www.cisco.com/warp/public/779/smbiz/service/troubleshooting/ts_ip.htm

Notes:

_____
_____
_____
_____
_____
_____
_____
_____
_____
_____
_____

Cisco Labs –Semester 3 – Routing and Switching
LAB 5.1 – ROUTED VS. ROUTING PROTOCOLS – WORKSHEET

Step 1. Review interior gateway routing protocols.

1. The following table lists some of the most common interior routing protocols. Fill in the table with the information requested based on your knowledge. You may look up answers in the text or online, or use the web site resources.

Interior Gateway Routing Protocols

Routing Protocol	Protocol Type (Distance Vector, Link State, Hybrid)	Developed By (Vendor/ Standards)	Characteristics/Notes
RIP v1 and v2 (Routing Information Protocol)			
IGRP (Interior Gateway Routing Protocol)			
OSPF (Open Shortest Path First)			
EIGRP (Enhanced Interior Gateway Routing Protocol)			

Step 2. Check to see which routing protocols the router can understand.
Routing protocols enable the router to learn about other routes. To see the list of IP routing protocols supported and the networks and routes that have been learned, use the **show IP route** command from user mode.

    Router> show IP route

2. What are some of the routing protocols supported? _____

    You can also see the routing protocols supported in an alphabetical list with definitions. Enter privileged mode, then configuration mode, and then use Help by typing **router ?**.

    Router#(config)# router ?

3. Are the routing protocols listed the same? _____

Cisco Labs – Semester 3 – Routing and Switching
LAB 5.1 – ROUTED VS. ROUTING PROTOCOLS – WORKSHEET

Step 3. Determine which routing protocols are in use.
You can see which interfaces and networks are defined for the routing protocols in use. This means that they will advertise and receive routing updates on those interfaces. Use the **show run** command to see which protocol is active and on which interfaces.

    Router# show run

4. What routing protocol is being used, and which networks will be advertised?

    _____

    _____

Step 4. Check to see which routed protocols the router can understand.
Routed (or routable) protocols enable packets to move from one network to another. To see the list of routed protocols supported, enter privileged mode and then configuration mode, and use Help by typing **?**. You will see many commands, but you should be able to pick out the routed protocols.

    Router(config)# ?

5. Which routed protocols can you see in the list? _____

Step 5. Determine which routed protocols are in use.
Each router in this lab is directly connected to at least one network, and most routers are connected to two or more networks.

    router> show protocols

6. Which routed protocols are in use? _____ On which interface(s)? _____

    _____

Cisco Labs – Semester 3 – Routing and Switching
LAB 5.1 – ROUTED VS. ROUTING PROTOCOLS – WORKSHEET

Step 6. Fill in the tree diagram of routed and routing protocols.

7. Fill in the boxes on the tree diagram showing the relationship and protocol names for the more common routed and routing protocols. This will help you visualize the tree when working with these protocols. Start at the top with routed and routing protocols, and then branch off into interior exterior, distance vector, link state, and so on. Use the abbreviations and acronyms in the legend at the bottom to fill in the boxes. You must use them all.

Legend:
IP = Internet Protocol, IPX = Internetwork Packet Exchange, A/T = AppleTalk,
D.V. = Distance Vector, L.S. = Link State, HYB = Hybrid, BGP = Border Gateway Protocol,
EGP = Exterior Gateway Protocol, RIP = Routing Information Protocol, IGRP = Interior
Gateway Routing Protocol, OSPF = Open Shortest Path First, EIGRP = Enhanced Interior
Gateway Routing Protocol

Cisco Labs –Semester 3 – Routing and Switching
LAB 5.1 – ROUTED VS. ROUTING PROTOCOLS – ANSWERS

Step 1. Review interior gateway routing protocols.

1. The following table lists some of the most common interior routing protocols. Fill in the table with the information requested based on your knowledge. You may look up answers in the text or online, or use the web site resources.

Interior Gateway Routing Protocols

Routing Protocol	Protocol Type (Distance Vector, Link State, Hybrid)	Developed By (Vendor/ Standards)	Characteristics/Notes
RIP v1 and v2 (Routing information protocol)	Distance vector	IP standard	Oldest, widely supported; uses only hop count as metric. Okay for simple networks. New version is RIP 2. Sends all or a portion of routing tables in routing-update messages to its neighbors.
IGRP (Interior Gateway Routing Protocol)	Distance vector	Cisco proprietary	Similar to RIP, but uses other metrics such as bandwidth and delay to determine the best path.
OSPF (Open Shortest Path First)	Link state	IP standard IETF	Sends link-state advertisements (LSAs) to other routers. Information on attached interfaces, the metrics used, and other variables is included in the OSPF LSAs. As the OSPF routers accumulate link-state information, they use the SPF algorithm to calculate the shortest path to each node.
EIGRP (Enhanced Interior Gateway Routing Protocol)	Hybrid	Cisco proprietary	EIGRP is an enhanced version of IGRP. The same distance vector technology found in IGRP is also used in EIGRP, and the underlying distance information remains unchanged. The convergence properties and the operating efficiency of this protocol have improved significantly.

Cisco Labs – Semester 3 – Routing and Switching
LAB 5.1 – ROUTED VS. ROUTING PROTOCOLS – ANSWERS

Step 2. Check to see which routing protocols the router can understand.
Routing protocols enable the router to learn about other routes. To see the list of IP routing protocols supported and the networks and routes that have been learned, use the **show IP route** command from user mode.

Router> show IP route

2. What are some of the routing protocols supported? **R (RIP), I (IGRP), E (EIGRP), O (OSPF), and so on**

Codes: C = Connected, S = Static, I = IGRP, R =RIP, M = Mobile, B = BGP,
D = EIGRP, EX - EIGRP external, O = OSPF, IA = OSPF interarea,
N1 - OSPF NSSA external type 1, N2 = OSPF NSSA external type 2,
E1 = OSPF external type 1, E2 = OSPF external type 2, E = EGP,
i = IS-IS, L1 = IS-IS level-1, L2 = IS-IS level-2, * = candidate default,
U = per-user static route, o = ODR
(Routing table omitted)

3. You can also see the routing protocols supported in an alphabetical list with definitions. Enter privileged mode and then configuration mode, and then use Help by typing **router ?**. Are the routing protocols listed the same? **Yes**

Router#config t

Router#(config)# router ?
bgp	Border Gateway Protocol (BGP)
egp	Exterior Gateway Protocol (EGP)
eigrp	Enhanced Interior Gateway Routing Protocol (EIGRP)
igrp	Interior Gateway Routing Protocol (IGRP)
isis	ISO IS-IS
iso-igrp	IGRP for OSI networks
mobile	Mobile routes
odr	On-demand stub routes
ospf	Open Shortest Path First (OSPF)
rip	Routing Information Protocol (RIP)
static	Static routes
traffic-engineering	Traffic engineered routes

Cisco Labs – Semester 3 – Routing and Switching
LAB 5.1 – ROUTED VS. ROUTING PROTOCOLS – ANSWERS

Step 3. Determine which routing protocols are in use.
You can see which interfaces and networks are defined for the routing protocols in use. This means that they will advertise and receive routing updates on those interfaces. Use the **show run** command to see which protocol is active and on which interfaces.

   Router# **show run**

4.   What routing protocol is being used, and which networks will be advertised? **RIP; networks 192.5.5.0, 201.100.11.0, 205.7.5.0 will be both sending and receiving RIP advertisements. (Answers will vary.)**

   (This is a portion of the **show run** command relating to routing protocols.)
   router rip
    network 192.5.5.0
    network 201.100.11.0
    network 205.7.5.0

Step 4. Check to see which routed protocols the router can understand.
Routed (or routable) protocols enable packets to move from one network to another. To see the list of routed protocols supported, enter privileged mode and then configuration mode, and use Help by typing **?**. You will see many commands, but you should be able to pick out the routed protocols.

   Router(config)# ?

5.   Which routed protocols can you see in the list? **AppleTalk, DECnet, IP, IPX**

Step 5. Determine which routed protocols are in use.
Each router in this lab is directly connected to at least one network, and most routers are connected to two or more networks.

   router> **show protocols**

6.   Which routed protocols are in use? **IP and IPX**   On which interface(s)? **Ethernet 0**
     (Answers will vary.)
     LAB-A#sh proto
     Global values:
       Internet Protocol routing is enabled
       IPX routing is enabled
     Ethernet0 is up, line protocol is down
       Internet address is 192.5.5.1/24
       IPX address is 9E.0000.0c76.e066
     Ethernet1 is up, line protocol is down
       Internet address is 205.7.5.1/24
     Serial0 is down, line protocol is down
       Internet address is 201.100.11.1/24
     Serial1 is administratively down, line protocol is down

Cisco Labs – Semester 3 – Routing and Switching
LAB 5.1 – ROUTED VS. ROUTING PROTOCOLS – WORKSHEET

Step 6. Fill in the tree diagram of routed and routing protocols.

7. Fill in the boxes on the tree diagram showing the relationship and protocol names for the more common routed and routing protocols. This will help you visualize the tree when working with these protocols. Start at the top with routed and routing protocols, and then branch off into interior exterior, distance vector, link state, and so on. Use the abbreviations and acronyms in the legend at the bottom to fill in the boxes. You must use them all.

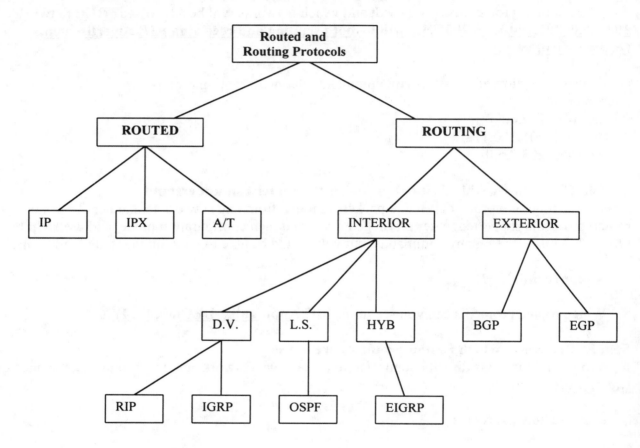

Legend:
IP = Internet Protocol, IPX = Internetwork Packet Exchange, A/T = AppleTalk, D.V. = Distance Vector, L.S. = Link State, HYB = Hybrid, BGP = Border Gateway Protocol, EGP = Exterior Gateway Protocol, RIP = Routing Information Protocol, IGRP = Interior Gateway Routing Protocol, OSPF = Open Shortest Path First, EIGRP = Enhanced Interior Gateway Routing Protocol

Cisco Labs –Semester 3 – Routing and Switching
LAB 5.2 – MIGRATING RIP TO IGRP – OVERVIEW
(Estimated time: 30 minutes)

Router Name - LAB A
Router Type - 2514
E 0 = 192.5.5.1
E 1 = 205.7.5.1
S 0 = 201.100.11.1
SM = 255.255.255.0

Router Name - LAB B
Router Type - 2503
E 0 = 219.17.100.1
S 0 = 199.6.13.1
S 1 = 201.100.11.2
SM = 255.255.255.0

Router Name - LAB C
Router Type - 2503
E 0 = 223.8.151.1
S 0 = 204.204.7.1
S 1 = 199.6.13.2
SM = 255.255.255.0

Router Name - LAB D
Router Type - 2501
E 0 = 210.93.105.1
S 1 = 204.204.7.2
SM = 255.255.255.0

Router Name - LAB E
Router Type - 2501
E 0 = 210.93.105.2
SM = 255.255.255.0

LEGEND

= ROUTER   User Exec Password = cisco

= HUB   Enable Secret Exec Password = class

= LAN SWITCH   Terminal vty Password = cisco

= CONSOLE CABLE

Objectives:
- Verify that the routing protocols are working properly
- Check routing table and interpret network entries
- Check for static routes, and remove them if necessary
- Compare RIP to IGRP based on administrative distance
- Convert a RIP-based router network to IGRP

Background:
In this lab, you will work with two dynamic interior routing protocols: Router Information Protocol (RIP) and Interior Gateway Routing Protocol (IGRP). Routing protocols are used by routers to communicate between themselves to dynamically exchange information about the networks they can reach and the desirability of the routes available. Routed protocols (such as IP and IPX) are those protocols that can be routed between networks to enable packets to get from one location to another. Routers can run multiple routing and routed protocols.

Cisco Labs – Semester 3 – Routing and Switching
LAB 5.2 – MIGRATING RIP TO IGRP – OVERVIEW

Both RIP and IGRP are distance-vector routing protocols. RIP is the oldest routing protocol and uses only hop count as a metric to determine the best path or route. IGRP is a Cisco proprietary protocol that uses hop count and other metrics such as bandwidth and delay to determine the best path. It may be desirable for a router network using RIP as the IP routing protocol to convert to IGRP, which has almost no hop count limitation and which uses bandwidth as a metric. This would bring about better routing decisions in an internetwork with alternative paths.

You will console into the router to check the status of the IP routing table and verify the networks that are reachable by each router. You will add IGRP to a router that has only RIP on it, and then you will remove RIP. The ability to both apply and interpret routing protocols is essential when maintaining internetworks.

Tools/Preparation:

Before you start the lab, the teacher or lab assistant should have the standard router lab with all five routers set up with RIP enabled. Workstations with HyperTerminal should be available to console into the routers. You may work individually or in teams. Before you begin this lab, you should read Chapter 5, "Routing Protocols: IGRP," of *Cisco Networking Academy Program: Second-Year Companion Guide*. You should also review Semester 3 online Lesson 5.

Required Resources:

- Standard Cisco five-router lab setup with hubs and switches
- Workstations to connect to the routers
- Console cable (rollover)
- CAT 5 Ethernet cable from the workstation to the hub or switch

Web Site Resources:

- **Routing basics** – http://www.cisco.com/univercd/cc/td/doc/cisintwk/ito_doc/routing.htm
- **General information on routers** – http://www.cisco.com/univercd/cc/td/doc/pcat/#2
- **2500 series routers** – http://www.cisco.com/warp/public/cc/cisco/mkt/access/2500/index.shtml
- **1600 series routers** – http://www.cisco.com/warp/public/cc/cisco/mkt/access/1600/index.shtml
- **Terms and acronyms** – http://www.cisco.com/univercd/cc/td/doc/cisintwk/ita/index.htm
- **IP routing protocol IOS command summary** –
  http://www.cisco.com/univercd/cc/td/doc/product/software/ios120/12cgcr/rbkixol.htm

Notes:

_____

_____

_____

_____

_____

_____

_____

Cisco Labs – Semester 3 – Routing and Switching
LAB 5.2 – MIGRATING RIP TO IGRP – WORKSHEET

Step 1. Verify that the routers have learned about the other networks in the lab.

1. To display the routing table and see the routing updates that have occurred and the networks the router knows about, issue the following command:

   router> **show IP route**

2. What letter appears in the first column of the routing table for any network/subnet directly connected to the router? _____

3. What letter(s) might appear in the first column of the routing table for any other networks *not* directly connected to the router? (Refer to the legend at the top of the display from the **show IP route** command.) _____

Step 2. Determine the directly connected networks.
Each router in this lab is directly connected to at least one network, and most routers are connected to two or more networks.

4. List below the networks (Class A, B, or C—*not* subnets) that each router is directly connected to. (You will be using this information when you enable IGRP.)

5. What is the difference between a router's interface address and the attached network address?
   _____

   Lab-A: _____   _____   _____

   Lab-B: _____   _____   _____

   Lab-C: _____   _____   _____

   Lab-D: _____   _____   _____

   Lab-E: _____   _____   _____

Step 3. Determine whether there are static routes, and remove them.

6. What letter would appear in the first column of the routing table for any network/subnet for which there is a static route? _____

7. If static routes are configured on the routers in this lab, they must be removed. The goal is for the routers to learn all routes via the IGRP routing protocol. To find the configuration statements for the static routes, issue the following command. Are there any static routes? _____

   router#**show running-config**

   (Notice any command of the form "**IP route …**"; they would be near the end of the output.)

Cisco Labs – Semester 3 – Routing and Switching
LAB 5.2 – MIGRATING RIP TO IGRP – WORKSHEET

8. Enter configuration mode before removing any static routes with this command:

   router#**config term**

9. Remove each of the static routes with a **no** command of this form:

   router(config)#**no IP route** …
   > (Be sure to enter exactly what you found in the **show running-config**, but with a "**no**" in front.)

Step 4. Identify routes learned with RIP and IGRP.

10. What letter appears in the first column of the routing table for any network or subnet learned via

    RIP? _____

When you have successfully and completely converted to IGRP, each of the entries learned via RIP should be replaced with a similar entry.

11. What will the letter in the first column be, to show that the network/subnet is now being learned via IGRP? _____

Step 5. Enable IGRP routing.

12. Issue the following commands:

    router(config)#**router igrp 100**
    router(config-router)#**network a.b.c.d**
(Add a network statement for each network directly connected to the router being configured; refer to the table you filled in above.)

Step 6. Verify that IGRP is now running and configured correctly.

13. Issue this command:

    Router> show IP protocol

14. At this point, you are still running two routing protocols for IP (RIP and IGRP), and both should be listed. The output includes the administrative distance of the two routing protocols; fill in those values: RIP _____ IGRP _____

Administrative distance is used to choose the routing protocol when more than one is in use, with the lowest value being preferred. IGRP has a lower administrative distance, so it will be preferred. However, if some of the routers in the lab are not yet configured correctly for IGRP, RIP information will still be learned and used. Continue to issue the command **show IP route** until there is no more RIP information in the table, and then turn off RIP.

Step 7. What is the command to turn off the RIP routing protocol? _____

Cisco Labs –Semester 3 – Routing and Switching
LAB 5.2 – MIGRATING RIP TO IGRP – ANSWERS

Step 1. Verify that the routers have learned about the other networks in the lab.

1. To display the routing table and see the routing updates that have occurred and the networks that the router knows about, issue the following command:

    router> **show IP route**

2. What letter appears in the first column of the routing table for any network/subnet directly connected to the router? **C**

3. What letter(s) might appear in the first column of the routing table for any other networks *not* directly connected to the router? (Refer to the legend at the top of the display from the **show IP route** command) **R (RIP), I (IGRP), E (EIGRP), O (OSPF), and so on**

Step 2. Determine the directly connected networks.
Each router in this lab is directly connected to at least one network, and most routers are connected to two or more networks.

4. List below the networks (Class A, B, or C—*not* subnets) that each router is directly connected to. (You will be using this information when you enable IGRP).

5. What is the difference between a router's interface address and the attached network address? **The interface has a valid IP host address using all four octets. The network address is not a valid host address and has at least one zero in it.**

Lab-A:	**192.5.5.0**	**205.7.5.0**	**201.100.11.0**
Lab-B:	**219.17.100.0**	**199.6.13.0**	**201.100.11.0**
Lab-C:	**223.8.151.0**	**204.204.7.0**	**199.6.13.0**
Lab-D:	**210.93.105.0**	**204.204.7.0**	
Lab-E:	**210.93.105.0**		

Step 3. Determine whether there are static routes, and remove them.

6. What letter would appear in the first column of the routing table for any network/subnet for which there is a static route? **S**

7. If static routes are configured on the routers in this lab, they must be removed. The goal is for the routers to learn all routes via the IGRP routing protocol. To find the configuration statements for the static routes, issue the following command. Are there any static routes? **Yes or No**

    router#**show running-config**

    (Notice any command of the form **"IP route ..."**; they would be near the end of the output.)

Cisco Labs – Semester 3 – Routing and Switching
LAB 5.2 – MIGRATING RIP TO IGRP – ANSWERS

8. Enter configuration mode before removing any static routes with this command:

   router#**config term**

9. Remove each of the static routes with a **no** command of this form:

   router(config)#**no IP route** …
   (Be sure to enter exactly what you found in the **show running-config**, but with a "**no**" in front.)

Step 4. Identify routes learned with RIP and IGRP.

10. What letter appears in the first column of the routing table for any network or subnet learned via RIP? **R**

When you have successfully and completely converted to IGRP, each of the entries learned via RIP should be replaced with a similar entry learned via IGRP.

11. What will the letter in the first column be, to show that the network/subnet was now being learned via IGRP? **I**

Step 5. Enable IGRP routing.

12. Issue the following commands:

   router(config)#**router igrp 100**
   router(config-router)#**network a.b.c.d**
(The autonomous system number is 100. Add a network statement for each network directly connected to the router being configured; refer to the table that you filled in above.)

Step 6. Verify that IGRP is now running and configured correctly.

13. Issue this command:

   Router> show IP protocol

14. At this point, you are still running two routing protocols for IP (RIP and IGRP), and both should be listed. The output includes the administrative distance of the two routing protocols. Fill in those values: RIP **120**   IGRP **100**

Administrative distance is used to choose the routing protocol when more than one is in use, with the lowest value being preferred. IGRP has a lower administrative distance, so it will be preferred. However, if some of the routers in the lab are not yet configured correctly for using IGRP, RIP information will still be learned and used. Continue to issue the command **show IP route** until there is no more RIP information in the table, and then turn off RIP.

Step 7. What is the command to turn off the RIP routing protocol? <u>router(config)# no router rip</u>

Cisco Labs – Semester 3 – Routing and Switching
LAB 5.3 – CONFIGURING IGRP – OVERVIEW
(Estimated time: 30 minutes)

Router Name - LAB A
Router Type - 2514
E 0 = 192.5.5.1
E 1 = 205.7.5.1
S 0 = 201.100.11.1
SM = 255.255.255.0

Router Name - LAB B
Router Type - 2503
E 0 = 219.17.100.1
S 0 = 199.6.13.1
S 1 = 201.100.11.2
SM = 255.255.255.0

Router Name - LAB C
Router Type - 2503
E 0 = 223.8.151.1
S 0 = 204.204.7.1
S 1 = 199.6.13.2
SM = 255.255.255.0

Router Name - LAB D
Router Type - 2501
E 0 = 210.93.105.1
S 1 = 204.204.7.2
SM = 255.255.255.0

Router Name - LAB E
Router Type - 2501
E 0 = 210.93.105.2
SM = 255.255.255.0

LEGEND

= ROUTER   User Exec Password = cisco

= HUB   Enable Secret Exec Password = class

= LAN SWITCH   Terminal vty Password = cisco

= CONSOLE CABLE

Objectives:
- Learn how to configure IGRP as the network's routing protocol
- Adjust configurable IGRP metrics

Background:
In this lab, you will work with Cisco's Interior Gateway Routing Protocol (IGRP). Routing protocols are used by routers to communicate between themselves to exchange information about the networks they can reach and the desirability of the routes available. Routed protocols (such as IP and IPX) are those protocols that can be routed between networks to enable packets to get from one location to another. Routers can run multiple routing and routed protocols.

IGRP is a dynamic distance-vector routing protocol developed by Cisco in the mid-1980s for routing in an autonomous system that contains large, complex networks with diverse bandwidth and delay characteristics. In this lab, your school district has decided to implement IGRP as the routing protocol. Several requests were made to InterNIC, which has issued an autonomous system number of 100 to your district office.

Cisco Labs – Semester 3 – Routing and Switching
LAB 5.3 – CONFIGURING IGRP – OVERVIEW

Cisco's IGRP Implementation

IGRP uses a combination of user-configurable metrics, including internetwork delay, bandwidth, reliability, and load. IGRP also advertises three types of routes: interior, system, and exterior. Interior routes are routes between subnets in the network attached to a router interface. If the network attached to a router is not subnetted, IGRP does not advertise interior routes. System routes are routes to networks within an autonomous system. The Cisco IOS software derives system routes from directly connected network interfaces and system route information provided by other routers or access servers that use IGRP. System routes do not include subnet information. Exterior routes are routes to networks outside the autonomous system that are considered when identifying a gateway of last resort. The IOS software chooses a gateway of last resort from the list of exterior routes that IGRP provides. The software uses the gateway (router) of last resort if it does not have a better route for a packet and if the destination is not a connected network. If the autonomous system has more than one connection to an external network, different routers can choose different exterior routers as the gateway of last resort.

Tools/Preparation:

Before you start the lab, the teacher or lab assistant should have the standard router lab with all five routers set up and all dynamic protocols and static routes removed. This is done issuing the **no router igrp xxx** and **no ip route xxx.xxx.xxx.xxx** commands from the **Router(config)#command** level of the enable exec user level. You may work individually or in teams. Before you begin this lab, you should read Chapter 5, "Routing Protocols: IGRP," of *Cisco Networking Academy Program: Second-Year Companion Guide*. You should also review Semester 3 online Lesson 4.

Required Resources:
- Standard Cisco five-router lab setup with hubs and switches
- Workstation connected to the router's console port
- Console cable (rollover)

Web Site Resources:
- **Routing basics** – http://www.cisco.com/univercd/cc/td/doc/cisintwk/ito_doc/routing.htm
- **General information on routers** – http://www.cisco.com/univercd/cc/td/doc/pcat/#2
- **2500 series routers** – http://www.cisco.com/warp/public/cc/cisco/mkt/access/2500/index.shtml
- **1600 series routers** – http://www.cisco.com/warp/public/cc/cisco/mkt/access/1600/index.shtml
- **Terms and acronyms** –http://www.cisco.com/univercd/cc/td/doc/cisintwk/ita/index.htm
- **IP routing protocol IOS command summary** – http://www.cisco.com/univercd/cc/td/doc/product/software/ios120/12cgcr/rbkixol.htm

Cisco Labs – Semester 3 – Routing and Switching
LAB 5.3 – CONFIGURING IGRP – WORKSHEET

Perform the following steps using one of the five lab routers. The router prompt shown here is the default prompt of "Router," assuming that no host name has been assigned to the router. The actual prompt will vary (LAB-A or LAB-B, and so on).

Step 1. Enter user exec mode with the Cisco password.

Step 2. Ping all IP interfaces on your router and all interfaces on the directly connected neighboring routers.
Document in your Lab Engineering Journal the responses from ICMP **ping** command.
Which router interfaces respond with a successful ping? _____

Step 3. Display the current routing protocols in use with the following command:
    Router>**show ip protocols**
Are any routing protocols defined? _____
(If so, these protocols should be removed. Repeat Steps 1 and 2 – refer to Lab 5.2, "Migrating from RIP to IGRP," for removal.)

Step 4. Enter privileged exec mode with the class password using the following command:
    Router>**enable**
    Password: **class**

Step 5. Display the current running configuration in RAM with the following command:
        Router#**show running-config**
Are static routes defined? _____
(If so, these routes should be removed; refer to Lab 5.2)

Step 6. Enter configure mode with the following command:
        Router#**config term**

Step 7. Enable IGRP on this router with the following command:
    Router(**config**)#**router igrp 100**
What changed on the router prompt? _____

Step 8. Define which networks are to use IGRP by entering the following command:
    Router(config-router)#**network xxx.xxx.xxx.xxx**
(Here, **xxx.xxx.xxx.xxx** is the IP address of one of the networks directly connected to the router.)

1.   What was the router response? _____

Step 9. Repeat Step 8 for all the networks directly connected to the router.

Step 10. Enter Exit.

Step 11. Enter Ctrl-Z.

Cisco Labs – Semester 3 – Routing and Switching
LAB 5.3 – CONFIGURING IGRP – WORKSHEET

Step 12. Display the current router configuration file in RAM with the following command:
   Router#**show running-config**
Is the router IGRP protocol turned on and advertising the networks you defined? _____

Step 13. Enter the following command at the privileged mode prompt:
      Router#**copy run start**
What does this command do? _____

Step 14. Display the current routing protocols in use with the following command:
   Router#**show ip protocols**
Enter in your Lab Engineering Journal any important information you have received from issuing this command. What routing protocol was shown? _____

Step 15. Display the IP routing table to show what networks are known to this router.
   Router#**show ip route**
Enter in your Lab Engineering Journal any important information you have received from issuing this command. What networks were listed? _____
_____

Step 16. Display the router interfaces and their statistics.
   Router#**show ip interface**
Enter in your Lab Engineering Journal any important information you have received from issuing this command. What interfaces are in use? _____

Step 17. Enable IGRP debugging with the following command:
   Router#**debug ip igrp transactions**
Enter in your Lab Engineering Journal any important information you have received from issuing this command. What was the effect of this command? _____

Step 18. Reset the IGRP network timers with the following series of commands:
   Router#**config term**
   Router(config)#**router igrp 100**
   Router(config-router)#**no timers basic**
What is the purpose of this command? _____

Step 19. Check the current default basic settings for the timers with the following command:
   Router#**show ip protocol**
What is the current setting for the four basic timers?
Update: _____   **Invalid:** _____   **Holddown:** _____   **Flushed:** _____

Cisco Labs – Semester 3 – Routing and Switching
LAB 5.3 – CONFIGURING IGRP – WORKSHEET

Step 20. Adjust the network timers using the following command.
All devices in an IGRP autonomous system must be consistent in their use of timers, such as how often they send updates and how long the holddown is. Use the following series of commands to adjust the timers to different settings than the default ones in Step 19:

    Router#**config term**
    Router(config)#**router igrp 100**
    Router(config-router)#**timers basic** *update invalid holddown flush* [*sleeptime*]

(Replace each of the italicized words with a number in seconds.)

Enter in your Lab Engineering Journal any important information you have received from issuing this command, and enter the significance of issuing this command.

Step 20. Enforce a maximum network diameter of two hops with the following series of commands:

    Router#**config term**
    Router(config)#**router igrp 100**
    Router(config-router)#**metric maximum-hops 2**

Step 21. Turn off IP protocol debugging with the following command:

    Router#**no debug ip igrp transactions**

Enter in your Lab Engineering Journal any important information that you have received from issuing this command.

Cisco Labs – Semester 3 – Routing and Switching
LAB 5.3 – CONFIGURING IGRP – ANSWERS

Perform the following steps using one of the five lab routers. The router prompt shown here is the default prompt of "Router," assuming that no host name has been assigned to the router. The actual prompt will vary (LAB-A or LAB-B, and so on).

Step 1. Enter user exec mode with the Cisco password.

Step 2. Ping all IP interfaces on your router and all interfaces on the directly connected neighboring routers.
Document in your Lab Engineering Journal what the responses were from ICMP **ping** command. Which router interfaces respond successfully? **Only those on directly connected networks**

Step 3. Display the current routing protocols in use with the following command:
    Router>**show ip protocols**
Are any routing protocols defined? **No response comes from command if there are none.**
(If so, the protocols should be removed. Repeat steps 1 and 2; refer to Lab 5.2 for removal.)

Step 4. Enter privileged exec mode with the class password using the following command:
    Router>**enable**
    Password: **class**

Step 5. Display the current running configuration in RAM with the following command:
    Router#**show running-config**
Are static routes defined? **There should be none.**
(If so, the routes should be removed; refer to Lab 5.2)

Step 6. Enter configure mode with the following command:
    Router#**config term**

Step 7. Enable IGRP on this router with the following command:
    Router**(config)#router igrp 100**
What changed on the router prompt? **Changed to Router(config-router)#**

Step 8. Define which networks are to use IGRP by entering the following command:
    Router(config-router)#**network xxx.xxx.xxx.xxx**
(Here, **xxx.xxx.xxx.xxx** is the IP address of one of the networks directly connected to the router.)

1. What was the router response? **The router is waiting for more networks to be entered.**
    Network numbers have a zero for the host portion of the address. Do not enter subnets.

Step 9. Repeat Step 8 for all the networks directly connected to the router.
Type in the directly attached network addresses (This example is for router Lab-B.)
        LAB-B(config-router)#network 199.6.13.0
        LAB-B(config-router)#network 219.17.100.0
        LAB-B(config-router)#network 201.100.11.0

Step 10. Enter Exit.

Cisco Labs – Semester 3 – Routing and Switching
LAB 5.3 – CONFIGURING IGRP – ANSWERS

Step 11. Enter **Ctrl-Z.**

Step 12. Display the current router configuration file in RAM with the following command.
Router#**show running-config**
Is the router IGRP protocol turned on and advertising the networks you defined? **Yes**

Step 13. Enter the following command at the privileged mode prompt:
Router#**copy run start**
What does this command do? **Copies the current configuration from RAM to NVRAM**

Step 14. Display the current routing protocols in use with the following command:
Router#**show ip protocols**
Enter in your Lab Engineering Journal any important information you have received from issuing this command. What routing protocol was shown? **IGRP**

Step 15. Display the IP routing table to show what networks are known to this router.
Router#**show ip route**
Enter in your Lab Engineering Journal any important information you have received from issuing this command. What networks were listed? _____

_____

Step 16. Display the router interfaces and their statistics.
Router#**show ip interface**
Enter in your Lab Engineering Journal any important information you have received from issuing this command. What interfaces are in use? **Serial 0, Serial 1, Ethernet 0 (and others, depending on the router)**

Step 17. Enable IGRP debugging with the following command:
Router#**debug ip igrp transactions**
Enter in your Lab Engineering Journal any important information you have received from issuing this command. What was the effect of this command? **Turns on igrp protocol debugging and displays Output of igrp transactions run on the router. This is sample output:**

        IGRP: sending update to 255.255.255.255 via Ethernet1 (205.7.5.1)
            network 204.204.7.0, metric=12476
            network 223.8.151.0, metric=10576
            network 201.100.11.0, metric=8476
            network 219.17.100.0, metric=8576
            network 199.6.13.0, metric=10476
            network 210.93.105.0, metric=12576
        IGRP: Update contains 0 interior, 6 system, and 0 exterior routes.
        IGRP: Total routes in update: 6
        IGRP: sending update to 255.255.255.255 via Serial0 (201.100.11.1)
            network 205.7.5.0, metric=1100
        IGRP: Update contains 0 interior, 1 system, and 0 exterior routes.
        IGRP: Total routes in update: 1

Cisco Labs –Semester 3 – Routing and Switching
LAB 5.3 – CONFIGURING IGRP – ANSWERS

Step 18. Reset the IGRP network timers to the defaults with the following series of commands:

    Router#**config term**
    Router(config)#**router igrp 100**
    Router(config-router)#**no timers basic**

What is the purpose of this command? **Resets the basic routing timer parameters**

Step 19. Check the current default basic settings for the timers with the following command:

    Router#**show ip protocol**

What is the current setting for the four basic timers for IGRP?
Update: 90   Invalid: 270   Holddown: 280   Flushed: 630

Default Timer Values for Routing Protocols:

Protocol	Update	Invalid	Holddown	Flush	Sleeptime
EGP	N/A	1080	N/A	1200	N/A
RIP	30	180	180	240	N/A
IGRP	90	270	280	630	0

Step 20.   Adjust the network timers using the following command.
All devices in an IGRP autonomous system must be consistent in their use of timers, such as how often they send updates and how long the holddown is. Use the following series of commands to adjust the timers to different settings than the default ones in Step 19:

    Router#**config term**
    Router(config)#**router igrp 100**
    Router(config-router)#**timers basic *update invalid holddown flush* [*sleeptime*]**

(Replace each of the italicized words with a number in seconds.)

Enter in your Lab Engineering Journal any important information you have received from issuing this command, and enter the significance of issuing this command.

Cisco Labs – Semester 3 – Routing and Switching
LAB 5.3 – CONFIGURING IGRP – ANSWERS

Definition of Timers:

Update	Rate in seconds at which updates are sent. This is the fundamental timing parameter of the routing protocol.
Invalid	Interval of time in seconds after which a route is declared invalid; it should be at least three times the value of the update. A route becomes invalid when there is an absence of updates that refresh the route. The route then enters holddown. The route is marked inaccessible and is advertised as unreachable. However, the route is still used for forwarding packets.
Holddown	Interval in seconds during which routing information regarding better paths is suppressed. It should be at least three times the value of the update. A route enters into a holddown state when an update packet is received to indicate that the route is unreachable. The route is marked inaccessible and is advertised as unreachable. However, the route is still used for forwarding packets. When holddown expires, routes advertised by other sources are accepted, and the route is no longer inaccessible.
Flush	Amount of time in seconds that must pass before the route is removed from the routing table; the interval specified must be at least the sum of the invalid and the holddown. If it is less than this sum, the proper holddown interval cannot elapse, which results in a new route being accepted before the holddown interval expires.
Sleeptime	(Optional) For IGRP only, interval in milliseconds for postponing routing updates in the event of a flash update. The sleeptime value should be less than the update time. If the sleeptime is greater than the update time, routing tables will become unsynchronized.

Step 20. Enforce a maximum network diameter of two hops with the following series of commands:

Router#**config term**
Router(config)#**router igrp 100**
Router(config-router)#**metric maximum-hops 2**

Step 21. Turn off IP protocol debugging with the following command:

Router#**no debug ip igrp transactions**

Enter in your Lab Engineering Journal any important information that you have received from issuing this command.

Cisco Labs – Semester 3 – Routing and Switching
LAB 5.4 – MULTIPATH IGRP – OVERVIEW
(Estimated time: 60 minutes)

Router Name - LAB A
Router Type - 2514
E 0 = 192.5.5.1
E 1 = 205.7.5.1
S 0 = 201.100.11.1
SM = 255.255.255.0

Router Name - LAB B
Router Type - 2503
E 0 = 219.17.100.1
S 0 = 199.6.13.1
S 1 = 201.100.11.2
SM = 255.255.255.0

Router Name - LAB C
Router Type - 2503
E 0 = 223.8.151.1
S 0 = 204.204.7.1
S 1 = 199.6.13.2
SM = 255.255.255.0

Router Name - LAB D
Router Type - 2501
E 0 = 210.93.105.1
S 1 = 204.204.7.2
SM =255.255.255.0

Router Name - LAB E
Router Type - 2501
E 0 = 210.93.105.2
SM = 255.255.255.0

LEGEND

= ROUTER	User Exec Password = cisco	
= HUB	Enable Secret Exec Password = class	
= LAN SWITCH	Terminal vty Password = cisco	
= CONSOLE CABLE		

Objectives:
- Work with IGRP metrics used in path selection
- Understand the path that is selected to route data to a particular host.

Background:
In a previous lab, you saw how to set up the RIP routing protocol on Cisco routers. In this lab, you will configure the routers to use IGRP and see how IGRP uses metrics to select the best path.

Initially, a router must refer to entries about networks or subnets that are directly connected to it. Each interface must be configured with an IP address and a subnet mask. The initial source of this information is from the user who types it into a configuration file. Interior Gateway Routing Protocol (IGRP) is a distance-vector routing protocol developed by Cisco to address problems associated with routing in large, heterogeneous networks.

RIP sends out routing updates every 30 seconds and uses only hop count to determine the best path. IGRP sends routing updates at 90 second intervals and uses a combination of variables in determining the best path to route packets. The variables that make up this composite metric include bandwidth, delay, load, reliability, and maximum transmission unit (MTU). Detailed information on how IGRP calculates the best path can be found at the IGRP Metrics site listed in the Web Site Resources section of this lab.

Cisco Labs – Semester 3 – Routing and Switching
LAB 5.4 – MULTIPATH IGRP – OVERVIEW

IGRP takes a more intelligent approach to determining the best route than RIP does. RIP counts only the number of routers (hops) from point A to point B, whereas IGRP looks at, among other factors, the speed of the various links before it determines the best path.

In this lab, you will add a WAN link between Lab A and Lab E. This link will be configured for 56 kbps speed. The other WAN links are configured for 1544 kbps (T1 speed) by default. You will examine the routing tables and determine what path the data will take. Finally, you will take down one of the fast links between routers and force the data to be routed through the 56 kbps WAN link.

Tools/Preparation:
Before you start this lab, you will need to have the equipment for the standard five-router lab available. The routers and workstations should be preconfigured by the instructor or lab assistant with the correct IP settings prior to starting the lab. Work in teams of three or more. Before beginning this lab, you should review Chapter 5, in *Cisco Networking Academy Program: Second-Year Companion Guide*, and Semester 3 online Chapter 5.

Required Resources:
- A minimum of five PC workstations, with both Windows operating system and HyperTerminal installed
- Five Cisco routers (model 1600 series or 2500 series, with IOS 11.2 or later)
- Four Ethernet hubs (10BaseT with four to eight ports)
- One Ethernet switch (Cisco Catalyst 1900 or comparable)
- Five serial console cables to connect the workstation to the router console port (with RJ45-to-DB9 converters)
- Four sets of V.35 WAN serial cables (DTE male/DCE female) to connect routers
- CAT5 Ethernet cables, wired straight through to connect routers and workstations to hubs and switches
- AUI (DB15) to RJ45 Ethernet transceivers (quantity depends on the number of routers with AUI ports) to convert router AUI interfaces to 10BaseT RJ45

Web Site Resources:
- **Routing basics** – http://www.cisco.com/univercd/cc/td/doc/cisintwk/ito_doc/routing.htm
- **General information on routers** – http://www.cisco.com/univercd/cc/td/doc/pcat/#2
- **2500 series routers** – http://www.cisco.com/warp/public/cc/cisco/mkt/access/2500/index.shtml
- **1600 series routers** – http://www.cisco.com/warp/public/cc/cisco/mkt/access/1600/index.shtml
- **Terms and acronyms** – http://www.cisco.com/univercd/cc/td/doc/cisintwk/ita/index.htm
- **IP routing protocol IOS command summary** – http://www.cisco.com/univercd/cc/td/doc/product/software/ios120/12cgcr/rbkixol.htm
- **Introduction to IGRP** – http://www.cisco.com/warp/public/103/5.html
- **IGRP metrics** – http://www.cisco.com/warp/public/103/3.html

Cisco Labs – Semester 3 – Routing and Switching
LAB 5.4 – MULTIPATH IGRP –WORKSHEET

Step 1. Connect router Lab-A to Lab-E.
Connect the DCE side of a V.35 WAN serial cable on port Serial 0 of Lab-E. Connect the other end of the cable (the DTE end) to port Serial 1 **of Lab-A.**

Step 2. Configure the serial port on Lab-E.
On Lab-E, enter the privileged EXEC mode by entering the command **enable**. If prompted, enter the password **class**. Enter global configuration mode by entering the command **configure terminal** (abbreviated **config t**). Enter the interface configuration mode for port Serial 0 by entering the command **interface Serial 0** (abbreviated **int s 0**). Assign the IP address of 220.68.33.1 to the serial port by entering the command **ip address 206.68.33.1 255.255.255.0**. This WAN link will be a 56 kbps circuit, so enter the command **bandwidth 56**. Assign the clock rate of 56000 bits per second by entering the command **clock rate 56000**. Bring up the interface by entering the command **no shutdown**. Type the key sequence Ctrl-Z to return to the command-line interface.

Step 3. Configure the serial port on Lab-A.
On Lab-A, enter the privileged EXEC mode by entering the command **enable**. If prompted, enter the password **class**. Enter global configuration mode by entering the command **configure terminal** (abbreviated **config t**). Enter the interface configuration mode for port Serial 1 by entering the command **interface Serial 1** (abbreviated **int s 1**). Assign the IP address of 220.68.33.2 to the serial port by entering the command **ip address 206.68.33.2 255.255.255.0**. This WAN link will be a 56 kbps circuit, so enter the command **bandwidth 56**. Bring up the interface by entering the command **no shutdown**. Type the key sequence Ctrl-Z to return to the command-line interface.

Step 4. Document the change to the network topology.
To successfully complete this lab, you will be referring to the topology diagram at the start of this lab. Draw a WAN link (indicated by a lightening bolt-style line) between Lab-A and Lab-E. Indicate the network number **220.68.33.0** above this link. Indicate the point at which the line connects to Lab-E as S0 (DCE) with the IP address of **220.68.33.1**. Indicate the point at which the line connects to Lab-A as S1 with an IP address of **220.68.33.2**.

Step 5. Configure IGRP routing on each router.
Each router in the lab must be configured with IGRP and the same autonomous system number. For purposes of this lab, use the number **10**. On each router, enter privileged EXEC mode by entering the command **enable**. If prompted, enter the password of **class**. Enter global configuration mode by entering the command **configure terminal** (abbreviated **config t**). To ensure that RIP routing is not in use on the lab routers, enter the command **no router rip**. To start to configure IGRP, enter the command **router igrp 10** (where 10 is the autonomous system number that you are assigned).

Cisco Labs – Semester 3 – Routing and Switching
LAB 5.4 – MULTIPATH IGRP – WORKSHEET

1. What does the prompt change to? **Router-name(config-router)#**

IGRP requires the router administrator to enter the network number of all networks that are physically connected to it. The command to do this is **network xxx.xxx.xxx.xxx** (where **xxx.xxx.xxx.xxx** is the IP address of the network connected to the interface, not the IP address of the interface itself). Refer to the network topology diagram at the start of this lab for these numbers. Be sure to include the IP address of the networks on the Ethernet ports as well as those on the serial ports (see example below). Type the key sequence Ctrl-Z to return to the command-line interface. Save the router configuration to NVRAM by entering the command **copy running-config startup-config** (abbreviated **copy run start**).

Example for Lab-A:

> **Lab-A(config)# router igrp 10**
> **Lab-A(config-router)# network 205.7.5.0**
> **Lab-A(config-router)# network 192.5.5.0**
> **Lab-A(config-router)# network 201.100.11.0**
> **Lab-A(config-router)# network 220.68.33.0**

Step 6. Examine a routing table.
Log on to the Lab-C router, and issue the command **show ip route**.

2. Record the results below:

_____
_____
_____
_____
_____
_____
_____
_____
_____
_____
_____

You will note that a "C" in the first column indicates that the network is directly connected to the router. An "I" in the first column indicates that the network was learned via IGRP. The first number in the square brackets indicates the calculated distance to the particular router. The second number indicates the calculated metric to the particular router.

Cisco Labs – Semester 3 – Routing and Switching
LAB 5.4 – MULTI-PATH IGRP – WORKSHEET

Step 7. Examine the path that data travels.
From Lab-C, follow the path that data travels to reach interface S0 on Lab-E. Issue the command **traceroute 220.68.33.1** (abbreviated **tr 220.68.33.1**).

3. What path does the data travel? _____

Step 8. Examine the path that data travels between two different routers.
Log on to Lab-E. Trace from Lab-E to the Ethernet 1 interface of the Lab-A router by entering the command **traceroute 192.5.5.1 (abbreviated tr 192.5.5.1)**.

4. What path did the **traceroute** command follow? _____

5. Why didn't the path travel from Lab-E to Lab-A ? _____
_____

Step 9. Shut down one of the fast links between routers.
The network of routers has more than one path to route data, so you have some redundancy in your system. If one of the links between routers goes down, data can be routed via the alternate path. This routing will occur when the network has converged.

From Lab-E, issue the command **show ip route**.

6. Record the results below.

_____
_____
_____
_____
_____
_____
_____
_____
_____
_____
_____
_____

Disconnect the cable from Lab-E's Ethernet 0 interface. The output of the **show ip route** command (above) indicated that all traffic from Lab-E was being routed through the Ethernet 0 interface.

Enter the command **traceroute 192.5.5.1 (abbreviated tr 192.5.5.1)**.

7. What path does the **traceroute** command now follow? _____
_____

Cisco Labs – Semester 3 – Routing and Switching
LAB 5.4 – MULTIPATH IGRP – WORKSHEET

Issue the command **show ip route**.

8. Record the results below.

_____

_____

_____

_____

_____

_____

_____

_____

_____

_____

_____

_____

Note that the IGRP metric (the second number in the square brackets) on each route has increased significantly from the results you recorded in question 6. This indicates that the 56 kbps WAN link, between Lab-E and Lab-A, is slower. Even though it is slower, this is the only way to route traffic out of Lab-E.

Step 10. Examine the routing of traffic from another router.
Log on to Lab-C. Note that it takes time for the network to converge between Steps 9 and 10. Enter the command **clear ip route *** to force the router to clear all routing table information and obtain new information from the other routers, via a broadcast. Issue the command **show ip route**, and compare the results to those you recorded in question 2.

9. Have any of the routes changed? _____

10. What interface does this route now use? _____

Examine the path data now takes to go to interface Serial 0 on Lab-E. Enter the command **traceroute 220.68.33.1** (abbreviated **tr 220.68.33.1**).

11. What path does the **traceroute** command now follow? _____

Cisco Labs – Semester 3 – Routing and Switching
LAB 5.4 – MULTIPATH IGRP – ANSWERS

1. What does the prompt change to? **Router-name(config-router)#**

2. Record the results below:
   C   204.204.7.0/24 is directly connected, Serial0
   C   223.8.151.0/24 is directly connected, Ethernet0
   I   201.100.11.0/24 [100/10476] via 199.6.13.1, 00:00:06, Serial1
   I   219.17.100.0/24 [100/8576] via 199.6.13.1, 00:00:07, Serial1
   I   220.68.33.0/24 [100/182671] via 204.204.7.2, 00:00:50, Serial0
   I   192.5.5.0/24 [100/10576] via 199.6.13.1, 00:00:07, Serial1
   C   199.6.13.0/24 is directly connected, Serial1
   I   210.93.105.0/24 [100/8576] via 204.204.7.2, 00:00:50, Serial0

3. What path does the data travel? **Lab-D, Lab-E**

4. What path did the **traceroute** command follow? **Lab-D, Lab-C, Lab-B, Lab-A**

5. Why didn't the path travel from Lab-E to Lab-A? **The WAN link from Lab-E to Lab-A is only 56 kbps and is slower than taking a path with more routers (more hops).**

6. Record the results below.
   I   204.204.7.0/24 [100/8576] via 210.93.105.1, 00:00:15, Ethernet0
   I   223.8.151.0/24 [100/8676] via 210.93.105.1, 00:00:15, Ethernet0
   I   201.100.11.0/24 [100/12576] via 210.93.105.1, 00:00:15, Ethernet0
   I   219.17.100.0/24 [100/10676] via 210.93.105.1, 00:00:15, Ethernet0
   C   220.68.33.0/24 is directly connected, Serial0
   I   192.5.5.0/24 [100/12676] via 210.93.105.1, 00:00:15, Ethernet0
   I   199.6.13.0/24 [100/10576] via 210.93.105.1, 00:00:15, Ethernet0
   C   210.93.105.0/24 is directly connected, Ethernet0

7. What path does the **traceroute** command now follow? **Directly to Lab-A via the 56 kbps link.**

8. Record the results below.
   I   204.204.7.0/24 [100/186571] via 220.68.33.2, 00:00:33, Serial0
   I   223.8.151.0/24 [100/184671] via 220.68.33.2, 00:00:33, Serial0
   I   201.100.11.0/24 [100/182571] via 220.68.33.2, 00:00:34, Serial0
   I   219.17.100.0/24 [100/182671] via 220.68.33.2, 00:00:34, Serial0
   C   220.68.33.0/24 is directly connected, Serial0
   I   192.5.5.0/24 [100/180671] via 220.68.33.2, 00:00:34, Serial0
   I   199.6.13.0/24 [100/184571] via 220.68.33.2, 00:00:34, Serial0
   C   210.93.105.0/24 is directly connected, Ethernet0

9. Have any of the routes changed? **Yes, the route to the 220.68.33.0 network has changed.**

10. What interface does this route now use? **It now uses interface S1.**

11. What path does the **traceroute** command now follow? **Lab-B, Lab-A, Lab-E**

Cisco Labs – Semester 3 – Routing and Switching
LAB 5.5 – NEOTRACE AND TRACEROUTE – OVERVIEW
(Estimated time: 15 minutes)

Objectives:

- Use the shareware program NeoTrace to verify the network path from source router to destination router with a graphical display.
- Verify that the network layer between source, destination, and each router along the way is working properly. Retrieve information to evaluate the end-to-end path reliability.
- Determine delays at each point over the path, and determine whether the host can be reached.

Background:

In this lab, you will use the shareware utility NeoTrace to determine the path that data travels through an internetwork. In Semester 2, you completed a lab using the Cisco IOS **traceroute** command. NeoTrace uses graphics to depict the results of the **traceroute** command. Additionally, NeoTrace displays the "Whois" information for each router, by looking up the domain name owner and labeling this information for each router on the data path.

The **traceroute** command uses ICMP packets and the error message generated by routers when the packet exceeds its Time To Live (TTL). When you initiate the **traceroute** command to a target host, the router sends an ICMP echo-request packet with the TTL set to 1. The first router in the path to the target host receives the ICMP echo-request packet and sets the TTL to 0. The first router then sends an ICMP Time-exceeded message back to the source. The source router then sends an ICMP echo-request packet with the TTL set to 2. The first router receives the ICMP echo-request, sets the TTL to 1, and sends it to the next router in the path to the target host. The second router receives the ICMP echo-request, sets the TTL to 0, and then sends an ICMP Time-exceeded message back to the source. The source then sends an ICMP echo-request with a TTL set to 3. This cycle continues until an ICMP echo-reply is received from the target host or until an ICMP destination-unreachable message is received. This allows you to determine the last router to be reached in the path to the target host. This is a troubleshooting technique called fault isolation.

Tools/Preparation:

Before you start the lab, you will need to connect a PC workstation with Internet access and NeoTrace installed. You will be able to download an evaluation version of NeoTrace. Please review the license provided with NeoTrace to ensure that you are abiding by the rules of its shareware use. The location of the NeoTrace program can be found later in the "Web Site Resources" section.

Required Resources:

- PC with monitor, keyboard, mouse, power cords, and other essentials
- Windows operating system (Windows 95, 98, NT, or 2000) installed on the PC
- PC with NeoTrace program installed connected to the lab routers
- PC with NeoTrace program installed, and access to the Internet

Cisco Labs – Semester 3 – Routing and Switching
LAB 5.5 – NEOTRACE AND TRACEROUTE – OVERVIEW

Web Site Resources:

- **Routing basics** – http://www.cisco.com/univercd/cc/td/doc/cisintwk/ito_doc/routing.htm
- **General information on routers** – http://www.cisco.com/univercd/cc/td/doc/pcat/#2
- **2500 series routers** –http://www.cisco.com/warp/public/cc/cisco/mkt/access/2500/index.shtml
- **1600 series routers** – http://www.cisco.com/warp/public/cc/cisco/mkt/access/1600/index.shtml
- **Terms and acronyms** –http://www.cisco.com/univercd/cc/td/doc/cisintwk/ita/index.htm
- **IP routing protocol IOS command summary** –
  http://www.cisco.com/univercd/cc/td/doc/product/software/ios120/12cgcr/rbkixol.htm
- **NeoTrace** – http://www.neotrace.com
- **Internet RFCs** – http://www.faq.org

Notes:

_____

_____

_____

_____

_____

_____

_____

Cisco Labs – Semester 3 – Routing and Switching
LAB 5.5 – NEOTRACE AND TRACEROUTE – WORKSHEET

Step 1. Run the NeoTrace program.
Start the NeoTrace program by clicking the Windows Start button and then clicking Programs. Click the NeoTrace program group, and then click the NeoTrace icon. If NeoTrace needs to be installed, download it from the web site listed previously.

If this is the first time the program has been run, you will need to fill in the blanks on the Home Location screen. This allows the program to look up the latitude and longitude for your location. Click the "Try NeoTrace" button to continue.

Step 2. Enter the address of an Internet resource to trace to.
In the address field, type **www.cisco.com** and press Enter. The address of the site you are tracing to could be any IP address or computer that is accessible from your location, either on the Internet or on your private LAN/WAN.

You will notice that as the process of tracing takes place, a series of dots and line segments is displayed. When the **traceroute** command is completed, the display shows a map with the approximate locations of the routers between your location and Cisco's web site.

Place the mouse pointer near the green dot near San Jose, California. Clicking the left mouse button zooms in, and clicking the right mouse button zooms out. Zoom in until you see the green circular dot with only one line segment connecting to it. Place the mouse pointer on this dot.

1. What information is displayed? (Answers may vary.) _____

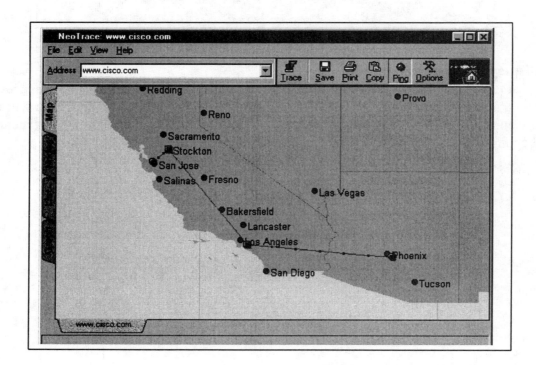

Cisco Labs – Semester 3 – Routing and Switching
LAB 5.5 – NEOTRACE AND TRACEROUTE – WORKSHEET

Step 3. Display information on the nodes.

Click the Nodes tab on the left side of the screen. A block diagram of the path taken to reach Cisco's web site is displayed. You will note that periodically the line segments between each node, or router, turn green. NeoTrace is running the **traceroute** command again to check the path to your destination because this path may change. You will notice that the average time (expressed in milliseconds) may change each time the **traceroute** command is executed. The DNS name of each node is also displayed.

Step 4. Display list information.

Click the List tab on the left side of the screen. NeoTrace displays the results of the **traceroute** command in a manner very similar to that of the Cisco IOS **traceroute** command. You will note that periodically an arrow shows up on the far left side of the list. NeoTrace is running the **traceroute** command again to check the path to your destination because this path may change.

Cisco Labs Workbook – Semester 3 – Routing and Switching
LAB 5.5 – NEOTRACE AND TRACEROUTE – WORKSHEET

#	IP Address	Name	ms	Network
1	140.198.131.57	C101-03	0	
2	140.198.128.1	e0.cg-cisco.cgc.maricopa.edu	1	Maricopa Community Coll...
3	140.198.254.25	atm1-0.8.do-cisco.dist.maricopa.edu	3	Maricopa Community Coll...
4	206.80.195.185	61.atm3-0-0.phnx-cust.phnx.uswest.net	5	U S WEST Internet Servi...
5	206.80.192.251	fa0-0-0.phnx-gw2.phnx.uswest.net	6	U S WEST Internet Servi...
6	206.80.192.251	fa0-0-0.phnx-gw2.phnx.uswest.net	4	U S WEST Internet Servi...
7	144.228.207.205	sl-gw12-ana-1-1-1.sprintlink.net	14	Sprint (NET-SPRINT-INN...
8	144.232.8.89	sl-bb10-stk-6-0.sprintlink.net	26	Sprint/United Information...
9	144.232.4.106	sl-bb11-stk-8-0.sprintlink.net	23	Sprint/United Information...
10	144.232.4.78	sl-gw10-stk-8-0-0.sprintlink.net	23	Sprint/United Information...
11	144.228.146.14	sl-ciscopsn2-4-0-0.sprintlink.net	28	Sprint (NET-SPRINT-INN...
12	192.31.7.9	pigpen.cisco.com	31	Cisco Systems, Inc. (NET...
13	198.133.219.25	www.cisco.com	31	Cisco Systems, Inc. (NET...

Step 5. Display graph information.
Click the Graph tab on the left side of the screen. NeoTrace displays the results of the **traceroute** command as a line graph. This graph shows the current time as a gray line, and the average time as a blue line. The vertical access represents each node or router in the path to your destination. Placing the mouse pointer over any of these nodes displays the "Whois" information found for that particular router. The horizontal access represents the time in milliseconds.

Cisco Labs – Semester 3 – Routing and Switching
LAB 5.5 – NEOTRACE AND TRACEROUTE – ANSWERS

1. What information is displayed? (Answers may vary.)

Node 13 of 13
Name: www.cisco.com
IP Address: 198.133.219.25
Location: 37.412N, 121.942W
Network: Cisco Systems, Inc. (NET-SWLAB1)4
Registrant:
 Cisco Systems (CISCO-DOM)
 170 W. Tasman Drive
 San Jose, CA 95134
 US

Cisco Labs – Semester 3 – Routing and Switching
LAB 6.1 – STANDARD ACLs – OVERVIEW
(Estimated time: 60 minutes)

Router Name - LAB A
Router Type - 2514
E 0 = 192.5.5.1
E 1 = 205.7.5.1
S 0 = 201.100.11.1
SM = 255.255.255.0

Router Name - LAB B
Router Type - 2503
E 0 = 219.17.100.1
S 0 = 199.6.13.1
S 1 = 201.100.11.2
SM = 255.255.255.0

Router Name - LAB C
Router Type - 2503
E 0 = 223.8.151.1
S 0 = 204.204.7.1
S 1 = 199.6.13.2
SM = 255.255.255.0

Router Name - LAB D
Router Type - 2501
E 0 = 210.93.105.1
S 1 = 204.204.7.2
SM = 255.255.255.0

Router Name - LAB E
Router Type - 2501
E 0 = 210.93.105.2
SM = 255.255.255.0

LEGEND

= ROUTER   User Exec Password = cisco

= HUB   Enable Secret Exec Password = class

= LAN SWITCH   Terminal vty Password = cisco

= CONSOLE CABLE

Objectives:

- Review the characteristics and capabilities of standard IP access control lists (ACLs)
- Construct a standard ACL to permit or deny specific traffic
- Apply a standard IP ACL to a router interface
- Test the ACL to determine whether the desired results were achieved
- Remove an ACL from a router interface
- Delete an ACL from a router

Background:

In this lab, you will work with standard access control lists (ACLs) to regulate the traffic that is allowed to pass through a router based on the source, either a specific host (typically a workstation or a server) or an entire network (any host or server on that network). A standard ACL is a simple and effective tool to control which packets should be allowed to pass through a router from one network to another. Standard ACLs are a basic form of control with limited capabilities. They can filter (permit or deny) packets coming into or going out of a router interface based only on the IP address of the source network or host. As a result, they should be applied near the destination address because you cannot specify the destination address.

Cisco Labs – Semester 3 – Routing and Switching
LAB 6.1 – STANDARD ACLs – OVERVIEW

Other routed (or routable) protocols such as IPX or AppleTalk can also have ACLs or filters, but this lab focuses on IP ACLs. When a standard IP ACL is applied, it will filter (permit or deny) the entire IP protocol suite (IP, TCP, SMTP, HTTP, Telnet, and so on). When creating standard IP ACLs, they are numbered from 1 to 99. In the next lab, you will work with extended IP ACLs, which are numbered from 100 to 199. Refer to the text or online lesson for IPX and AppleTalk ACL numbering.

These are the steps necessary to use ACLs effectively:
1. Determine the ACL requirements (based on security needs and other considerations).
2. Construct the ACL.
3. Verify the statements in the ACL.
4. Apply the ACL to a router interface.
5. Verify that the ACL is applied correctly to the intended interface.
6. Verify that the ACL is functioning properly.

Tools/Preparation:
Before you start the lab, the teacher or lab assistant should have the standard router lab with all five routers set up. You may work individually or in teams. Before beginning this lab you should read Chapter 6, "ACLs," in *Cisco Networking Academy Program: Second-Year Companion Guide*. You should also review Semester 3 online Chapter 6.

Required Resources:
- Standard Cisco five-router lab setup with hubs and switches
- Workstation connected to the router's console port with a rollover cable

Web Site Resources:
- **Routing basics** – http://www.cisco.com/univercd/cc/td/doc/cisintwk/ito_doc/routing.htm
- **General information on routers** – http://www.cisco.com/univercd/cc/td/doc/pcat/#2
- **2500 series routers** – http://www.cisco.com/warp/public/cc/cisco/mkt/access/2500/index.shtml
- **1600 series routers** – http://www.cisco.com/warp/public/cc/cisco/mkt/access/1600/index.shtml
- **Terms and acronyms** – http://www.cisco.com/univercd/cc/td/doc/cisintwk/ita/index.htm
- **IP routing protocol IOS command summary** –
  http://www.cisco.com/univercd/cc/td/doc/product/software/ios120/12cgcr/rbkixol.htm
- **Access control lists – overview and guidelines** –
  www.cisco.com/univercd/cc/td/doc/product/software/ios113ed/113ed_cr/secur_c/scprt3/scacls.htm

Notes:
_____
_____
_____
_____
_____
_____
_____
_____

Cisco Labs – Semester 3 – Routing and Switching
LAB 6.1 – STANDARD ACLs – WORKSHEET

In this lab, you will construct, apply, and test a standard IP ACL. Exercise A is required, and Exercise B is optional but recommended. Exercise A is intended to block packets from a specific host on one network from getting to any host on another network. Exercise B will block traffic from all hosts on a specific network from getting to any host on an entire network. Answers are provided for both exercises. Refer to the standard lab diagram in the overview section.

Exercise A (Required)
ACL 1 prevents IP traffic from a specific host (workstation with 192.5.5.2 IP address) attached to the Ethernet hub off router Lab-A interface E0, from reaching an entire network (210.93.105.0, the network between routers Lab-D and Lab-E).

Exercise B (Optional)
ACL 2 prevents IP traffic from all hosts on a specific network 219.17.100.0 (an Ethernet network off router Lab-B) from reaching an entire network 223.8.151.0 (an Ethernet network off router Lab-C).

Step 1. Determine the ACL requirements.
Which traffic (packets) from which hosts or networks will be blocked (denied) or allowed (permitted)? You will use a standard IP ACL, so you can filter only on the source address. With Exercise A, you wish to block traffic from host address 192.5.5.2 from an Ethernet on router Lab-A. With Exercise B, you wish to block traffic from network address 219.17.100.0 on router Lab-B.

Step 2. Construct the ACL.
Define the ACL statements in **Router(config)#** mode. ACL statements are additive, which means that each statement adds to the ACL. If there is more than one statement in the ACL (typical) and you want to change a prior statement, you must delete the ACL and start again. In these examples, you are blocking packets from only one host IP address or one network. The format or syntax of the standard IP ACL statement is shown below:

access-list   list#   {permit / deny}   source IP address   [wildcard mask]   [log]

(Note: Any number between 1 and 99 can be used for a standard IP ACL. To delete the ACL, repeat the **access-list # portion** of the command with the word **NO** in front.)

Complete the ACL command with the correct source address and wildcard mask that would accomplish the requirements for either Exercise A or B (or both). The first statement would be used for ACL 1. The second statement would be used for ACL 2.

     Exercise A.   access-list 1 deny   _____   _____

     Exercise B.   access-list 2 deny   _____   _____

Cisco Labs – Semester 3 – Routing and Switching
LAB 6.1 – STANDARD ACLs – WORKSHEET

1. What is the purpose of a zero (0) in a wildcard mask? _____
2. How many bits does each decimal zero in the wildcard mask above represent? _____
3. What is the purpose of a 255 in a wildcard mask? _____
4. How many bits does the 255 represent? _____

5. Because ACLs always end with an implicit "deny any," using just one of the previous statements would cause this list to deny a single source address but then implicitly deny any other source address. The objective is to only deny access from a single host, so you need to add a second statement to allow all other traffic. Enter the second ACL statement that would allow all other traffic (the same statement would be used for Exercise A or B):

    _____

6. Why are both statements using the same ACL number (1) ?

    _____

7. What would happen if the first statement was "Access-list 1" and the second "Access-list 2"?

    _____

Step 3. Verify the statements in the ACL.
Use the following command to check your statements and verify that everything was typed in correctly. If you want to correct a mistake or change an existing statement, you must delete the ACL and start again. To delete the ACL, repeat the **access-list # portion** with the word **NO** in front.

   Router#show access-list 1

8. How many statements are in your ACL? _____

Step 4. Apply the ACL to a router interface.
Because standard ACLs can only specify or check source addresses, you must apply the filter as close to the destination as possible. On which router and which interface would you apply the ACL for each of the sample Exercises A or B? Refer to the standard lab diagram, and fill in the following table with the IP address(es) to be blocked, the network you wish to keep them out of, the router where the ACL will be applied, the interface it will be applied to, and whether it will block incoming or outgoing packets.

Exercise	IP Host or Network to Be Denied (Blocked)	Network to Keep Packets Out Of	Router Where ACL Will Be Applied	Interface Where ACL Will Be Applied (S0, S1, E0 etc.)	Block Incoming or Outgoing? (IN or OUT)
A (ACL 1)					
B (ACL 2)					

Note: Remember to put standard ACLs close to the destination.

Cisco Labs – Semester 3 – Routing and Switching
LAB 6.1 – STANDARD ACLs – WORKSHEET

Enter the following commands to apply ACL 1 to interface S1 to block incoming packets on interface S1 for router Lab-D. The real router name (Lab-D), would appear instead of "Router" in the prompt. For ACL 2, the ACL would be applied to interface E0 on Lab-C for outgoing packets.

Router(config)#interface Serial 1
Router(config-if)#ip access-group 1 in

Step 5. Verify the ACL is applied correctly to the intended interface.
Use this command to check that the ACL is applied to the correct interface on the correct router:

Router#show running-config

9. What results were displayed that proves that the ACL is applied correctly?

_____

Note: To remove an ACL from an interface, first configure the interface as with Step 4, and then repeat the second command with the word NO in front (no ip access-group 1).

Step 6. Verify that the ACL is functioning properly.
Test the ACL by trying to send packets from the source network that is to be permitted or denied. Issue several **ping** commands to test these ACLs. Several tests are given for each exercise.

Exercise	Test #	Ping From	To	Should Be Successful?	Was It?
A	1	Workstation (192.5.5.2) off router Lab-A	Workstation (210.93.105.2) off router Lab-E		
	2	Workstation (192.5.5.2) off router Lab-A	Router Lab-C, interface S0 (204.204.7.1)		
B	1	Workstation (219.17.100.X) off router Lab-B	Router Lab-E, interface E0 (210.93.105.2), or workstation (210.93.105.X)		
	2	Workstation (219.17.100.X) off router Lab-B	Router Lab-C, interface E0 (223.8.151.1)		
	3	Workstation (219.17.100.X) off router Lab-B	Workstation (223.8.151.2) off router Lab-C		

Cisco Labs – Semester 3 – Routing and Switching
LAB 6.1 – STANDARD ACLs – ANSWERS

In this lab, you will construct, apply, and test a standard IP ACL. Exercise A is required, and Exercise B is optional but recommended. Exercise A is intended to block packets from a specific host on one network from getting to any host on another network. Exercise B will block traffic from all hosts on a specific network from getting to any host on an entire network. Answers are provided for both exercises. Refer to the standard lab diagram in the overview section

Exercise A (Required)
ACL 1 prevents IP traffic from a specific host (workstation with 192.5.5.2 IP address) attached to the Ethernet hub off router Lab-A interface E0, from reaching an entire network (210.93.105.0, the network between routers Lab-D and Lab-E).

Exercise B (Optional)
ACL 2 prevents IP traffic from all hosts on a specific network 219.17.100.0 (an Ethernet network off router Lab-B) from reaching an entire network 223.8.151.0 (an Ethernet network off router Lab-C).

Step 1. Determine the ACL requirements.
Which traffic (packets) from which hosts or networks will be blocked (denied) or allowed (permitted)? You will use a standard IP ACL, so you can filter only on the source address. With Exercise A, you wish to block traffic from host address 192.5.5.2 from an Ethernet on router Lab-A. With Exercise B, you wish to block traffic from network address 219.17.100.0 on router Lab-B.

Step 2. Construct the ACL.
Define the ACL statements in **Router(config)#** mode. ACL statements are additive, which means that each statement adds to the ACL. If there is more than one statement in the ACL (typical) and you want to change an existing statement, you must delete the ACL and start again. In these examples, you are blocking packets from only one host IP address or one network. The format or syntax of the standard IP ACL statement is this:

access-list   list#   {permit / deny}   source IP address   [wildcard mask]   [log]

(Note: Any number between 1 and 99 can be used for a standard IP ACL. To delete the ACL, repeat the **access-list # portion** of the command with the word **NO** in front.)

Complete the ACL command with the correct source address and wildcard mask that would accomplish the requirements for either Exercise A or B (or do both). The first statement would be used for ACL 1. The second statement would be used for ACL 2.

Exercise A.	**access-list 1 deny**	<u>**192.5.5.2**</u>	<u>**0.0.0.0**</u>
Exercise B.	**access-list 2 deny**	<u>**219.17.100.0**</u>	<u>**0.0.0.255**</u>

Cisco Labs – Semester 3 – Routing and Switching
LAB 6.1 – STANDARD ACLs – ANSWERS

1. What is the purpose of a zero (0) in a wildcard mask? **Source address bits must match.**

2. How many bits does each decimal zero in the wildcard mask above represent? **8**

3. What is the purpose of a 255 in a wildcard mask? **Source address bits can be anything.**

4. How many bits does the 255 represent? **8**

5. Because ACLs always end with an implicit "deny any," using just one of the previous statements would cause this list to deny a single source address but then implicitly deny any other source address. The objective is to only deny access from a single host, so you need to add a second statement to allow all other traffic. Enter the second ACL statement that would allow all other traffic (the same statement would be used for Exercise A or B):

    access-list 1 permit any

6. Why are both statements using the same ACL number (1)? **To be part of the same ACL**

7. What would be the implication if the first statement was "Access-list 1" and the second was "Access-list 2"? **Each statement would be part of a different ACL, and ACL 1 would still block all traffic because of the implicit "deny any." Only one of the ACLs could have been applied to a single interface.**

Step 3. Verify the statements in the ACL.
Use the following command to check your statements and verify that everything was typed in correctly. If you want to correct a mistake or change an existing statement, you must delete the ACL and start again. To delete the ACL, repeat the **access-list #** portion with the word **NO** in front.

    Router#show access-list 1

8. How many statements are in your ACL? **2**

Step 4. Apply the ACL to a router interface.
Because our standard ACLs can check only source addresses, you must apply the filter as close to the destination as possible. On which router and which interface would you apply the ACL for each of the sample Exercises A or B? Refer to the standard lab diagram and fill in the following table with the IP address(es) to be blocked, the network you wish to keep them out of, the router where the ACL will be applied, and the interface it will be applied to.

Exercise	IP Host or Network to Be Denied (Blocked)	Network to Keep Packets Out Of	Router Where ACL Will Be Applied	Interface Where ACL Will Be Applied (S0, S1, E0 etc.)	Block Incoming or Outgoing? (IN or OUT)
A (ACL 1)	192.5.5.2 (host)	210.93.105.0	Lab-D	S1	IN
B (ACL 2)	219.17.100.0 (network)	223.8.151.0	Lab-C	E0	OUT

Note: Remember to put standard ACLs close to the destination.

Cisco Labs – Semester 3 – Routing and Switching
LAB 6.1 – STANDARD ACLs – ANSWERS

Enter the following commands to apply ACL 1 to interface S1 to block incoming packets on interface S1 for router Lab-D. The real router name (Lab-D), would appear instead of "Router" in the prompt. For ACL 2, The access list would be applied to interface E0 on Lab-C for outgoing packets.

> **Router(config)#interface Serial 1**
> **Router(config-if)#ip access-group 1 in**

(Note: The ACL can be applied to incoming or outgoing packets. If you do not specify the word IN, then the ACL applies only to outgoing packets. OUT is the default.)

Step 5. Verify that the ACL is applied to the correct interface.
Use this command to check that the ACL is applied to the correct interface on the correct router:

> **Router#show running-config**

9. What results were displayed that proves that the ACL is applied correctly? **Standard IP ACL 1 is listed, and then the statements that are in it are displayed.**

Note: To remove an ACL from an interface, first configure the interface as with Step 4, and then repeat the second command with the word **NO** in front (**no ip access-group 1 out**). If the ACL was applied to incoming packets, then the command is **no ip access-group 1 in**.

Step 6. Verify that the ACL is functioning properly.
Test the ACL by trying to send packets from the source network that is to be permitted or denied. Issue several **ping** commands to test these ACLs. Several tests are given for each exercise.

Exercise	Test #	Ping From	To	Should Be Successful?	Was It?
A	1	Workstation (192.5.5.2) off router Lab-A	Workstation (210.93.105.2) off router Lab-E	No	No
	2	Workstation (192.5.5.2) off router Lab-A	Router Lab-C, interface S0 (204.204.7.1)	Yes	Yes
B	1	Workstation (192.5.5.2) off router Lab-A	Router Lab-E, interface E0 (210.93.105.2), or workstation (210.93.105.X)	Yes	Yes
	2	Workstation (192.5.5.2) off router Lab-A	Router Lab-C, interface E0 (223.8.151.1)	*Yes	Yes
	3	Workstation (192.5.5.2) off router Lab-A	Workstation (223.8.151.2) off router Lab-C	No	No

* With test no. 2, the packet has not yet come out of the E0 interface, so it will not be blocked until the ping destination is for a workstation on the 223.8.151.2 network (test no. 3).

Cisco Labs – Semester 3 – Routing and Switching
LAB 6.2 – EXTENDED ACLs – OVERVIEW
(Estimated time: 60 minutes)

Objectives:
- Review the characteristics and capabilities of extended IP access control lists (ACLs)
- Construct an extended IP ACL to permit or deny specific traffic
- Apply an extended IP ACL to a router interface
- Test the ACL to determine whether the desired results were achieved

Background:
Extended ACLs are a more advanced form of control with more flexibility in the way packets are controlled. Extended ACLs can filter (permit or deny) packets based on source or destination address and on the type of traffic (FTP, Telnet, HTTP, and so on). Because extended ACLs can block traffic based on destination address, they can be placed near the source, which helps to reduce network traffic.

In this lab, you will work with extended ACLs to regulate the traffic that is allowed to pass through the router based on the source and type of traffic. ACLs are an important tool to control which packets and what particular type of packets should be allowed to pass through a router from one network to another.

There are different types of ACLs for different routed protocols, such as IP, Novell IPX, and AppleTalk. With this lab, you will work only with extended IP ACLs that are created with a number from 100 to 199.

Cisco Labs – Semester 3 – Routing and Switching
LAB 6.2 – EXTENDED ACLs – OVERVIEW

These are the steps necessary to use ACLs effectively:
1. Determine the ACL requirements (based on company security needs and considerations).
2. Construct the ACL.
3. Verify the statements in the ACL.
4. Apply the ACL to a router interface.
5. Verify that the ACL is applied correctly to the intended interface.
6. Verify that the ACL is functioning properly.

Tools/Preparation:
Before you start the lab, the teacher or lab assistant should have the standard router lab with all five routers set up. You may work individually or in teams. Before beginning this lab, you should read Chapter 6 of *Cisco Networking Academy Program: Second-Year Companion Guide*. You should also review Semester 3 online Chapter 6.

Required Resources:
- Standard Cisco five-router lab setup with hubs and switches
- Workstation connected to the router's console port with a rollover cable

Web Site Resources:
- **Routing basics** – http://www.cisco.com/univercd/cc/td/doc/cisintwk/ito_doc/routing.htm
- **General information on routers** – http://www.cisco.com/univercd/cc/td/doc/pcat/#2
- **2500 series routers** – http://www.cisco.com/warp/public/cc/cisco/mkt/access/2500/index.shtml
- **1600 series routers** – http://www.cisco.com/warp/public/cc/cisco/mkt/access/1600/index.shtml
- **Terms and acronyms** – http://www.cisco.com/univercd/cc/td/doc/cisintwk/ita/index.htm
- **IP routing protocol IOS command summary** –
  http://www.cisco.com/univercd/cc/td/doc/product/software/ios120/12cgcr/rbkixol.htm
- **Access control lists – overview and guidelines** –
  www.cisco.com/univercd/cc/td/doc/product/software/ios113ed/113ed_cr/secur_c/scprt3/scacls.htm

Notes:
_____
_____
_____
_____
_____
_____
_____
_____
_____

Cisco Labs – Semester 3 – Routing and Switching
LAB 6.2 – EXTENDED ACLs – WORKSHEET

In this lab, you will construct, apply, and test an extended IP ACL using the following standard lab setup. You may do either Exercise A or Exercise B, as outlined in Step 1.

Step 1. Determine the ACL requirements.
Which traffic (packets) will be blocked (denied) or allowed (permitted)? You will use an extended IP ACL, so you can control not only the source address but also the destination address. You can also pick and choose the specific protocols in the IP protocol suite that you want to allow or prevent from entering the destination network (TCP, UDP, ICMP, HTTP, Telnet, and so on).

Exercise A: Prevent Telnet traffic from a specific host 192.5.5.2 (a workstation off router Lab-A) from reaching an entire network 210.93.105.0 (the network between routers Lab-D and Lab-E).

Exercise B: Prevent Telnet traffic from a specific host 210.93.105.2 (a workstation off router Lab-E) from reaching an entire network 192.5.5.0 (off router Lab-A).

Step 2. Construct the ACL.
Define the ACL statements in **Router(config)#** mode. ACL statements are additive, which means that each statement adds to the ACL. If there is more than one statement in the ACL (typical) and you want to change the prior statement, you must delete the ACL and start again. In these examples, you will be blocking packets from only one host IP address or one network based on the destination network and higher-level IP protocol (such as Telnet) being used. The format or syntax of the extended IP ACL statements that you will be using is shown below:

access-list   list#   {permit/deny}   [protocol]   source IP   wildcard mask   [port]
**   dest. IP   wildcard mask   [port]   [established]   [log]   [other options]**
(Note: Any number from 100 and 199 can be used for an extended IP ACL.)

Complete the ACL command with the correct source and destination addresses that would accomplish the requirements for Exercise A or B (or both). With extended ACLs, you must also specify the protocol (IP, TCP, UDP, ICMP). Because you are filtering telnet, which uses TCP, you must remember to include **TCP** in the command.

Exercise A (ACL 101)
access-list 101 deny ____   _____   _____   _____   _____   _____

Exercise B (ACL 102)
access-list 102 deny ____   _____   _____   _____   _____   _____

1. Why is the source wildcard mask given as 0.0.0.0?

    _____

2. Why is the destination wildcard mask given as 0.0.0.255?

    _____

3. What are you checking with the "eq telnet"?

    _____

Cisco Labs – Semester 3 – Routing and Switching
LAB 6.2 – EXTENDED ACLs – WORKSHEET

4. What would it mean if you left off the "eq telnet"?

    _____

5. Because ACLs always end with an implicit "deny any," using just one of the previous statements would cause this list to deny a single source address but then implicitly deny any other source address. The objective is to deny access to only a single host, so you need to add a second statement to allow all other traffic. Enter the second ACL statement that would allow all other traffic (the same statement would be used for Exercise A or B):

    _____

Step 3. Verify the statements in the ACL.
Use the following command to check your statements and verify that everything was typed in correctly. If you want to correct a mistake or change an existing statement, you must delete the ACL and start again. To delete the ACL, repeat the **access-list #** portion with the word **NO** in front.

    Router#show access-list 101

6. How many statements are in your ACL? _____

Step 4. Apply the ACL to a router interface.
Because you are now using extended ACLs and can filter on both the source and the destination addresses, you can apply the filter as close to the source as possible, saving on bandwidth. Also remember that you can decide to apply the ACL to incoming packets or outgoing packets. Unless IN is specified, the ACL will be applied to OUT packets only (IN and OUT are always viewed from outside the router). Which router and which interface would you apply the ACL to for each of the sample Exercises A or B? Refer to the extended lab diagram and answer the following questions.

Exercise A.
7. On which router, Lab-B or Lab-D, would you apply the filter that would prevent router Lab-A's Telnet packets from being transmitted to the D/E LAN (network 210.93.105.0)? _____

8. On which interface would this list be applied? _____

9. Complete the commands that would apply this list to that interface:

    Router(config)# _____
    Router(config-if)# _____

Cisco Labs – Semester 3 – Routing and Switching
LAB 6.2 – EXTENDED ACLs – WORKSHEET

Exercise B.

10. On which router, Lab-B or Lab-D, would you apply the filter that would prevent router Lab-E's packets from being transmitted to the A LAN (network 201.100.11.0)? _____

11. On which interface would this list be applied? _____

12. Complete the commands that would apply this list to that interface:
    Router(config)#_____
    Router(config-if)#_____

Step 5. Verify that the ACL is applied to the correct interface.
Use this command to check that the ACL is applied to the correct interface on the correct router:
    Router#show running-config

13. What results were displayed that prove that the ACL is applied correctly?
    _____

Note: To remove an ACL from an interface, first configure the interface as with Step 4, and then repeat the second command with the word **NO** in front (**no ip access-group 101 in**).

Step 6. Verify that the ACL is functioning properly.
Test the ACL by trying to send packets from the source network that is to be permitted or denied. Issue several **ping** commands to test these ACLs. Several tests are given for each exercise.

Exercise	Test #	Telnet From	To	Should Be Successful?	Was It?
A (ACL 101)	1	Workstation (192.5.5.2) off router Lab-A	Workstation (210.93.105.2) off router Lab-E		
	2	Workstation (192.5.5.2) off router Lab-A	Workstation (223.8.151.2) off router Lab-C		

Exercise	Test #	Telnet From	To	Should Be Successful?	Was It?
B (ACL 102)	1	Workstation (210.93.105.2) off router Lab-E	Workstation (192.5.5.2) off router Lab-A		
	2	Workstation (210.93.105.2) off router Lab-E	Workstation (219.17.100.2) off router Lab-B		

Use the following command with one of the routers where the ACL was applied to verify that packets are being blocked:
    Router#show access-list 101

14. What was the result of the command? How could you tell that the ACL was working?

_____

_____

Cisco Labs – Semester 3 – Routing and Switching
LAB 6.2 – EXTENDED ACLs – ANSWERS

In this lab you will construct, apply, and test an extended IP ACL using the following standard lab setup. You may do either Exercise A or Exercise B, as outlined in Step 1.

Step 1. Determine the ACL requirements.
Which traffic (packets) will be blocked (denied) or allowed (permitted)? You will use an extended IP ACL, so you can control not only the source address but also the destination address. You can also pick and choose the specific protocols in the IP protocol suite that you want to allow or prevent from entering the destination network TCP, UDP, ICMP, Telnet, and so on).

Exercise A: Prevent Telnet traffic from a specific host 192.5.5.2 (a workstation off router Lab-A) from reaching an entire network 210.93.105.0 (the network between routers Lab-D and Lab-E).

Exercise B: Prevent Telnet traffic from a specific host 210.93.105.2 (a workstation off router Lab-E) from reaching an entire network 192.5.5.0 (off router Lab-A).

Step 2. Construct the ACL.
Define the ACL statements in **Router(config)#** mode. ACL statements are additive, which means that each statement adds to the ACL. If there is more than one statement in the ACL (typical) and you want to change the prior statement, you must delete the ACL and start again. In these examples, you will be blocking packets from only one host IP address or one network based on the destination network and higher-level IP protocol (such as Telnet) being used. The basic format or syntax of the extended IP ACL statements that you will be using is this:

access-list list# {permit/deny} [protocol] source IP wildcard mask [port] dest. IP wildcard mask [port] [established] [log] [other options]
(Note: Any number from 100 and 199 can be used for an extended IP ACL)

Complete the ACL command with the correct source and destination addresses that would accomplish the requirements for Exercise A or B (or both). With extended ACLs, you must also specify the protocol (IP, TCP, UDP, ICMP). Because you are filtering telnet, which uses TCP, you must remember to include **TCP** in the command.

Exercise A. (ACL 101)
access-list 101 deny **tcp** **192.5.5.2** **0.0.0.0** **210.93.105.0** **0.0.0.255** **eq telnet**

Exercise B. (ACL 102)
access-list 102 deny **tcp** **210.93.105.2** **0.0.0.0** **192.5.5.0** **0.0.0.255** **eq telnet**

1. Why is the source wildcard mask given as 0.0.0.0?
   All four octets (32 bits) in the source host IP address must match the IP address in the ACL.

2. Why is the destination wildcard mask given as 0.0.0.255?
   The first three octets (24 bits) in the destination network must match the IP address in the ACL, but the last octet can be any host on that network.

Cisco Labs – Semester 3 – Routing and Switching
LAB 6.2 – EXTENDED ACLs – ANSWERS

3. What are you checking with the "eq telnet"?
The incoming packet, to see if the Layer 4 protocol is Telnet (TCP port 23)

4. What would it mean if you left off the "eq telnet"?
All other TCP traffic would be blocked, which includes FTP and e-mail, because they both use the TCP transport protocol.

5. Because ACLs always end with an implicit "deny any," using just one of the previous statements would cause this list to deny a single source address but then implicitly deny any other source address. The objective is to deny access to only a single host, so you need to add a second statement to allow all other traffic. Enter the second ACL statement that would allow all other traffic (the same statement would be used for Exercise A [ACL 101] or B [ACL 102]):

access-list 101 permit ip any any

Step 3. Verify the statements in the ACL.
Use the following command to check your statements and verify that everything was typed in correctly. If you want to correct a mistake or change an existing statement, you must delete the ACL and start again. To delete the ACL, repeat the **access-list #** portion with the word **NO** in front.

Router#show access-list 101

6. How many statements are in your ACL? **2**

Step 4. Apply the ACL to a router interface.
Because you are now using extended ACLs and can filter on both the source and the destination addresses, you can apply the filter as close to the source as possible, saving on bandwidth. Also remember that you can decide to apply the ACL to incoming packets or outgoing packets. Unless IN is specified, the ACL will be applied to OUT packets only (IN and OUT are always viewed from outside the router). Which router and which interface would you apply the ACL to for each of the sample Exercises A or B? Refer to the extended lab diagram and answer the following questions.

Exercise A.
7. On which router, Lab-A or Lab-D, would you apply the filter that would prevent Telnet packets from the workstation 192.5.5.2 off router Lab-A from being transmitted to the D/E LAN (network 210.93.105.0)? **Lab-A**

8. On which interface would this list be applied? **Serial S0**

9. Complete the commands that would apply this list to that interface:

Router(config)#interface   Serial 0
Router(config-if)#ip access-group   101   out

Cisco Labs – Semester 3 – Routing and Switching
LAB 6.2 – EXTENDED ACLs – ANSWERS

Exercise B.

10. On which router, Lab-B or Lab-D, would you apply the filter that would prevent router Lab-E's telnet packets from being transmitted to the A LAN (network 192.5.5.0)? **Lab-D**

11. On which interface would this list be applied? **Ethernet 0**

12. Complete the commands that would apply this list to that interface:

   Router(config)#interface   Ethernet   0
   Router(config-if)#ip access-group   102   in

Step 5. Verify that the ACL is applied to the correct interface.
Use this command to check that the ACL is applied to the correct interface on the correct router:

   Router#show running-config

13. What results were displayed that prove that the ACL is applied correctly?
   You should see the ACL listed with the interface where it was applied (as IN or OUT).

Note: To remove an ACL from an interface, first configure the interface as with Step 4, and then repeat the second command with the word **NO** in front (**no ip access-group 101 in**).

Step 6. Verify that the ACL is functioning properly.
Test the ACL by trying to send packets from the source network that is to be permitted or denied. Issue several **ping** commands to test these ACLs. Several tests are given for each exercise.

Exercise	Test #	Telnet From	To	Should Be Successful?	Was It?
A	1	Workstation (192.5.5.2) off router Lab-A	Workstation (210.93.105.2) off router Lab-E	No	No
	2	Workstation (192.5.5.2) off router Lab-A	Workstation (223.8.151.2) off router Lab-C	Yes	Yes

Exercise	Test #	Telnet From	To	Should Be Successful?	Was It?
B	1	Workstation (210.93.105.2) off router Lab-E	Workstation (192.5.5.2) off router Lab-A	No	No
	2	Workstation (210.93.105.2) off router Lab-E	Workstation (219.17.100.2) off router Lab-B	Yes	Yes

Cisco Labs – Semester 3 – Routing and Switching
LAB 6.2 – EXTENDED ACLs – ANSWERS

Use the following command with one of the routers where the ACL was applied to verify that packets are being blocked:

Router#show access-list 101

14. What was the result of the command? How could you tell that the ACL was working?
Access list and statements should be listed with counters indicating how many packets were filtered by each ACL statement, similar to the following:

Router#show access-list 101
Extended IP access list 101
      deny ip host 192.5.5.2   210.93.105.0   0.0.0.255 (5 matches)
      permit ip any any (5 matches)

Cisco Labs – Semester 3 – Routing and Switching
LAB 6.3 – EXTENDED ACLs INTERNET – OVERVIEW
(Estimated time: 90 minutes)

Router Name - LAB A
Router Type - 2514
E 0 = 192.5.5.1
E 1 = 205.7.5.1
S 0 = 201.100.11.1
SM = 255.255.255.0

Router Name - LAB C
Router Type - 2503
E 0 = 223.8.151.1
S 0 = 204.204.7.1
S 1 = 199.6.13.2
SM = 255.255.255.0

Router Name - LAB E
Router Type - 2501
E 0 = 210.93.105.2
SM = 255.255.255.0

Router Name - LAB B
Router Type - 2503
E 0 = 219.17.100.1
S 0 = 199.6.13.1
S 1 = 201.100.11.2
SM = 255.255.255.0

Router Name - LAB D
Router Type - 2501
E 0 = 210.93.105.1
S 1 = 204.204.7.2
SM = 255.255.255.0

LEGEND

= ROUTER   User Exec Password = cisco

= HUB   Enable Secret Exec Password = class

= LAN SWITCH   Terminal vty Password = cisco

= CONSOLE CABLE

Objectives:
- Design an ACL plan based on specific security requirements
- Work with the more advanced capabilities of extended IP access control lists (ACLs)
- Construct an extended ACL with multiple statements
- Construct an extended ACL to control Internet traffic using one or more routers
- Construct an extended ACL to permit or deny other specific IP protocol traffic

Background:
This lab is a practice exercise that simulates a real-world example. You will work with multiple extended access control lists (ACLs) to simulate regulating the traffic that is allowed to pass through multiple routers to various servers and the Internet. This is primarily a paper-based exercise to practice the analysis of security requirements and design an ACL plan. You can configure most of the ACLs on the routers indicated in the answer section, but you may not be able to actually test some of the ACLs filtering capabilities in some cases.

Cisco Labs – Semester 3 – Routing and Switching
LAB 6.3 – EXTENDED ACLs INTERNET – OVERVIEW

Extended ACLs provide a more advanced form of filtering, with more flexibility in the way that packets are controlled. Extended ACLs can filter (permit or deny) packets based on source or destination address and also on the type of traffic (FTP, Telnet, HTTP, and so on). Because extended ACLs can block based on destination address, they can be placed near the source, which helps to reduce network traffic.

In this lab, you will work with multiple extended access control lists (ACLs) to regulate the traffic that is allowed to pass through multiple routers based on the source, destination, and type of traffic.

These are the steps necessary to use ACLs effectively:
1. Determine the ACL requirements (based on security needs and other considerations).
2. Construct one or more ACLs.
3. Verify the statements in the ACL.
4. Apply the ACLs to the necessary router interfaces.
5. Verify that the ACL is applied correctly to the intended interfaces.
6. Verify that the ACL is functioning properly.

Tools/Preparation:
This is primarily a paper-based practice exercise, but access to the five-router labs is desirable. A white board should be available to brainstorm the different ways to provide the required security. Work in teams of two or three. Before beginning this lab, you should read Chapter 6, "ACLs," in *Cisco Networking Academy Program: Second-Year Companion Guide*. You should also review Semester 3 online Chapter 6.

Required Resources:
- Standard Cisco five-router lab setup with hubs and switches
- Workstation connected to the router's console port with a rollover cable

Web Site Resources:
- **Routing basics** – http://www.cisco.com/univercd/cc/td/doc/cisintwk/ito_doc/routing.htm
- **General information on routers** – http://www.cisco.com/univercd/cc/td/doc/pcat/#2
- **2500 series routers** – http://www.cisco.com/warp/public/cc/cisco/mkt/access/2500/index.shtml
- **1600 series routers** – http://www.cisco.com/warp/public/cc/cisco/mkt/access/1600/index.shtml
- **Terms and acronyms** – http://www.cisco.com/univercd/cc/td/doc/cisintwk/ita/index.htm
- **IP routing protocol IOS command summary** –
  http://www.cisco.com/univercd/cc/td/doc/product/software/ios120/12cgcr/rbkixol.htm
- **Access control lists – overview and guidelines** –
  www.cisco.com/univercd/cc/td/doc/product/software/ios113ed/113ed_cr/secur_c/scprt3/scacls.htm

Notes:
_____
_____
_____
_____
_____

Cisco Labs – Semester 3 – Routing and Switching
LAB 6.3 – EXTENDED ACLs INTERNET – WORKSHEET

In this lab, you will design a security plan using multiple extended ACLs and determine where they should be applied based on the following standard router lab setup. There is more than one correct answer.

Start with the standard lab setup shown in the overview, and then draw a detailed diagram of all routers, servers, and networks to help work out the requirements. Use the space provided on the next page to diagram the requirements listed below and to help determine what ACLs are needed and where they should go.

Step 1. Define the ACL requirements.
The requirements and some assumptions for this lab are given below. In general, it is best to try to use the fewest ACLs possible while minimizing network traffic and allowing for potential network growth. You will use extended ACLs for this exercise.

Assume that your enterprise servers are located on network 219.17.100.0 (off LAB-B).

1. Allow everyone Web access (http protocol) to your web server 219.17.100.80.
2. Allow everyone DNS access to your DNS server 219.17.100.53.
3. Allow faculty from network 223.8.151.0 full access to any of these servers.
4. Allow no other access to any server on the 219.17.100.0 network.

Assume that students are all on network 210.93.105.0, and control access to or from their network. Assume that router Lab-A belongs to your ISP and that you do not have control over it.

4. Do *not* allow students to use FTP to the Internet (virus alert!).
5. Allow students all other access to the Internet.
6. Permit student access to the faculty network 223.8.151.0 for e-mail (SMTP).
7. Deny all other student access to the faculty network 223.8.151.0.

Step 2. Construct one or more ACLs.
Group the statement above based on common characteristics and where you think the ACL should be applied. Try to create the fewest ACLs possible and still be flexible. The format or syntax of the extended IP ACL statements that you will be using is shown below:

**access-list list# {permit/deny} [protocol] source IP wildcard mask [port]
       dest. IP wildcard mask [port] [established] [log] [other options]**
(Note: Any number from 100 and 199 can be used for an extended IP ACL.)

Step 3. Apply and check the ACLs with lab routers (if available).
If you have access to the routers in the lab, you can apply and check the ACLs you have created. You may not be able to test all the ACL filtering capabilities because you will not have an HTTP or DNS server or access to the Internet, but you can test most of the filtering. Remember that only one ACL can be applied per protocol (such as IP) per direction (in or out).

Cisco Labs – Semester 3 – Routing and Switching
LAB 6.3 – EXTENDED ACLs INTERNET – WORKSHEET

Diagram the routers and servers, and show the location of ACLs (router and interface, in or out) based on the security requirement.

Cisco Labs – Semester 3 – Routing and Switching
LAB 6.3 – EXTENDED ACLs INTERNET – ANSWERS

This is a suggested solution to the requirements. There are other possible solutions.

EXTENDED ACL 101
Assume that your enterprise servers are located on network 219.17.100.0 (off Lab-B).

1. Allow everyone Web access (http protocol) to your web server 219.17.100.80.
   Access-list 101 permit TCP any 219.17.100.80 eq HTTP

2. Allow everyone DNS access to your DNS server 219.17.100.53.
   Access-list 101 permit UDP any 219.17.100.53 eq DNS

3. Allow faculty from network 223.8.151.0 full access to any of these servers.
   Access-list 101 permit IP 223.8.151.0 0.0.0.255 219.17.100.0 0.0.0.255

4. Allow no other access to any server on the 219.17.100.0 network.
   Access-list 101 deny IP any 219.17.100.0 0.0.0.255

Apply this list to the appropriate router and interface on router Lab-B, interface E0.
   ip access-group 101

Note: With all ACLs, if the direction (in/out) is not specified, the packets will be filtered outgoing. Out is the default. In this case, you will filter packets coming out of interface E0.

EXTENDED ACL 102
Assume that students are all on network 210.93.105.0, and control access to or from their network. Assume that router Lab-A belongs to your ISP and that you do not have control over it.

1. Do *not* allow students to use FTP to the Internet (virus alert!).
   Access-list 102 deny TCP 210.93.105.0 0.0.0.255 any eq FTP

2. Allow students all other access to the Internet.
   Access-list 102 permit IP 210.93.105.0 0.0.0.255 any

Apply this list to the appropriate router and interface on router Lab-B, interface S1.
   Ip access-group 102

EXTENDED ACL 103
3. Permit student access to the faculty network 223.8.151.0 for e-mail (SMTP).
   Access-list 103 permit TCP 210.93.105.0 0.0.0.255 223.8.151.0 eq SMTP

4. Deny all students any other access to the faculty network 223.8.151.0.
   Access-list 103 deny IP 210.93.105.0 0.0.0.255 223.8.151.0 any

Apply this list to the appropriate router and interface on router Lab-C, interface E0.
   Ip access-group 103

Cisco Labs – Semester 3 – Routing and Switching
LAB 7.1 – IPX ROUTING – OVERVIEW
(Estimated time: 90 minutes)

Router Name - LAB A
Router Type - 2514
E 0 = 192.5.5.1
E 1 = 205.7.5.1
S 0 = 201.100.11.1
SM = 255.255.255.0

Router Name - LAB B
Router Type - 2503
E 0 = 219.17.100.1
S 0 = 199.6.13.1
S 1 = 201.100.11.2
SM = 255.255.255.0

Router Name - LAB C
Router Type - 2503
E 0 = 223.8.151.1
S 0 = 204.204.7.1
S 1 = 199.6.13.2
SM = 255.255.255.0

Router Name - LAB D
Router Type - 2501
E 0 = 210.93.105.1
S 1 = 204.204.7.2
SM = 255.255.255.0

Router Name - LAB E
Router Type - 2501
E 0 = 210.93.105.2
SM = 255.255.255.0

LEGEND

= ROUTER   User Exec Password = cisco

= HUB   Enable Secret Exec Password = class

= LAN SWITCH   Terminal vty Password = cisco

= CONSOLE CABLE

Objectives:

- To become familiar with Novell NetWare IPX protocol and its use in internetworks
- To configure the lab routers to route the Novell IPX protocol as well as IP
- To provide support for NetWare clients and servers running IPX

Background:

In previous labs, you have been working with the TCP/IP routed protocol or the Internet Protocol (IP). In this lab, you will work with Novell's Internetwork Packet Exchange (IPX) routed protocol. OSI Layer 3 protocols such as IP and IPX contain information in their packets to indicate what network the packet came from and what network it is going to. Routable protocols (such as IP and IPX) are those protocols that are capable of allowing packets to be routed between networks and that enable them to get from one location to another. Routers can run multiple routing (RIP or IGRP) and routed (IP and IPX) protocols. To be capable of routing both IP and IPX, the router must maintain multiple routing tables, one for each type of routed protocol being supported.

Cisco Labs - Semester 3 – Routing and Switching
LAB 7.1 – IPX ROUTING – OVERVIEW

Novell's IPX/SPX Implementation
IPX is a proprietary routed protocol developed by Novell Inc. for use with its NetWare Network Operating System. It is very widely used with private local- and wide-area networks that have Novell NetWare servers. Earlier versions of NetWare (3.x and most 4.x versions) used IPX as their primary protocol. To support these servers, it is necessary to run the IPX protocol on routers, servers, and workstations. Newer versions such as NetWare 5.0 can use IP natively. It is possible to have a multirouter Novell network using only the IPX protocol, but IP is still required to access the Internet. IPX does not support subnets and cannot be routed over the Internet.

The Novell network operating system uses two main protocols, IPX and SPX, to help ensure delivery of packets. IPX is responsible for Layer 3 routing to get packets from one network to another. Sequential Packet Exchange (SPX) is a connection-oriented packet delivery protocol similar to TCP. There are two parts to an IPX address: a network portion and a host portion. The network portion of the IPX address is a 32-bit hexadecimal number, and the host portion is the 48-bit MAC address of the NIC (for the server, workstation, and so on). Because the host or node address is its MAC address, it is not necessary to assign a host address as with IP. ARP is not required because the MAC address is known.

Tools/Preparation:
Before you start the lab, the teacher or lab assistant should have the standard router lab with all five routers set up. Before beginning this lab, you should read Chapter 7, "Novell IPX," in *Cisco Networking Academy Program: Second-Year Companion Guide*. You should also review Semester 3 online Chapter 7.

Required Resources:
- Standard Cisco five-router lab setup with hubs and switches
- Workstation connected to the router's console port
- Console cable (rollover)

Web Site Resources:
- **Routing basics** – http://www.cisco.com/univercd/cc/td/doc/cisintwk/ito_doc/routing.htm
- **General information on routers** – http://www.cisco.com/univercd/cc/td/doc/pcat/#2
- **2500 series routers** – http://www.cisco.com/warp/public/cc/cisco/mkt/access/2500/index.shtml
- **1600 series routers** – http://www.cisco.com/warp/public/cc/cisco/mkt/access/1600/index.shtml
- **Terms and acronyms** – http://www.cisco.com/univercd/cc/td/doc/cisintwk/ita/index.htm
- **Routing Novell IPX** –
  http://www.cisco.com/univercd/cc/td/doc/product/software/ssr90/rpc_r/54040.htm
- **Troubleshooting Novell IPX** –
  http://www.cisco.com/univercd/cc/td/doc/cisintwk/itg_v1/tr1908.htm
- **Novell IPX commands** –
  http://www.cisco.com/univercd/cc/td/doc/product/access/acs_fix/750/700cr44/700cripx.htm

Cisco Labs – Semester 3 – Routing and Switching
LAB 7.1 – IPX ROUTING – WORKSHEET

The following IOS IPX-related commands will help you with IPX connectivity information and troubleshooting:

IPX Connectivity/Troubleshooting Commands

show ipx interface	Shows the status of IPX interfaces and IPX configured parameters (frame type) on each interface
show ipx route	Displays the contents of the IPX routing table with known IPX networks
show ipx servers	Lists the Novell servers running IPX that are discovered through SAP advertisements
show ipx traffic	Shows IPX traffic information, including the number and type of IPX packets transmitted and received by the router
debug ipx routing activity	Displays dynamic information about IPX routing update packets that are transmitted and received (every 60 seconds)
debug ipx sap	Displays dynamic information about IPX Service Advertising Protocol (SAP) packets that are transmitted or received
ping	Use extended version (**ping** and then press Enter) to specify an IPX node address

Step 1. Determine the number of networks needed.
How many IPX networks will you need (LAN and WAN networks) for a five-router lab? _____
(Refer to the standard five-router diagram. How many IP networks are there?)

Step 2. Review proper IPX addressing.
Review the structure of the IPX addressing scheme and answer the following questions:

1. Would 6F be a valid IPX network number? _____   Why or why not? _____
    _____
    (Hint: Are IPX network numbers represented in decimal or in hex?)

2. Would 1a2b3c4d5e be a valid IPX network number? _____   Why or why not? _____
    _____
    (Hint: How long are IPX network numbers? How many bits? How many hex digits is that?)

Step 3. Enable IPX routing.
Use the following command to enable IPX routing for each router. This enables IPX RIP and SAP. After enabling IPX on the router, and while still in IPX configuration mode, go to Step 4 and select the interfaces that will route IPX and assign them network numbers.

   Router(config)# ipx routing

Cisco Labs – Semester 3 – Routing and Switching
LAB 7.1 – IPX ROUTING – WORKSHEET

Step 4. Create IPX network numbers.

Use the standard five-router diagram as a guide for creating unique network numbers for each "wire" or network. Fill in the table below with the model number of each router and the IPX network addresses you will use. Not all routers will have or use all the interfaces shown. Remember that serial interfaces between two routers will share the same network number. Hexadecimal IPX network numbers can contain numbers 0 through 9 and letters A to F, and can range from 1 to FFFFFFFF.

Router Name	Model Number	Ethernet 0 IPX Network	Ethernet 1 IPX Network	Serial 0 IPX Address	Serial 1 IPX Address
Lab-A					
Lab-B					
Lab-C					
Lab-D					
Lab-E					

Step 5. Assign IPX network numbers to interfaces.

On each interface on each router, configure the IPX network number from the table above:

    Router(config)# interface E0   (Selects the Ethernet interface E0)
    Router(config-if)# ipx network A2C   (A2C = unique IPX network number)

Step 6. Check for redundant paths.

3. Are there any redundant paths in the lab? That is, are there two or more ways for packets to get from one place to another? _____

4. If there are redundant paths (2), and you want IPX traffic load sharing over those two possible paths, you need to tell the router to accept multiple paths. Complete the command you would use:

    Router(config)# ipx _____ _____

Step 7. Check routing tables.

IPX RIP is automatically enabled when you enable IPX routing, so you can now check each router's routing table to verify that all routers have learned all the IPX networks:

    Router# show ipx route

Cisco Labs – Semester 3 – Routing and Switching
LAB 7.1 – IPX ROUTING – WORKSHEET

Step 8. Telnet to a neighboring router.
Telnet to another router and issue a **show running-config** command to see which interfaces are in use. Use the following command to find the IPX address of one of the Ethernet interfaces.

    Router# show ipx interface e0

5. What was the IPX address of the interface? _____

6. What portion is the network address? _____

7. What portion is the interface MAC address? _____

Step 9. Ping the neighboring Router interface.
Return to the router you were on, and issue the **ping** command, remembering to use a dot between the network number and the MAC address, and again after every four digits of the MAC address. Enter a sample IPX **ping** command here.

    Router# ping ipx _____

Step 10. Reflect.
In your journal, write about the differences between IPX and IP routing tables.

Cisco Labs – Semester 3 – Routing and Switching
LAB 7.1 – IPX ROUTING – ANSWERS

The following IOS IPX-related commands will help you with IPX connectivity information and troubleshooting:

IPX Connectivity/Troubleshooting Commands

show ipx interface	Shows the status of IPX interfaces and IPX configured parameters (frame type) on each interface
show ipx route	Displays the contents of the IPX routing table with known IPX networks
show ipx servers	Lists the Novell servers running IPX that are discovered through SAP advertisements
show ipx traffic	Shows IPX traffic information, including the number and type of IPX packets transmitted and received by the router
debug ipx routing activity	Displays dynamic information about IPX routing update packets that are transmitted and received (every 60 seconds)
debug ipx sap	Displays dynamic information about IPX Service Advertising Protocol (SAP) packets that are transmitted or received
ping	Use extended version (**ping** and then press Enter) to specify an IPX node address

Step 1. Determine the number of networks needed.
How many IPX networks will you need (LAN and WAN networks) for a five-router lab? **8**
(Refer to the standard five-router diagram on the next page. How many IP networks are there?)

Step 2. Review proper IPX addressing.
Review the structure of the IPX addressing scheme and answer the following questions:

1. Would 6F be a valid IPX network number? **Yes**   Why or why not? **IPX network numbers are expressed in hex and with 32 bits; anything less than FFFFFFFF would be valid.**
    (Hint: are IPX network numbers represented in decimal or in hex?)

2. Would 1a2b3c4d5e be a valid IPX network number? **No**   Why or why not? **There are too many hex digits (each hex digit is 4 bits).** (Hint: how long are IPX network numbers? How many bits? How many hex digits would that be?)

Step 3. Enable IPX routing.
Use the following command to enable IPX routing for each router. This enables IPX RIP and SAP. After enabling IPX on the router, and while still in IPX configuration mode, go to Step 4 and select the interfaces that will route IPX and assign them network numbers.

   Router(config)# ipx routing

Cisco Labs – Semester 3 – Routing and Switching
LAB 7.1 – IPX ROUTING – ANSWERS

Step 4. Create IPX network numbers.

Use the standard five-router diagram below as a guide for creating unique network numbers for each "wire" or network. Fill in the table below with the model number of each router and the IPX network addresses you will use. Not all routers will have or use all the interfaces shown. Remember that serial interfaces between two routers will share the same network number. Hexadecimal IPX network numbers can contain numbers 0 through 9 and letters A to F, and can range from 1 to FFFFFFFF.

Router Name	Model Number	Ethernet 0 IPX Network	Ethernet 1 IPX Network	Serial 0 IPX Address	Serial 1 IPX Address
Lab-A	2514	AA1	AA2	AB3	(Not used)
Lab-B	2503	BB1	(Not used)	BC3	AB3
Lab-C	2503	CC1	(Not used)	CD3	BC3
Lab-D	2501	DD1	(Not used)	(Not used)	CD3
Lab-E	2501	DD1	(Not used)	(Not used)	(Not used)

Step 5. Assign IPX network numbers to interfaces.

On each interface on each router, configure the IPX network number from the table above:

> **Router(config)# interface E0**   (Selects the Ethernet interface E0)
> **Router(config-if)# ipx network A2C**   (A2C = unique IPX network number)

Step 6. Check for redundant paths.

3. Are there any redundant paths in the lab? That is, are there two or more ways for packets to get from one place to another? **No**

4. If there are redundant paths (2), and you want IPX traffic load sharing over those two possible paths, you need to tell the router to accept multiple paths. Complete the command you would use:

> **Router(config)# ipx maximum-paths   2**

Step 7. Check routing tables.

IPX RIP is automatically enabled when you enable IPX routing, so you can now check each router's routing table to verify that all routers have learned all the IPX networks:

> **Router# show ipx route**

Cisco Labs – Semester 3 – Routing and Switching
LAB 7.1 – IPX ROUTING – ANSWERS

Step 8. Telnet to a neighboring router.
Telnet to another router and issue a **show running-config** command to see which interfaces are in use. Use the following command to find the IPX address of one of the interfaces.

    Router# show ipx interface e0

5. What was the IPX address of the interface? **DD1.1234.1234.1234** (Answers will vary.)

6. What portion is the network address? **DD1**

7. What portion is the interface MAC address? **1234.1234.1234**

Step 9. Ping the neighboring router interface.
Return to the router you were on and issue the **ping** command, remembering to use a dot between the network number and the MAC address, and again after every four digits of the MAC address. Enter a sample IPX **ping** command here

    Router# ping ipx DD1.1234.1234.1234
(This is a sample only; it will *not* be a valid address for the lab.)

Step 10. Reflect.
In your journal, write about the differences between IPX and IP routing tables.

Semester 4 Labs

Cisco Labs – Semester 4 – Wide-Area Networking
LAB 8.1 – WAN COMMANDS – OVERVIEW
(Estimated time: 60 minutes)

Router Name - LAB A
Router Type - 2514
E 0 = 192.5.5.1
E 1 = 205.7.5.1
S 0 = 201.100.11.1
SM = 255.255.255.0

Router Name - LAB B
Router Type - 2503
E 0 = 219.17.100.1
S 0 = 199.6.13.1
S 1 = 201.100.11.2
SM = 255.255.255.0

Router Name - LAB C
Router Type - 2503
E 0 = 223.8.151.1
S 0 = 204.204.7.1
S 1 = 199.6.13.2
SM = 255.255.255.0

Router Name - LAB D
Router Type - 2501
E 0 = 210.93.105.1
S 1 = 204.204.7.2
SM = 255.255.255.0

Router Name - LAB E
Router Type - 2501
E 0 = 210.93.105.2
SM = 255.255.255.0

LEGEND
= ROUTER   User Exec Password = cisco
= HUB   Enable Secret Exec Password = class
= LAN SWITCH   Terminal vty Password = cisco
= CONSOLE CABLE

Objectives:
- Explore the WAN capabilities of the router
- Use the terminology from the Semester 4 online chapters on WANs
- Experiment with some WAN-related IOS commands

Background:

LANs vs. WANs
This lab is an introduction to wide-area networks (WANs) and the part routers play in them. Local-area networks (LANs) typically consist of a group of computers that are interconnected with hubs or switches using physical cable (twisted-pair copper and multimode fiber). WANs are made up of two or more LANs that are geographically separate sites. They typically use services provided by a long-distance carrier with transmission over fiber or microwave to connect the sites. An organization can own the equipment that interconnects its WAN sites, but most often WAN links are leased from a service provider.

Cisco Labs – Semester 4 – Wide-Area Networking
LAB 8.1 – WAN COMMANDS – OVERVIEW

Routers and WANs

Although routers can be used to subdivide campus LANs to limit the size of broadcast domains and help maintain security, they are most commonly used to interconnect LANs to make WANs. The router is the interface or gateway from the LAN to the WAN. With most organizations' WANs, each location will have at least one router with an interface or link to one or more other locations in the WAN. This is usually done through a channel service unit/data service unit (CSU/DSU). Even small organizations with a single location today need a router to connect them to the largest WAN in the world, the Internet.

WANs and the OSI Model

WAN links typically operate at OSI Layer 2 (the data link layer) and convert the LAN frame encapsulation, such as Ethernet or Token Ring, to a wide-area Layer 2 frame encapsulation such as HDLC, PPP, or Frame Relay. As an example, let's say that you have two Ethernet LANs interconnected by a WAN link (such as a T1 line), and a workstation in LAN A needs to connect to a server in LAN B. The workstation sends a packet to the Ethernet interface (for example, E0) of the router in LAN A. That router removes the Ethernet LAN frame header, replaces it with a WAN frame header (such as Frame Relay or PPP), and sends it out one of its serial interfaces (for example, S0). When the router on LAN B receives the packet on its serial interface, it strips off the WAN frame header and replaces it with the LAN Ethernet frame header. The packet is delivered to the local server on LAN B through the router's Ethernet interface.

Tools/Preparation:

Before you start the lab, the teacher or lab assistant should have the standard router lab with all five routers set up. Before beginning this lab, you should read Chapter 8, "WANs," and Chapter 9, "WAN Design," in *Cisco Networking Academy Program: Second-Year Companion Guide*. You should also review the Semester 4 online chapters "WANs" and "WAN Design." Work individually or in teams.

Resources Required:

- Standard Cisco five-router lab setup with hubs and switches
- Workstation connected to the router's console port
- Router manuals and access to the Cisco web site (www.cisco.com)

Web Site Resources:

- **Routing basics** – http://www.cisco.com/univercd/cc/td/doc/cisintwk/ito_doc/routing.htm
- **General information on routers** – http://www.cisco.com/univercd/cc/td/doc/pcat/#2
- **2500 series routers** –http://www.cisco.com/warp/public/cc/cisco/mkt/access/2500/index.shtml
- **1600 series routers** – http://www.cisco.com/warp/public/cc/cisco/mkt/access/1600/index.shtml
- **Terms and acronyms** – http://www.cisco.com/univercd/cc/td/doc/cisintwk/ita/index.htm
- **IP routing protocol IOS command summary** –
  http://www.cisco.com/univercd/cc/td/doc/product/software/ios120/12cgcr/rbkixol.htm
- **Introduction to WAN technologies** –
  http://www.cisco.com/univercd/cc/td/doc/cisintwk/ito_doc/introwan.htm

Cisco Labs – Semester 4 – Wide-Area Networking
LAB 8.1 – WAN COMMANDS – WORKSHEET

Step 1. Review router lab WAN physical connections.

The standard five-router lab setup uses WAN serial cables to simulate three wide-area network connections between four of the routers (A, B, C, and D). These four routers could all belong to corporation XYZ and could be located in different cities across the United States (Lab-A = Anaheim, California; Lab-B = Boise, Idaho; Lab-C = Chicago, Illinois; Lab-D = Dallas, Texas). Routers D and E are attached to a common Ethernet LAN. Normally, the cable from the router in each location would connect to a channel service unit/data service unit (CSU/DSU) and then to a WAN link, such as a T1 (1.544 Mbps) line from a service provider. With some routers, the CSU is built in or can be installed in a modular slot.

One end of each cable is a DB60 (60-pin) connector that attaches to a synchronous serial interface on the router (S0 or S1, in most cases). The other end is a V.35 connector that normally attaches to the CSU/DSU. The CSU/DSU then connects to the digital data line (such as a 56 K or T1 link) via a network interface unit (NIU) at the demarc (demarcation point). This is the separation point between customer premises equipment (CPE) and the WAN link service provider's connection. The standard five-router lab setup simulates the CSU/DSUs on point-to-point WAN links by crossing the connections between the V.35 cables, which eliminates the need for the CSU/DSUs.

The router is typically the data-circuit terminating equipment (DTE) and the CSU/DSU is normally the data communications equipment (DCE). Because there is no CSU/DSU, one of the routers on each simulated WAN link must play the role of the DCE to provide the synchronous clocking signal. With the standard lab setup, router Lab-A serial interface 0 is the DCE, and the clock rate is set to 56000 bps on that interface, simulating a 56 K digital data circuit. You must attach the DCE (female) cable to this router interface. The DTE (male) serial cable is attached to the Serial 1 interface on the next router Lab-B. No clock is set on the Lab-B S1 interface. Serial interface S0 on router Lab-B then becomes the DCE for the next router.

Step 2. Identify the router lab WAN connections.

Use the standard lab diagram to identify the wide-area network (WAN) links. Fill in the table below with WAN information contained in the diagram, including the number of the WAN IP network between each pair of routers, the router names that have WANs between them, the interfaces in use on each router, and the characteristics of the WAN interface cable.

1. Fill in the following WAN connection table.

WAN IP Network Number	Connects <u>from</u> Which Router and Interface?	DCE or DTE?	Connects <u>to</u> Which Router and Interface?	DCE or DTE?

Cisco Labs – Semester 4 – Wide-Area Networking
LAB 8.1 – WAN COMMANDS – WORKSHEET

Step 3. Diagram the lab WAN connections.

Use the standard lab diagram as a starting point, and draw the physical and logical WAN topology of the existing lab setup. The main purpose is to identify the routers and WAN links. Identify and label all WAN connections (identify DCE and DTE cables, clock rate, and so on).

2. Diagram the WAN links and their characteristics in the standard lab setup.

Cisco Labs – Semester 4 – Wide-Area Networking
LAB 8.1 – WAN COMMANDS – WORKSHEET

Step 4. Review WAN connection options.
Refer to the Cisco online documentation (www.cisco.com) and the hardware manuals, such as the _Cisco 2500 Installation and Configuration Guide_, for the routers you are working with.

3. What are common options or types of router WAN connections?

   _____

   _____

   _____

   _____

   _____

   _____

   _____

4. What router features and/or additional hardware would you need to use ISDN, PPP, Frame-Relay, or dial-up WAN connections?

   _____

   _____

   _____

   _____

   _____

   _____

   _____

   _____

   _____

Step 5. Review WAN encapsulation types.
The frame encapsulation used at the data link layer (OSI Layer 2) will vary depending on the WAN technology used between networks connected by routers. The data link encapsulation places a header and a trailer on the packet. Layer 2 framing on a LAN is different than that on a WAN, and the router must convert between the two.

Check the WAN encapsulation on Lab-A serial interface 0 using the following command:

   Router# show interface s0

5. What is the default WAN encapsulation currently in use on the interface between routers Lab-A and Lab-B? _____

To see what WAN encapsulation options are available, use the following commands:

   Router(config)# interface Serial 0
   Router(config-if) #encapsulation ?

6. What are some of the data link layer WAN encapsulation types available?

   _____

   _____

Cisco Labs – Semester 4 – Wide-Area Networking
LAB 8.1 – WAN COMMANDS – WORKSHEET

Step 6. Review WAN-related router commands.
The following **router show** commands can help to explore the WAN capabilities of the router. On a router with standard configurations, try the following **show** commands from the privileged EXEC mode, note the results, and answer the questions.

7. **show interfaces**
    What does this command tell you about WAN connections?

    _____

    _____

    _____

8. **show int s0, show int s1, show int bri0, show int e0, show int e1**, and so on
    What do these commands tell you about WAN connections?

    _____

    _____

    _____

9. **show protocols**
    What does this command tell you about WAN connections?

    _____

    _____

    _____

10. **show ip route**
    What does this command tell you about WAN connections?

    _____

    _____

    _____

11. **show cdp neighbors**
    What does this command tell you about WAN connections?

    _____

    _____

Step 7. Explore WAN protocol commands.
Try some of these additional WAN protocol-related commands. Be sure to use a space and a "?" at the end of the command to see the options available. If the WAN option is not available, you will not get an error, but no information will be displayed. Write down some of the options that are displayed.

12. **show frame-relay ?** _____

13. **show dialer ?** _____

14. **show ppp ?** _____

15. **show smds ?** _____

16. **show x25 ?** _____

Cisco Labs – Semester 4 – Wide-Area Networking
LAB 8.1 – WAN COMMANDS – ANSWERS

1. Fill in the following WAN connection table.

WAN IP Network Number	Connects from Which Router and Interface?	DCE or DTE?	Connects to Which Router and Interface?	DCE or DTE?
201.100.11.0	Lab-A: Serial 0	DCE	Lab-B: Serial 1	DTE
199.6.13.0	Lab-B: Serial 0	DCE	Lab-C: Serial 1	DTE
204.204.7.0	Lab-C: Serial 0	DCE	Lab-D: Serial 1	DTE

2. Diagram the WAN links and their characteristics in the standard lab setup.
   The diagram should show only the routers with WAN connections and only WAN-related information.

3. What are common options or types of router WAN connections?
   Most routers have the capability to support various types of WAN connections, depending on the model and interfaces provided. Some of the more common WAN interfaces discussed in Semester 4 labs, online lessons, and *Cisco Networking Academy Program: Second-Year Companion Guide* are PPP, ISDN, Frame Relay, and dial-up.

4. What router features and/or additional hardware would you need to use ISDN, PPP, Frame-Relay, or dial-up WAN connections?
   In most cases, the router is purchased with specific WAN interfaces such as serial or BRI ISDN. These interfaces can also be added later with some routers by inserting modular cards. Additional external hardware is frequently required, as is the specific service such as an ISDN line or a T1 circuit to the premises. Synchronous serial router interfaces can support PPP and Frame Relay with the addition of a CSU/DSU, and ISDN interfaces can support Basic Rate Interface (BRI) with the addition of a network termination 1 (NT1) device. Asynchronous router interfaces such as the AUX port require a modem to be attached. Refer to manuals and online documentation for additional details.

Check the WAN encapsulation on Lab-A serial interface 0 using the following command:

   Router# show interface s0

5. What is the default WAN encapsulation currently in use on the interface between routers Lab-A and Lab-B? **High Level Data Link Control (HDLC), Cisco proprietary version**

To see what WAN encapsulation options are available, use the following commands:

   Router(config)# interface Serial 0
   Router(config-if)# encapsulation ?

6. What are some of the data link layer WAN encapsulation types available?
   Frame-Relay, HDLC, LAPB, PPP, SDLC, and SMDS, among others

7. **show interfaces**
   What does this command tell you about WAN connections? **Displays all ports with line protocol status, the IP address, bandwidth, encapsulation type, and interface counters with packets sent and received. E0 and E1 are LAN connections. BRI0 may not exist.**

8. **show int s0, show int s1, show int bri0, show int e0, show int e1**, and so on
   What do these commands tell you about WAN connections?
   Displays a specific port with line protocol status, the IP address, bandwidth, encapsulation type, and interface counters with packets sent and received. E0 and E1 are LAN connections. BRI0 is a WAN connection but may not exist or may not be in use.

9. **show protocols**
   What does this command tell you about WAN connections?
   Displays a list of all interfaces (LAN and WAN) and tells whether the line protocol for each is up or down

10. **show ip route**
    What does this command tell you about WAN connections?
    Displays a list of all known networks that are active, and indicates how they were learned (directly connected, RIP, IGRP, and so on)

11. **show cdp neighbors**
    What does this command tell you about WAN connections?
    Displays a list of neighboring attached devices with the device ID, the local interface, and information on what type and model of device it is (router, switch, and so on)

Try some of these additional WAN protocol-related commands. Be sure use a space and a "?" at the end of the command to see the options available. If the WAN option is not available or is not being used, you will not get an error, but no information will be displayed. Write down some of the options that are displayed.

12. **show frame-relay ? IP, LMI, MAP, PVC, route, traffic**

13. **show dialer ? Interface**

14. **show ppp ? Multilink**

15. **show smds ? Addresses, map, traffic**

16. **show x25 ? Map, PAD, Remote Red, route, VC**

Cisco Labs – Semester 4 – Wide-Area Networking
EXERCISE 8.2 – WAN ACRONYMS – OVERVIEW
(Estimated time: 60 minutes)

Router Name - LAB A
Router Type - 2514
E 0 = 192.5.5.1
E 1 = 205.7.5.1
S 0 = 201.100.11.1
SM = 255.255.255.0

Router Name - LAB C
Router Type - 2503
E 0 = 223.8.151.1
S 0 = 204.204.7.1
S 1 = 199.6.13.2
SM = 255.255.255.0

Router Name - LAB E
Router Type - 2501
E 0 = 210.93.105.2
SM = 255.255.255.0

Router Name - LAB B
Router Type - 2503
E 0 = 219.17.100.1
S 0 = 199.6.13.1
S 1 = 201.100.11.2
SM = 255.255.255.0

Router Name - LAB D
Router Type - 2501
E 0 = 210.93.105.1
S 1 = 204.204.7.2
SM = 255.255.255.0

LEGEND

= ROUTER   User Exec Password = cisco

= HUB   Enable Secret Exec Password = class

= LAN SWITCH   Terminal vty Password = cisco

= CONSOLE CABLE

Objectives:
- Review some of the more common WAN-related acronyms and terminology
- Check your knowledge of WAN acronym definitions

Background:
The computer and networking field uses an incredible number of acronyms and abbreviations, some-times called TLAs (for three-letter acronyms). Many of these are related to wide-area networking (WAN, another TLA!). When discussing WANs with a coworker or an industry representative, you should understand the meaning of these acronyms, or at least define the words that make them up. This exercise will highlight some of the more common acronyms and terminology used.

Tools/Preparation:
Before beginning this lab, you should read Chapter 8, "WANs," and Chapter 9, "WAN Design," in *Cisco Networking Academy Program: Second-Year Companion Guide.* You should also review Semester 4 online chapters "WANs" and "WAN Design." Complete in teams or work alone.

Resource Required:
- Semester 4 online glossary and the *Cisco Networking Academy Program: Second-Year Companion Guide* glossary

Web Site Resources:
- **Terms and acronyms** – http://www.cisco.com/univercd/cc/td/doc/cisintwk/ita/index.htm
- **Introduction to WAN technologies** –
  http://www.cisco.com/univercd/cc/td/doc/cisintwk/ito_doc/introwan.htm

Cisco Labs – Semester 4 – Wide-Area Networking
EXERCISE 8.2 – WAN ACRONYMS – WORKSHEET

Step 1. Define the following WAN acronyms and terms.

Try to define as many of these WAN-related acronyms as possible as a pretest, and then take this challenge again at the end of the semester to see how many more you know. Give yourself a point for the definition of the acronym and a point for related terms or a more detailed definition.

Acronym	Definition	Related Terms/Devices/Examples or Additional Explanation
2B+D		
ATM		
BECN		
BRI		
CHAP		
CIR		
CO		
CPE		
CSU/DSU		
DCE		
DDR		
DEMARC		
DLCI		
DTE		
FECN		
Frame Relay		
IETF		
ISDN		
LAPB		
LAPD		
LCP		
LMI		
MAN		
NCP		

Cisco Labs – Semester 4 – Wide-Area Networking
EXERCISE 8.2 – WAN ACRONYMS – WORKSHEET

Acronym	Definition	Related Terms/Devices/Examples or Additional Explanation
NT1		
NT2		
PAP		
PBX		
PDN		
POP		
PPP		
PRI		
PSTN		
PVC		
RBOC		
SDLC		
SLIP		
SMDS		
SOHO		
SPID		
SS7		
SVC		
T1		
T3		
TA		
TDM		
TE1		
TE2		
X.25		

Cisco Labs – Semester 4 – Wide-Area Networking
EXERCISE 8.2 – WAN ACRONYMS – ANSWERS

Step 1. Define the following WAN acronyms and terms.

Try to define as many of these WAN-related acronyms as possible as a pretest, and then take this challenge again at the end of the semester to see how many more you know. Indicate the definition of the acronym, and then list related terms or a more specific definition.

Acronym	Definition	Related Terms/Devices/Examples or Additional Explanation
2B+D	2 bearer + 1 delta	Channels for BRI ISDN
ATM	Asynchronous Transfer Mode	Fixed cell length, packet-switched network
BECN	Backward Explicit Congestion Acknowledgement	Frame Relay term
BRI	Basic Rate Interface	ISDN (narrowband) – 2 x 64 Kbps bearer channels and 1 16 Kbps delta (or control) channel
CHAP	Challenge Handshake Authentication Protocol	Security protocol for network communications
CIR	committed information rate	Frame Relay term
CO	central office	Telephone company switch location
CPE	customer premises equipment	Equipment owned by the customer
CSU/DSU	channel service unit/data service unit	Interface device for a digital data circuit (56 K or T1)
DCE	data circuit-terminating equipment (or data communications equipment)	Examples: modem or CSU/DSU
DDR	dial-on-demand routing	Dials WAN connection when needed
DEMARC	demarcation point	Point where service provider portion of WAN link begins
DLCI	data link connection identifier	Frame Relay term
DTE	data terminal equipment	Examples: PC, terminal, router
FECN	forward explicit congestion notification	Frame Relay term
Frame Relay	Frame Relay	Newer WAN packet-switching protocol suited to digital phone lines
IETF	Internet Engineering Task Force	Develops most OSI Layer 3 and higher protocols and standards
ISDN	Integrated Services Digital Network	Types: BRI and PRI – voice, video, and data
LAPB	Link Access Procedure – Balanced	X.25 data link protocol
LAPD	Link Access Procedure – D Channel	ISDN data link protocol
LCP	Link Control Protocol	Frame Relay term
LMI	Local Management Interface	Frame Relay term
MAN	metropolitan-area network	Developed by RBOCs – IEEE 802.6

Cisco Labs – Semester 4 – Wide-Area Networking
EXERCISE 8.2 – WAN ACRONYMS – ANSWERS

NCP	Network Control Program	Frame Relay term
NT1	Network Termination Device – Type 1	ISDN term – single connection to ISDN network
NT2	Network Termination Device – Type 2	ISDN term – multiple connections to ISDN network (like ISDN hub)
PAP	Password Authentication Protocol	Older, less secure network security
PBX	private branch exchange	Local customer-owned phone switch
PDN	public data network	LD carriers and switching equipment
POP	point of presence	Point (room) at which the telco enters the customer site
PPP	Point-to-Point Protocol	WAN data link encapsulation; successor to SLIP
PRI	Primary Rate Interface	ISDN (broadband) – 23 x 64 Kbps bearer channels, and 1 x 64 Kbps delta channel
PSTN	Public Switched Telephone Network	Central-office-to-central-office circuit-switched network
PVC	permanent virtual circuit	Frame Relay and others; more common than SVC
RBOC	Regional Bell Operating Company	Subdivision of AT&T breakup
SDLC	Synchronous Data Link Control	IBM WAN data link protocol
SLIP	Serial Line Internet Protocol	Precursor to PPP
SMDS	Switched Multimegabit Data Service	RBOC-developed MAN packet-switching protocol for digital lines
SOHO	small office/home office	Market segment for WANs
SPID	service profile identifier	ISDN term
SS7	Signaling System 7	Independent PSTN call setup and control network
SVC	switched virtual circuit	Frame Relay and others; less common than PVC
T1	Trunk Carrier 1	Basic unit of digital service – 1.544 Mbps over four copper wires
T3	Trunk Carrier 3	Basic unit of digital service – About 45 Mbps over fiber
TA	terminal adapter	Converts non-ISDN TE2 device (analog phone) to connect to ISDN
TDM	time-division multiplexing	T1 method of combining multiple channels (24) on one set of wires
TE1	Terminal Equipment Type 1	Native ISDN device (ISDN phone or PBX)
TE2	Terminal Equipment Type 2	Non-native ISDN device (analog phone)
X.25	X.25	Older WAN packet-switching protocol suited to analog phone lines

Cisco Labs – Semester 4 – Wide-Area Networking
LAB 10.1 – PPP CONFIGURATION – OVERVIEW
(Estimated time: 60 minutes)

Router Name - LAB A
Router Type - 2514
E 0 = 192.5.5.1
E 1 = 205.7.5.1
S 0 = 201.100.11.1
SM = 255.255.255.0

Router Name - LAB B
Router Type - 2503
E 0 = 219.17.100.1
S 0 = 199.6.13.1
S 1 = 201.100.11.2
SM = 255.255.255.0

Router Name - LAB C
Router Type - 2503
E 0 = 223.8.151.1
S 0 = 204.204.7.1
S 1 = 199.6.13.2
SM = 255.255.255.0

Router Name - LAB D
Router Type - 2501
E 0 = 210.93.105.1
S 1 = 204.204.7.2
SM = 255.255.255.0

Router Name - LAB E
Router Type - 2501
E 0 = 210.93.105.2
SM = 255.255.255.0

LEGEND

= ROUTER   User Exec Password = cisco

= HUB   Enable Secret Exec Password = class

= LAN SWITCH   Terminal vty Password = cisco

= CONSOLE CABLE

Objectives:
- Understand how WAN encapsulation types affect synchronous serial connections
- Convert from HDLC to PPP encapsulation on a WAN connection
- Use the terminology of the Semester 4 online lesson on WANs

Background:
This lab focuses on Point-to-Point Protocol (PPP). PPP is a wide-area network (WAN) protocol that provides OSI Layer 2 (data link layer) services for router-to-router and host-to-network connections over synchronous and asynchronous circuits using a serial interface. It is commonly used by PCs to connect to an Internet service provider (ISP) via a dial-up phone line (asynchronous host-to-network) or as a WAN encapsulation method between LANs (synchronous router-to-router). PPP is an international, standardized, and widely used protocol developed by the Internet Engineering Task Force (IETF). PPP is considered a part of the TCP/IP protocol suite and supports a number of LAN protocols such as IP and IPX, and various methods of security authentication such as PAP and CHAP. PPP can be used on various physical media, including twisted-pair, fiber, or satellite transmission. It uses a variation of High-Speed Data Link Control (HDLC) for packet encapsulation.

Cisco Labs – Semester 4 – Wide-Area Networking
LAB 10.1 – PPP CONFIGURATION – OVERVIEW

Synchronous Serial Ports

Nearly all wide-area network (WAN) links used with internetworks are serial, meaning that they transmit bits one after another in a series along a wire or fiber cable. Routers have synchronous serial ports for WAN connections. They are not the same as the asynchronous serial connection ports found on PCs, and they are capable of much higher data rates. Most routers have at least one synchronous serial port for WAN connections and two asynchronous serial ports; a console port for local connection and an AUX port for remote configuration of the router.

The WAN connections between the routers in the standard Cisco lab setup are synchronous serial links. Speeds for serial digital WAN links can range from a 56 Kbps circuit to a T1 (about 1.5 Mbps) or a T3 (about 45 Mbps). When setting up the serial WAN links for the router lab, the default Layer 2 encapsulation is a Cisco proprietary version of High-Level Data Link Control (HDLC) protocol. PPP is more standardized, providing better security and support for dial-up connections. With this lab, you will convert the WAN links between the lab routers from HDLC to PPP. The PPP encapsulation must be set on both ends of the WAN connection.

Tools/Preparation:

Before you start the lab, the teacher or lab assistant should have the standard router lab with all five routers set up. Before beginning this lab, you should read Chapter 10, "PPP," in *Cisco Networking Academy Program: Second-Year Companion Guide*. You should also review the Semester 4 online chapter on PPP. Work individually or in teams.

Resources Required:

- Standard Cisco five-router lab setup with hubs and switches
- Two routers with a WAN link between them and HDLC encapsulation (default)
- Workstation connected to the router's console port
- Router manuals

Web Site Resources:

- **Routing basics** – http://www.cisco.com/univercd/cc/td/doc/cisintwk/ito_doc/routing.htm
- **General information on routers** – http://www.cisco.com/univercd/cc/td/doc/pcat/#2
- **2500 series routers** – http://www.cisco.com/warp/public/cc/cisco/mkt/access/2500/index.shtml
- **1600 series routers** – http://www.cisco.com/warp/public/cc/cisco/mkt/access/1600/index.shtml
- **Terms and acronyms** – http://www.cisco.com/univercd/cc/td/doc/cisintwk/ita/index.htm
- **IP routing protocol IOS command summary** –
  http://www.cisco.com/univercd/cc/td/doc/product/software/ios120/12cgcr/rbkixol.htm
- **Introduction to WAN technologies** –
  http://www.cisco.com/univercd/cc/td/doc/cisintwk/ito_doc/introwan.htm

Notes:

_____

_____

_____

Cisco Labs – Semester 4 – Wide-Area Networking
LAB 10.1 – PPP CONFIGURATION – WORKSHEET

Select a pair of routers that have a WAN serial link between them, such as Lab-A and Lab-B, before starting the lab. You could also use Lab-B and Lab-C, or Lab-C and Lab-D. Connect your workstation to the console port connection of the first router (Lab-A).

Step 1. Use the lab diagram and the show running-config command to answer the following questions about the Lab-A router:

 Lab-A# show running-config

1. Which serial interface is used for the WAN link? _____
2. What is the IP address of this interface? _____
3. What is the subnet mask of this interface? _____
4. Is this interface a DCE or DTE connection? _____
5. How do you know whether it is DCE or DTE? _____
6. What is the clock rate set to for his interface? _____
7. What is the bandwidth to set for this interface (if set)? _____
8. What would the bandwidth be set to if this were a T1 interface? _____

Step 2. Examine the WAN cables attached to router Lab-A, and answer the following three questions:

9. To which interface is the cable attached on router Lab-A? _____
10. What type of physical connector is the serial port on the router? _____
11. What type of physical connector is on the other end of the cable? _____

Step 3. Use the show interface command, and answer the following questions:

 Lab-A# show interface serial 0

12. What is the status of the interface and the line protocol? _____
13. How are the IP address and subnet mask displayed? _____
14. What is the maximum transmission unit (MTU)? _____
15. What is the bandwidth set to? _____
16. What is the purpose of setting the bandwidth? _____
17. What is the encapsulation currently set to? _____

Step 4. Remove the bandwidth setting from Serial S0 with the following series of commands:

 Lab-A# config t
 Lab-A(config)# int s0
 Lab-A(config-if)# no bandwidth

18. Use the **show interface s0** command again. What is the default bandwidth set to now?

 _____

Cisco Labs – Semester 4 – Wide-Area Networking
LAB 10.1 – PPP CONFIGURATION – WORKSHEET

19. Why do you think this is? _____

Change the bandwidth back to 56 Kb with the following series of commands:

Lab-A# config t
Lab-A(config)# int s0
Lab-A(config-if)# bandwidth 56

Use the **show interface s0** command again to verify that the bandwidth has been changed.

Step 5. Use the show cdp neighbors command, and answer the following questions:

Lab-A# show cdp neighbors

20. What is the device ID of the neighboring router? _____
21. What is the local interface on which this device was discovered? _____
22. What is the capability of the device? _____
23. What model platform number is it? _____
24. What is the port ID for the neighboring router interface? _____

Step 6. Check the configuration of the WAN interface on router Lab-B.
Telnet from router Lab-A to router Lab-B, and use the lab diagram and the **show running-config**
command to answer the following questions (either Telnet to the router name or the IP address of the
serial interface):

Lab-B# show running-config

25. Which serial interface is used for the WAN link? _____
26. What is the IP address of this interface? _____
27. What is the subnet mask of this interface? _____
28. Is this interface a DCE or a DTE connection? _____
29. How do you know whether it is DCE or DTE? _____
30. What is the clock rate set to for this interface? _____
31. What is the bandwidth set to for this interface? _____

**Step 7. Examine the WAN cables attached to router Lab-B, and answer the following
three questions:**

32. What interface is the cable attached to on router Lab-B? _____
33. What type of physical connector is the serial port on the router? _____
34. What type of physical connector is on the other end of the cable? _____

Cisco Labs – Semester 4 – Wide-Area Networking
LAB 10.1 – PPP CONFIGURATION – WORKSHEET

Step 8. Use the show interface command, and answer the following questions:

Lab-B# show interface serial 1

35. What is the status of the interface and the line protocol? _____
36. How is the IP address and subnet mask shown? _____
37. What is the maximum transmission unit (MTU)? _____
38. What is the bandwidth set to? _____
39. What is the encapsulation currently set to? _____

Step 9. Use the show cdp neighbors command, and answer the following questions:

Lab-A# show cdp neighbors

40. What is the device ID of the neighboring router? _____
41. What is the local interface that this device was discovered on? _____
42. What is the capability of the device? _____
43. What model platform number is it? _____
44. What is the port ID for the neighboring router interface? _____

Step 10. Change the WAN encapsulation on router Lab-A from HDLC to PPP.
Connect your workstation to the console port connection on router Lab-A, and use the following
commands to change the WAN encapsulation on router Lab-A serial interface 0. Then answer the
following questions:

Lab-A# config t
Lab-A(config)# interface serial 0
Lab-A(config-if)# encapsulation ppp

45. Use the **show interface s0** command. What is the status of the interface and the line
protocol now? _____
46. What does this mean? _____

_____

_____
47. What was the encapsulation previously set to? _____
48. What is the encapsulation set to now? _____
49. Can you ping or Telnet from router Lab-A to router Lab-B? _____
50. Why or why not? _____

_____

_____

Cisco Labs – Semester 4 – Wide-Area Networking
LAB 10.1 – PPP CONFIGURATION – WORKSHEET

Step 11. Change the WAN encapsulation on router Lab-B from HDLC to PPP.
Connect your workstation to the console port connection on router Lab-B (because you can no longer
Telnet to it), and use the following commands to change the WAN encapsulation on router Lab-B
serial interface 1. Then answer the following questions:

    Lab-B# config t
    Lab-B(config)# interface serial 1
    Lab-B(config-if)# encapsulation ppp

51. Use the **show interface s1** command. What is the status of the interface and the line
    protocol now? _____
52. What is the encapsulation currently set to? _____
53. Can you ping or Telnet from router Lab-A to router Lab-B? _____
54. Why or why not? _____
    _____
    _____
    _____

Cisco Labs – Semester 4 – Wide-Area Networking
LAB 10.1 – PPP CONFIGURATION – ANSWERS

Step 1. Use the lab diagram and the show running-config command to answer the following questions about the Lab-A router:

Lab-A# show running-config

1. Which serial interface is used for the WAN link? **Serial 0**
2. What is the IP address of this interface? **201.100.11.1**
3. What is the subnet mask of this interface? **255.255.255.0**
4. Is this interface a DCE or a DTE connection? **DCE**
5. How do you know whether it is DCE or DTE? **Check clock rate and cable type female**
6. What is the clock rate set to for this interface? **56000**
7. What is the bandwidth set for this interface (if set)? **56 Kb (for routing metric)**
8. What would the bandwidth be set to if this were a T1 interface? **1544 K**

Step 2. Examine the WAN cables attached to router Lab-A, and answer the following three questions:

9. To what interface is the cable attached on router Lab-A? **Serial 0**
10. What type of physical connector is the serial port on the router? **DB60 female**
11. What type of physical connector is on the other end of the cable? **V.35 DCE (female)**

Step 3. Use the show interface command, and answer the following questions:

Lab-A# show interface serial 0

12. What is the status of the interface and the line protocol? **Serial 0 is up, line protocol is up.**
13. How are the IP address and subnet mask displayed? **201.100.11.1 / 24 (Class C 24 bits)**
14. What is the maximum transmission unit (MTU)? **1500 (bytes)**
15. What is the bandwidth set to? **56 Kbit**
16. What is the purpose of setting the bandwidth? **Sets a metric that can be used by a routing protocol such as IGRP to determine the best path.**
17. What is the encapsulation currently set to? **HDLC (Cisco proprietary, by default)**

Step 4. Remove the bandwidth setting from Serial S0 with the following series of commands:

Lab-A# config t
Lab-A(config)# int s0
Lab-A(config-if)# no bandwidth

18. Use the **show interface s0** command again. What is the default bandwidth set to now? **1544 Kbit (or 1.544 Mbps)**
19. Why do you think this is? **This is the bandwidth (speed) of a standard T1, the most common digital WAN data link.**

Change the bandwidth back to 56 Kbits using instructions in the worksheet.

Cisco Labs – Semester 4 – Wide-Area Networking
LAB 10.1 – PPP CONFIGURATION – ANSWERS

Step 5. Use the show cdp neighbors command, and answer the following questions:

    Lab-A# show cdp neighbors

20. What is the device ID of the neighboring router? **Lab-B**
21. What is the local interface that this device was discovered on? **Serial 0**
22. What is the capability of the device? **R = Router**
23. What model platform number is it? **2500**
24. What is the port ID for the neighboring router interface? **Serial 1**

Step 6. Check the configuration of the WAN interface on router Lab-B.
Telnet from router Lab-A to router Lab-B, and use the **show running-config** command to answer the
following questions (Telnet to either the router name or the IP address of the serial interface):

    Lab-B# show running-config

25. Which serial interface is used for the WAN link? **Serial 1**
26. What is the IP address of this interface? **201.100.11.2**
27. What is the subnet mask of this interface? **255.255.255.0**
28. Is this interface a DCE or a DTE connection? **DTE**
29. How do you know whether it is DCE or DTE? **No clock rate and cable type male (DTE)**
30. What is the clock rate set to for his interface? **Not set**
31. What is the bandwidth set to for this interface? **56**

**Step 7. Examine the WAN cables attached to router Lab-B, and answer the following
three questions:**
32. Which interface is the cable attached to on router Lab-B? **Serial 1**
33. What type of physical connector is the serial port on the router? **DB60 female**
34. What type of physical connector is on the other end of the cable? **V.35 DTE (male)**

Step 8. Use the show interface command, and answer the following questions:

    Lab-B# show interface serial 1

35. What is the status of the interface and the line protocol? **Serial 1 is up, line protocol is up.**
36. How are the IP address and subnet mask shown? **201.100.11.2 / 24 (Class C = 24 bits)**
37. What is the maximum transmission unit (MTU)? **1500 (bytes)**
38. What is the bandwidth set to? **56 Kbit**
39. What is the encapsulation currently set to? **HDLC (Cisco proprietary, by default)**

Cisco Labs – Semester 4 – Wide-Area Networking
LAB 10.1 – PPP CONFIGURATION – ANSWERS

Step 9. Use the show cdp neighbors command, and answer the following questions:

    Lab-A# show cdp neighbors

40. What is the device ID of the neighboring router? **Lab-A**
41. What is the local interface that this device was discovered on? **Serial 1**
42. What is the capability of the device? **R = Router**
43. What model platform number is it? **2500**
44. What is the port ID for the neighboring router interface? **Serial 0**

Step 10. Change the WAN encapsulation on router Lab-A from HDLC to PPP.
Connect your workstation to the console port connection on router Lab-A, and use the following commands to change the WAN encapsulation on router Lab-A serial interface 0. Then answer the following questions:

    Lab-A# config t
    Lab-A(config)# interface serial 0
    Lab-A(config-if)# encapsulation ppp

45. Use the **show interface s0** command. What is the status of the interface and the line protocol?
    Serial 1 is up, line protocol is down.
46. What does this mean? **The Layer 1 physical link (cable) is okay (carrier detect is up), but the Layer 2 data-link protocols are not communicating (are not receiving keepalive messages).**
47. What was the encapsulation previously set to? **HDLC (Cisco proprietary, by default)**
48. What is the encapsulation now set to? **PPP**
49. Can you ping or Telnet from router Lab-A to router Lab-B? **No**
50. Why or why not? **The WAN encapsulation on Lab-A Serial 0 is now PPP, and the WAN encapsulation on Lab-B Serial 1 is still the default of HDLC. These are two different WAN data-link protocols and are incompatible.**

Step 11. Change the WAN encapsulation on router Lab-B from HDLC to PPP.
Connect your workstation to the console port connection on Router Lab-B (since you can no longer telnet to it) and use the following commands to change the WAN encapsulation on Router Lab-B serial interface 1. Then answer the following questions:

    Lab-B# config t
    Lab-B(config)# interface serial 1
    Lab-B(config-if)# encapsulation ppp

51. Use the **show interface s1** command. What is the status of the interface and the line protocol?
    Serial 1 is up, line protocol is up.
52. What is the encapsulation currently set to? **PPP**
53. Can you ping or Telnet from router Lab-A to router Lab-B? **Yes**
54. Why or why not? **The WAN encapsulation on both Lab-A Serial 0 and Lab-B Serial 1 are now set to the same data-link protocol (PPP).**

Cisco Labs – Semester 4 – Wide-Area Networking
EXERCISE 11.1 – ISDN TERMS AND DEVICES – OVERVIEW
(Estimated time: 45 minutes)

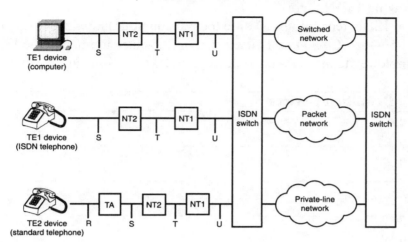

Objectives:
- Review ISDN-related acronyms and terminology
- Relate ISDN terms to specific devices

Background:
The Integrated Services Digital Network (ISDN) was developed to provide digital services over existing telephone wiring. These services can include voice, data, and video. ISDN was intended to be the replacement for the standard analog phone system of the Public Switched Telephone Network (PSTN). ISDN standards define the hardware and call setup schemes for end-to-end digital connectivity. This is a dial-up service that is widely used not only in the United States, but also internationally. There are two basic types of ISDN: Basic Rate Interface (BRI) and Primary Rate Interface (PRI). BRI is the slower of the two and is an alternative to dial-up modems. BRI provides 2 x 64 Kbps bearer (B) channels for voice and data, and a 16 Kbps delta (D) channel for control and signaling information. This gives a total of 144 Kbps for BRI ISDN. PRI typically runs over a T1 physical carrier and provides 23 x 64 Kbps B channels and 1 x 64 Kbps D channel (for a total of 1.544 Mbps). PRI is considered an alternative to dedicated standard leased lines. This exercise serves as a study guide to reinforce your understanding of basic ISDN terms and devices to which they relate.

Tools/Preparation:
Before beginning this lab, you should read Chapter 11 in *Cisco Networking Academy Program: Second-Year Companion Guide*. You should also review the Semester 4 online chapters on ISDN. You may compete in teams or work alone.

Required Resources:
- Semester 4 online ISDN chapter and glossary
- *Cisco Networking Academy Program: Second-Year Companion Guide*: Chapter 11, glossary

Web Site Resources:
- **Terms and acronyms** – http://www.cisco.com/univercd/cc/td/doc/cisintwk/ita/index.htm
- **Introduction to WAN technologies** –
  http://www.cisco.com/univercd/cc/td/doc/cisintwk/ito_doc/introwan.htm
- **Integrated Services Digital Network (ISDN) overview and components** –
  http://www.cisco.com/univercd/cc/td/doc/cisintwk/ito_doc/isdn.htm

Cisco Labs – Semester 4 – Wide-Area Networking
EXERCISE 11.1 – ISDN TERMS AND DEVICES – WORKSHEET

Step 1. Define the following ISDN terms.

These terms are related to ISDN technology. Define them using your knowledge, _Cisco Networking Academy Program: Second-Year Companion Guide_, the online curriculum, and the ISDN web site. Use the previous diagram to relate these terms to devices and connections in the ISDN network.

ISDN Term	Definition/Devices
2B+D	
BRI	
DCE	
DDR	
DTE	
LAPD	
NT1	
NT2	
PPP	
PRI	
R Reference point	
S Reference point	
T Reference point	
U Reference point	
SPID	
T1	
T3	
TA	
TE1	
TE2	

Cisco Labs – Semester 4 – Wide-Area Networking
EXERCISE 11.1 – ISDN TERMS AND DEVICES – ANSWERS

ISDN Term	Definition/Devices
2B+D	2 bearer (data) + 1 delta (control) channels for BRI ISDN.
BRI	Basic Rate Interface. ISDN (narrowband) – 2 x 64 Kbps bearer channels, and 1 x 16 Kbps delta channel.
DCE	Data circuit-terminating equipment (or data communications equipment), for ISDN switches.
DDR	Dial-on-demand routing (required for routers to place ISDN calls).
DTE	Data terminal equipment (PC, terminal, router).
LAPD	Link Access Procedure – D channel (ISDN data link layer protocol).
NT1	Network Termination Device – Type 1. Device that connects four-wire ISDN wiring to the two-wire local loop ISDN network.
NT2	Network Termination Device – Type 2. Directs traffic to and from different subscriber devices and the NT1; performs switching and concentrating, like an ISDN hub.
PPP	Point-to-Point Protocol (WAN data link encapsulation used by ISDN).
PRI	Primary Rate Interface. ISDN (broadband) – 23 x 64 Kbps bearer channels and 1 x 64 Kbps delta channel.
R Reference point	Reference connection between a device that is not ISDN-compatible and a terminal adapter (TA).
S Reference point	References the points that connect into the NT2 or customer switching device. This is the interface that enables calls between the various parts of the customer premises equipment (CPE).
T Reference point	Electrically identical to the S interface, a T interface references the outbound connection from the NT2 to the ISDN network or NT1.
U Reference point	References connections between the NT1 and the ISDN network owned by the phone company. The U interface point is relevant only in North America, where the NT1 function is not provided by the service provider.
SPID	Service profile identifier. Number used to define subscriber services (such as a phone number). An ISDN device uses the SPID to access the switch.
T1	Trunk Carrier1. Basic unit of digital service – 1.544 Mbps over four copper wires. PRI ISDN runs over T1.
T3	Trunk Carrier 3. Basic unit of digital service – about 45 Mbps over fiber (28 T1s).
TA	Terminal adapter. Converts non-ISDN TE2 device (analog phone or PC) to connect to the ISDN network. Essentially an ISDN modem.
TE1	Terminal Equipment Type 1. Native ISDN device (ISDN phone or PBX).
TE2	Terminal Equipment Type 2. Non-native ISDN device (analog phone or PC). Requires a TA to connect to the ISDN network.

Cisco Labs – Semester 4 – Wide-Area Networking
LAB 12.1 – FRAME RELAY CONFIGURATION – OVERVIEW
(Estimated time: 60 minutes)

Objectives:
- Become familiar with WAN terminology related to Frame Relay
- Understand the requirements and options for Frame Relay communications
- Simulate the configuration of a Frame Relay switch and links between two routers

Background:

This lab focuses on the Frame Relay Packet Switching Protocol for connecting devices on a wide-area network (WAN). Frame Relay is an industry-standard, switched data link layer protocol that handles multiple virtual circuits using HDLC encapsulation between connected devices (routers). Frame Relay is more efficient than X.25, the protocol for which it is generally considered a replacement. Frame Relay is a very widely used and important WAN communication technology. With this lab, you will use a router to create a Frame Relay switch (the cloud) and connect two other routers through it to simulate a wide-area link between two LANs.

Cisco Labs – Semester 4 – Wide-Area Networking
LAB 12.1 – FRAME RELAY CONFIGURATION – OVERVIEW

Point-to-Point vs. Frame Relay
Two of the most common types of WAN communication links in use today are leased dedicated point-to-point permanent circuits and Frame Relay packet-switched circuits. The prior labs used PPP (and Cisco HDLC) over a (simulated) leased dedicated point-to-point circuit. This assumes that the organization leasing the circuit is paying for the full dedicated bandwidth (such as a T1 at 1.544 Mbps) 24 hours a day, 7 days a week whether it actually uses the full bandwidth or not. Packet-switched networks enable end stations to dynamically share the network medium (sometimes referred to as "the cloud") and the available bandwidth, and it is possible to pay only for the bandwidth you need. This is referred to as a committed information rate (CIR).

Potential Bandwidth Sharing
Frame Relay uses variable-length packets for more efficient and flexible transfers. These packets then are switched between the various network segments (usually phone company central offices [COs]) until the destination is reached. Statistical multiplexing techniques control network access in a packet-switched network. The advantage of this technique is that it accommodates more flexibility and more efficient use of bandwidth, especially between switches within the cloud. Frame Relay is a way of sharing existing T1 and T3 lines owned by service providers and potentially getting better use from them. Most telephone companies now provide Frame Relay service for customers who want connections at 56 Kbps to T1 speeds.

Frame Relay Devices – DTE and DCE
Devices attached to a Frame Relay WAN fall into two general categories: data terminal equipment (DTE) and data circuit-terminating equipment (DCE). DTEs are typically located on the premises of and are owned by a customer. Examples of DTE devices are terminals, personal computers, routers, and bridges. DCEs are usually carrier-owned (phone company) internetworking devices but can be owned by the customer. The purpose of DCE equipment is to provide clocking and switching services in a network, which are the devices that actually transmit data through the WAN cloud. In most cases, these are Frame Relay packet switches themselves. CSU/DSUs are considered DCE.

The connection between a DTE device and a DCE device consists of both a physical-layer component and a data link layer component. The physical component defines the mechanical, electrical, functional, and procedural specifications for the connection between the devices. One of the most commonly used physical-layer interface specifications is the Recommended Standard (RS)-232 specification. The link-layer component defines the protocol that establishes the connection between the DTE device, such as a router, and the DCE device, such as a Frame Relay switch (usually at the phone company CO).

Virtual Circuits
Frame Relay provides connection-oriented data link layer communication. This means that a defined communication exists between each pair of devices and that these connections are associated with a connection identifier. This service is implemented by using a Frame Relay virtual circuit, which is a logical connection created between two data terminal equipment (DTE) devices across a Frame Relay packet-switched network (PSN). Virtual circuits provide a bidirectional communications path from one DTE device to another and are identified by a data-link connection identifier (DLCI).

Cisco Labs – Semester 4 – Wide-Area Networking
LAB 12.1 – FRAME RELAY CONFIGURATION – OVERVIEW

A number of virtual circuits can be multiplexed into a single physical circuit for transmission across the network. This capability often can reduce the equipment and network complexity required to connect multiple DTE devices. A virtual circuit can pass through any number of intermediate DCE devices (switches) located within the Frame Relay packet-switched network (PSN) or cloud. Frame Relay virtual circuits fall into two categories: switched virtual circuits (SVCs) and permanent virtual circuits (PVCs). PVCs are the most common.

Tools/Preparation:

Before you start the lab, the teacher or lab assistant should have at least three of the five routers in the standard router lab available. The middle router will act as the Frame Relay switch, and the other routers will connect through it. The middle router must have DCE clock rate and DCE cable ends on both serial ports (S0 and S1). Before beginning this lab, you should read Chapter 12, "Frame Relay," in *Cisco Networking Academy Program: Second-Year Companion Guide*. You should also review the Semester 4 online chapter on Frame Relay.

Note: This is a simulated lab because there will not likely be a real circuit with a Frame Relay cloud available for attachment and testing of the configuration changes made to the routers. The purpose of this lab is to practice the process of configuring the routers to connect to a Frame Relay WAN link.

Resources Required:
- Three Cisco routers with IOS 11.2 or later
- Middle router serial ports connected to DCE serial cables
- Hubs and/or switch attached to the end routers
- Workstation connected to each router's console port

Web Site Resources:
- **Routing basics** – http://www.cisco.com/univercd/cc/td/doc/cisintwk/ito_doc/routing.htm
- **General information on routers** – http://www.cisco.com/univercd/cc/td/doc/pcat/#2
- **2500 series routers** – http://www.cisco.com/warp/public/cc/cisco/mkt/access/2500/index.shtml
- **1600 series routers** – http://www.cisco.com/warp/public/cc/cisco/mkt/access/1600/index.shtml
- **Terms and acronyms** – http://www.cisco.com/univercd/cc/td/doc/cisintwk/ita/index.htm
- **IP routing protocol IOS command summary** –
  http://www.cisco.com/univercd/cc/td/doc/product/software/ios120/12cgcr/rbkixol.htm
- **Introduction to WAN technologies** –
  http://www.cisco.com/univercd/cc/td/doc/cisintwk/ito_doc/introwan.htm

Notes:

_____

_____

_____

_____

Cisco Labs – Semester 4 – Wide-Area Networking
LAB 12.1 – FRAME RELAY CONFIGURATION – WORKSHEET

Select three routers that have WAN serial links between them. The middle router will simulate a Frame Relay switch, and the end routers will simulate geographically separate sites connected through the Frame Relay cloud. This lab worksheet uses routers Lab-A, Lab-B, and Lab-C. You will configure the two remote routers (Lab-A and Lab-C) first, and then the middle Frame Relay router (Lab B).

Step 1. Configure the physical three-router setup.
The two cables connected to the middle router (Lab-B) should both be DCE to have this router simulate the Frame Relay switch (the DCE cables are labeled on one end). On router Lab-B, connect one of the DCE cables to Serial 0 and the other to Serial 1. The DCE cable from Lab–B Serial 1 will connect to a DTE cable going to router Lab-A Serial 0, and the Lab-B serial 1 cable will go to the router Lab-C DTE cable on Serial 1. Use the tables below for cabling and interfaces.

Router Frame Relay Switch	From Serial Interface Number and Type (DCE/DTE)	To Remote Router Name	To Serial Interface Number and Type (DCE/DTE)
Lab-B	Serial 0/DCE	Lab-C	Serial 1/DTE
Lab-B	Serial 1/DCE	Lab-A	Serial 0/DTE

Use the **show controller** command to check the DCE/DTE connections.

Lab-A#show controller Serial 0

1. What does the **show controller** command for S0 indicate? _____

Router	Interface Ethernet 0	Interface Serial 0	Interface Serial 1	Subnet Mask
Lab-A (remote)	192.5.5.1	201.100.11.1	Not used	255.255.255.0
Lab-B (switch)	Not used	DLCI 21	DLCI 20	N/A
Lab-C (remote)	223.8.151.1	Not used	200.100.11.2	255.255.255.0

2. In the space below, draw the three-router setup showing cabling, interfaces, IP addresses, and DLCIs.

Cisco Labs – Semester 4 – Wide-Area Networking
LAB 12.1 – FRAME RELAY CONFIGURATION – WORKSHEET

Step 2. Check the WAN interface on remote router Lab-A.

Connect your workstation to the console port connection on router Lab-A, and use the
show interface command to answer the following questions:

Lab-A# show interface serial 0

3. What is the IP address and number of subnet bits for this interface? _____

4. What is the status of the interface and the line protocol? _____

5. What is the encapsulation currently set to? _____

Step 3. Configure the serial interface on Lab-A for a Frame Relay connection.

Connect your workstation to the console port connection on router Lab-A, and use the following
commands to set up Frame Relay on interface serial 0. Note that if you are using Cisco IOS version
11.2 or newer, the Frame Relay DLCI and LMI type can be detected automatically and will not need
to be configured manually.

Lab-A – Remote Router Frame Relay Configuration

Prompt and Command	Purpose
*** Configure Interface S0 ***	
Lab-A#config t	Configure from terminal
Lab-A(config)# interface Serial0	Select interface S0 to configure
Lab-A(config-if)# ip address 201.100.11.1 255.255.255.0	Set the IP address and subnet mask for S0 (use the standard router lab IP)
Lab-A(config-if)# encapsulation frame-relay	Change data-link encapsulation from HDLC to Frame Relay. Use ietf if connecting to a non-Cisco router. Default is Cisco encapsulation
Lab-A(config-if)# no shutdown	Bring up interface S0
*** Configure Interface E0 ***	
Lab-A(config)# interface Ethernet0	Select interface E0
Lab-A(config-if)# ip address 192.5.5.1 255.255.255.0	Set the IP address and subnet mask for E0 (use the standard router lab IP)
Lab-A(config-if)# no shutdown	Bring up interface E0
*** Configure IGRP Routing Protocol ***	
Lab-A(config)# router igrp 100	Enables IGRP routing protocol process
Lab-A(config-router)# network 201.100.11.0	Selects network 210.100.11.0 to broadcast and receive IGRP updates
Lab-A(config-router)# network 192.5.5.0	Selects network 192.5.5.0 to broadcast and receive IGRP updates

Cisco Labs – Semester 4 – Wide-Area Networking
LAB 12.1 – FRAME RELAY CONFIGURATION – WORKSHEET

Step 4. Use the show running-config interface command to verify the configuration of S0.

Lab-A#sh run

6. What information was displayed about Lab-A interface S0? _____

_____

Step 5. Check the WAN interface on remote router Lab-C.

Connect your workstation to the console port connection on Router Lab-C, and use the **show interface** command to answer the following questions:

Lab-C# show interface serial 1

7. What is the IP address and number of subnet bits for this interface? _____
8. What is the status of the interface and the line protocol? _____
9. What is the encapsulation currently set to? _____

Step 6. Configure the serial interface on Lab-C for a Frame Relay connection.

Connect your workstation to the console port connection on router Lab-C, and use the following commands to set up Frame Relay on interface serial 1. Note that if you are using Cisco IOS version 11.2 or newer, the Frame Relay DLCI and LMI type can be detected automatically.

Lab-C – Remote Router Frame Relay Configuration

Prompt and Command	Purpose
*** Configure Interface S1 ***	
Lab-C#config t	Configure from terminal
Lab-C(config)# interface Serial1	Select interface S1 to configure
Lab-C(config-if)# ip address 201.100.11.2 255.255.255.0	Set the IP address and subnet mask for S1 (use the standard router lab IP)
Lab-C(config-if)# encapsulation frame-relay	Change data-link encapsulation from HDLC to Frame Relay. Use ietf if connecting to a non-Cisco router; default is Cisco encapsulation.
Lab-C(config-if)# no shutdown	Bring up interface S1
*** Configure Interface E0 ***	
Lab-C(config)# interface Ethernet0	Select interface E0
Lab-C(config-if)# ip address 223.8.151.1 255.255.255.0	Set the IP address and subnet mask for E0 (use the standard router lab IP)
Lab-C(config-if)# no shutdown	Bring up interface E0
*** Configure IGRP Routing Protocol ***	
Lab-C(config)# router igrp 100	Enables IGRP routing protocol process
Lab-C(config-router)# network 201.100.11.0	Selects network 201.100.11.0 to broadcast and receive IGRP updates
Lab-C(config-router)# network 223.8.151.0	Selects network 223.8.151.0 to broadcast and receive IGRP updates

Cisco Labs – Semester 4 – Wide-Area Networking
LAB 12.1 – FRAME RELAY CONFIGURATION – WORKSHEET

Step 7. Use the show running-config interface command to verify the configuration of S1.

Lab-C#sh run

10. What information was displayed about Lab-C interface S1? _____

_____

Step 8. Configure Lab-B as a Frame Relay switch.

Connect your workstation to the console port on Router Lab-B, and use the following commands to enable Frame Relay switching and define interfaces Serial 0 and Serial 1 as DCE.

Lab-B – Frame Relay Switch Configuration

Prompt and Command	Purpose
*** Enable Frame Relay Switching ***	
Lab-B#config t	Configure from terminal
Lab-B(config)# frame-relay switching	Start the Frame Relay switching process
*** Configure Interface S0 ***	
Lab-B(config)# interface Serial0	Select interface E0
Lab-B(config-if)# no ip address	Specify no IP address for S0
Lab-B(config-if)# encapsulation frame-relay	Change the Layer 2 data-link encapsulation from HDLC to Frame Relay
Lab-B(config-if)# clock rate 56000	Specify the synchronous clock rate for the DCE side of the interface
Lab-B(config-if)# frame-relay intf-type dce	Specify the interface as a DCE device
Lab-B(config-if)# frame-relay route 21 interface serial 1 20	Define the frame route so that packets coming in on S0 DLCI 21 should go to S1 DLCI 20
Lab-B(config-if)# no shutdown	Bring up interface S0
*** Configure Interface S1 ***	
Lab-B(config)# interface Serial1	Select interface S1
Lab-B(config-if)# no ip address	Specify no IP address for S1
Lab-B(config-if)# encapsulation frame-relay	Change the Layer 2 data-link encapsulation from HDLC to Frame Relay
Lab-B(config-if)# clock rate 56000	Specify the synchronous clock rate for the DCE side of the interface
Lab-B(config-if)# frame-relay intf-type dce	Specify the interface as a DCE device
Lab-B(config-if)# frame-relay route 20 interface serial 0 21	Define the frame route so that packets coming in on S1 DLCI 20 should go to S0 DLCI 21
Lab-B(config-if)# no shutdown	Bring up interface S0

Cisco Labs – Semester 4 – Wide-Area Networking
LAB 12.1 – FRAME RELAY CONFIGURATION – WORKSHEET

Step 9. **Use the show running-config interface command to verify the configuration of S0 and S1. Note that there are several commands added by the router.**
   Lab-B#sh run
11. What information was displayed about Lab-B interface S0? _____

   _____

12. What information was displayed about Lab-B interface S1? _____

   _____

Step 10. **Confirm that the line is up by entering the show interface serial 0 command:**
   Lab-A# show interface serial 0
13. What is the status of the serial frame link? _____

14. How many LMI messages were sent and received? _____
   What does this mean? _____
15. What is the LMI type? _____

Step 11. **Verify the Frame Relay PVC status for router Lab-A (remote router).**
   Lab-A# show frame pvc
16. What is the DLCI number of the connection? _____
17. What is the status of the PVC? _____

Step 12. **Check the Frame Relay map for router Lab-A (remote router).**
   Lab-A# show frame map
18. What is the local interface number, IP address of the switch interface, and the DLCI of
   the connection? _____
19. What is the status of the PVC? _____

Step 13. **Check the LMI status for router Lab-A (remote router).**
   Lab-A# show frame lmi
20. What is the local interface number, and is it DCE or DTE? _____

Step 14. **Verify the Frame Relay PVC status for router Lab-B (the switch).**
   Lab-B# show frame pvc
21. What are the DLCI numbers of the connections? _____
22. What is the status of the PVCs? _____

Step 15. **Verify the Frame Relay routing table for router Lab-B (the switch).**
   Lab-B# show frame route
23. What information is shown? _____

Step 16. **Verify that you can ping from router Lab-A through the switch to router Lab-B.**
   Lab-A# ping 201.100.11.2
24. What was the result? _____

Cisco Labs – Semester 4 – Wide-Area Networking
LAB 12.1 – FRAME RELAY CONFIGURATION – ANSWERS

1. What does the **show controller** command for S0 indicate? **V.35 DTE cable**

2. In the space below, draw the three-router setup showing cabling, interfaces, IP addresses, and DLCIs.

Lab-A# show interface serial 0

3. What is the IP address and number of subnet bits for this interface? **201.100.11.1 / 24**
4. What is the status of the interface and the line protocol? **Serial0 is up, line protocol is up**
5. What is the encapsulation currently set to? **Encapsulation HDLC**

Lab-A#sh run

6. What information was displayed about Lab-A interface S0?
    interface Serial0
    ip address 201.100.11.1 255.255.255.0
    encapsulation frame-relay

Lab-C# show interface serial 1

7. What is the IP address and number of subnet bits for this interface? **201.100.11.2 / 24**
8. What is the status of the interface and the line protocol? **Serial1 is up, line protocol is up**
9. What is the encapsulation currently set to? **Encapsulation HDLC**

Lab-C#sh run

10. What information was displayed about Lab-C interface S1?
    interface Serial1
    ip address 201.100.11.2 255.255.255.0
    encapsulation frame-relay

Cisco Labs – Semester 4 – Wide-Area Networking
LAB 12.1 – FRAME RELAY CONFIGURATION – ANSWERS

Lab-B#sh run

11. What information was displayed about Lab-B interface S0?
    interface Serial0
    no ip address
    no ip directed-broadcast
    encapsulation frame-relay
    no ip route-cache
    no ip mroute-cache
    no fair-queue
    clockrate 56000
    frame-relay intf-type dce
    frame-relay route 21 interface Serial1 20

12. What information was displayed about Lab-B interface S1?
    interface Serial1
    no ip address
    no ip directed-broadcast
    encapsulation frame-relay
    no ip route-cache
    no fair-queue
    clockrate 56000
    frame-relay intf-type dce
    frame-relay route 20 interface Serial0 21

Lab-A# show interface serial 0
Confirm that the following information appears in the command output. Write the message that relates to each question.

13. What is the status of the serial frame link? **Serial0 is up, line protocol is up; the Frame Relay connection is active.**

14. How many LMI messages were sent and received? **LMI enq sent: 1477, LMI stat received: 1458** What does this mean? **The connection is sending and receiving data.**

15. What is the LMI type? **LMI type is CISCO; the Local Management Interface (LMI) type is configured correctly for the router.**

Cisco Labs – Semester 4 – Wide-Area Networking
LAB 12.1 – FRAME RELAY CONFIGURATION – ANSWERS

```
Serial0 is up, line protocol is up
  Hardware is HD64570
  Internet address is 201.100.11.1/24
  MTU 1500 bytes, BW 1544 Kbit, DLY 20000 usec, rely 255/255, load 1/255
  Encapsulation FRAME-RELAY, loopback not set, keepalive set (10 sec)
  LMI enq sent  1477, LMI stat recvd 1458, LMI upd recvd 0, DTE LMI up
  LMI enq recvd 0, LMI stat sent  0, LMI upd sent  0
  LMI DLCI 1023  LMI type is CISCO  frame relay DTE
  Broadcast queue 0/64, broadcasts sent/dropped 190/0, interface broadcasts 185
  Last input 00:00:09, output 00:00:09, output hang never
  Last clearing of "show interface" counters never
  Input queue: 0/75/0 (size/max/drops); Total output drops: 0
  Queueing strategy: weighted fair
  Output queue: 0/1000/64/0 (size/max total/threshold/drops)
     Conversations  0/1/256 (active/max active/max total)
     Reserved Conversations 0/0 (allocated/max allocated)
  5 minute input rate 0 bits/sec, 0 packets/sec
  5 minute output rate 0 bits/sec, 0 packets/sec
     1925 packets input, 49357 bytes, 0 no buffer
     Received 0 broadcasts, 0 runts, 0 giants, 0 throttles
     0 input errors, 0 CRC, 0 frame, 0 overrun, 0 ignored, 0 abort
     1697 packets output, 33272 bytes, 0 underruns
     0 output errors, 0 collisions, 9 interface resets
     0 output buffer failures, 0 output buffers swapped out
     23 carrier transitions
     DCD=up  DSR=up  DTR=up  RTS=up  CTS=up
```

Lab-A# show frame pvc

16. What is the DLCI number of the connection? **20**
17. What is the status of the PVC? **Active**

```
PVC Statistics for interface Serial0 (Frame Relay DTE)

DLCI = 20, DLCI USAGE = LOCAL, PVC STATUS = ACTIVE, INTERFACE = Serial0

  input pkts 55        output pkts 41        in bytes 3317
  out bytes 2570       dropped pkts 0        in FECN pkts 0
  in BECN pkts 0       out FECN pkts 0       out BECN pkts 0
  in DE pkts 0         out DE pkts 0
  out bcast pkts 31    out bcast bytes 1530
  pvc create time 00:40:27, last time pvc status changed 00:40:27
```

Cisco Labs – Semester 4 – Wide-Area Networking
LAB 12.1 – FRAME RELAY CONFIGURATION – ANSWERS

Lab-A# show frame map

18. What is the local interface number, IP address of the switch interface, and the DLCI of the connection? **Serial 0, 201.100.11.2, DLCI 20**
19. What is the status of the PVC? **Defined, active**

Serial0 (up): ip 201.100.11.2 dlci 20(0x14,0x440), dynamic, broadcast, status defined, active

(Note that IP address 201.100.11.2 is the other router)

Lab-A# show frame lmi

20. What is local interface number, and is it DCE or DTE? **Serial 0, DTE**

LMI Statistics for interface Serial0 (Frame Relay DTE) LMI TYPE = CISCO	
Invalid Unnumbered info 0	Invalid Prot Disc 0
Invalid dummy Call Ref 0	Invalid Msg Type 0
Invalid Status Message 0	Invalid Lock Shift 0
Invalid Information ID 0	Invalid Report IE Len 0
Invalid Report Request 0	Invalid Keep IE Len 0
Num Status Enq. Sent 1496	Num Status msgs Rcvd 1477
Num Update Status Rcvd 0	Num Status Timeouts 19

Lab-B# show frame pvc for Lab-B

21. What are the DLCI numbers of the connections? **20 and 21**
22. What is the status of the PVCs? **Active on both**

PVC Statistics for interface Serial0 (Frame Relay DCE)
DLCI = 21, DLCI USAGE = SWITCHED, PVC STATUS = ACTIVE, INTERFACE = Serial0

input pkts 399	output pkts 186	in bytes 22016
out bytes 10010	dropped pkts 1	in FECN pkts 0
in BECN pkts 0	out FECN pkts 0	out BECN pkts 0
in DE pkts 0	out DE pkts 0	
out bcast pkts 0	out bcast bytes 0	Num Pkts Switched 399

pvc create time 03:45:00, last time pvc status changed 03:44:38

PVC Statistics for interface Serial1 (Frame Relay DCE)
DLCI = 20, DLCI USAGE = SWITCHED, PVC STATUS = ACTIVE, INTERFACE = Serial1

input pkts 188	output pkts 399	in bytes 10090
out bytes 22016	dropped pkts 0	in FECN pkts 0
in BECN pkts 0	out FECN pkts 0	out BECN pkts 0
in DE pkts 0	out DE pkts 0	
out bcast pkts 0	out bcast bytes 0	Num Pkts Switched 187

pvc create time 03:45:04, last time pvc status changed 03:44:52

Cisco Labs – Semester 4 – Wide-Area Networking
LAB 12.1 – FRAME RELAY CONFIGURATION – ANSWERS

Lab-B# show frame route

23. What information is shown? **Input/output interfaces, DLCIs, and status**

Input Intf	Input Dlci	Output Intf	Output Dlci	Status
Serial0	21	Serial1	20	active
Serial1	20	Serial0	21	active

Lab-A# ping 201.100.11.2

24. What was the result? **Success**

> Sending 5, 100-byte ICMP Echos to 201.100.11.2, timeout is 2 seconds: !!!!! Success rate is
> 100 percent (5/5), round-trip min/avg/max = 68/68/72 ms

Cisco Labs – Semester 4 – Wide-Area Networking
LAB 13.1 – AUX DIAL-UP – OVERVIEW
(Estimated time: 30 minutes)

Objectives:

- Understand both in-band and out-of-band router management techniques
- Compare synchronous serial interfaces with asynchronous serial interfaces
- Learn the requirements for using a dial-up link with a modem to configure a router
- Become familiar with the use of the router AUX port for out-of-band management
- Use ConfigMaker to create a dial-up asynchronous WAN link

Background:

Wide Area Network Scenario

This lab focuses out-of-band router management using the AUX port on the router and a modem. You can configure and monitor routers and other networking equipment using both in-band and out-of-band techniques. For example, let's say that router Lab-A is in Anaheim, California, and router Lab-B is in Boise, Idaho. They are connected via a wide-area link, such as T1 Frame Relay, PRI ISDN, or PPP over T1. Regardless of which you use , your WAN link has the bandwidth, or "speed," of a T1 (1.544 Mbps). You are a network administrator in Anaheim and wish to make some configuration changes or check the status for the Lab-B router in Boise.

In-Band Network Management

If you are attached to the console of router Lab-A and telnet to router Lab-B across the wide-area link, your connection to router Lab-B is considered in-bandwidth or "in-band" because you are using the same WAN link that the data travels on to manage the Lab-B router. If the WAN link goes down or there is a problem with the configuration of the Lab-B router that contributes to the down WAN link, you cannot get to the Lab-B router to monitor or change its configuration because the WAN link is down. In-band management is very common and is preferred if the WAN link is up.

Out-of Band Network Management

If the Wan link is down, you need a back-door or out-of-band method to get to the router and check it out to help troubleshoot the problem. This can be provided by redundant synchronous WAN serial links to other interfaces on the router. They can be the same as the existing high-speed WAN link or can be slower, such as BRI ISDN or perhaps a synchronous 56 Kbps digital data circuit. You can also get to the router by use of its asynchronous serial ports. Most routers have two asynchronous ports in order to manage the router out-of-band: the console port and the AUX (auxiliary) port. The use of the asynchronous console port or the AUX port is considered out-of-band management.

The Console Port vs. the AUX Port

The primary method of configuring routers with these labs has been with the console port. With the console port, your workstation is directly attached to the router with a special rollover cable and bypasses any other interfaces on the router. The console port is normally set to run at 9600 bps (8 data bits, no parity, and 2 stop bits, or 8-N-2) and does not support hardware flow control. The AUX port requires that a modem be attached and allows you to dial into the router from home or any other location. The AUX port can run at the same speed as the fastest modems, up to 56 Kbps, and supports hardware flow control. The console and AUX ports normally use RS-232 serial DB25 connectors (converted to RJ-45).

Cisco Labs – Semester 4 – Wide-Area Networking
LAB 13.1 – AUX DIAL-UP – OVERVIEW

Synchronous vs. Asynchronous Serial Interfaces

Nearly all wide-area network links (WAN) links used in internetworking are serial, meaning that they transmit bits one after another in a series down the wire or fiber cable. They are not the same as the asynchronous serial connection ports found on the back of most PCs and those used with modems. The console connection from a workstation to the console port on the router is an asynchronous connection that uses start and stop bits to separate the data bits in the stream. The bit rate on the asynchronous router console port is set to 9600 bits per second (bps). Asynchronous serial connections are commonly used with short-distance connections for terminals (to routers and switches) or for dial-in modem connections limited to 56 Kbps (kilobits per second, or 56,000 bits per second). A modem can be connected to the AUX port on the router to allow you to dial in asynchronously and diagnose problems. With this lab, you will practice setting up a modem with the router and dialing in from another location to configure it remotely. Note that the AUX port can also be used for dial-on-demand routing in case the main WAN serial link is down.

Tools/Preparation:

Before you start the lab, the teacher or lab assistant should have a router available and preferably two phone lines into the router that can function with an analog phone connection. (Some phone switches will not work for this lab.) If a connection can be made to the phone jack and you have a dial tone, then one line will work if the lab can be done from home or another location. This is a hands-on lab and assumes that the phone lines are available for dial-in to the router. If phone lines are not available, it is still worthwhile to work through the lab and do those portions that are possible. If a phone line is not available, it may be possible to simulate this lab with a modem eliminator between the COM port of the PC dialing in and the router's AUX port. **Note: You can use ConfigMaker to set up a dial-in port or an asynchronous WAN backup port to simulate this lab.**

Resources Required:

- Cisco router with AUX port (Note: Some routers do not have an AUX port)
- Standard asynchronous analog modem (USR 56 K or similar)
- Rollover cable with DB25 modem connector and RJ-45 router connector
- Phone cable from modem to phone jack
- Two direct inward dial-up analog phone lines (preferably)
- Router manuals and modem manuals
- Remote PC with modem to dial in to the router
- Workstation with HyperTerminal and a console connection

Web Site Resources:

- **Terms and acronyms** – http://www.cisco.com/univercd/cc/td/doc/cisintwk/ita/index.htm
- **IP routing protocol IOS command summary** – http://www.cisco.com/univercd/cc/td/doc/product/software/ios120/12cgcr/rbkixol.htm
- **Introduction to WAN technologies** – http://www.cisco.com/univercd/cc/td/doc/cisintwk/ito_doc/introwan.htm
- **Cisco ConfigMaker information and download** – http://www.cisco.com/warp/public/cc/cisco/mkt/enm/config/index.shtml

Cisco Labs – Semester 4 – Wide-Area Networking
LAB 13.1 – AUX DIAL-UP – WORKSHEET

Step 1. Prepare the router configuration for AUX dial-in.

A. Verify that you have a router with an AUX port. Look at the back of the router, and check to see that there is an AUX port next to the console port. Some routers, such as the 1600 series, do not have an AUX port.

B. Provide password security for dial-in to the AUX port.

    1. Connect to the router with a workstation using the console port and HyperTerminal.
    2. Set a password for the AUX port, as follows:
    Router# Config t
    Router(config)# line aux 0
    Router(config-line)# password cisco
    Router(config-line)# login

C. Discover the modem automatically. The Cisco IOS software contains a database of modem capabilities for most modems. You can configure a router to automatically attempt to discover what kind of modem is connected to the line and then to configure that modem. To automatically discover which of the supported modem strings properly initializes your modem and then initialize the modem, enter these lines:
Router(config-line)# modem autoconfigure discovery
Router(config-line)# modem dialin

D. Set the router port transmission speed (try not to use the **baud** command if you do not need to, because it can cause problems with the router).

    1. Enter the following command to set the speed:
    Router(config-line)# speed 38400
    2. Enter the following command to hang up the modem automatically:
    Router(config-line)# autohangup

E. Verify that hardware flow control is used with data carrier detect (DCD) and data terminal ready (DTR) operations.

    1. Enter the following command to set flow control:
    Router(config-line)# flowcontrol hardware

F. Configure the line asynchronous data transmission parameters to 8 data bits, no parity, and 2 stop bits (8, none, and 2 or 8-N-2)

    1. Enter the following command to set the number of data bits to 8:
    Router(config-line)# databits 8
    2. Enter the following command to set the parity to None:
    Router(config-line)# parity none
    3. Enter the following command to set the number of data bits to 8:
    Router(config-line)# stopbits 2

Cisco Labs – Semester 4 – Wide-Area Networking
LAB 13.1 – AUX DIAL-UP – WORKSHEET

G. Check the configuration of the AUX port with the **show running-config** command. The output from the command should show the following port characteristics:
line aux 0
 password cisco
 login
 autohangup
 flowcontrol hardware

H. Copy the running configuration to the startup configuration to save the AUX port configuration commands you have entered.
Router# copy run start

I. Plug the rollover cable RJ-45 connector into the AUX port on the back of the router.

Step 2. Prepare the workstation used for dial-in.
A. Review the workstation's HyperTerminal configuration. Click Start, Programs, Accessories, and then HyperTerminal. Right-click the icon that is defined for AUX access to the Cisco router, and then click Properties. If an icon does not exist. you can create it using the settings shown in the answers to the worksheet. On the Properties screen, click the Phone Number tab, and then click on the Configure button. Fill in the following table with the information indicated.

B. Configure the workstation modem (internal or external) to match the transmission settings (speed, data bits, parity, stop bits, and flow control) for the router AUX port. Fill in the following table with the settings and values you used:

Configuration Option	Current Setting(s)
COM port	Modem driver name
Bits per second (baud)	34800
Data bits	8
Parity	None
Stop bits	2
Flow control	Hardware

Step 3. Dial in to the router.
Use the phone number of the line to the router or a modem eliminator (null modem) cable connected to the router. You should get a prompt and be able to configure it remotely.

Step 4. Use ConfigMaker to create a dial-in asynchronous WAN link.
Start ConfigMaker and select a Cisco 2501 router. Select Dial-in PC with Modem for dial-in, and add an asynchronous link between them. Double-click on the router to see the configuration generated.

Cisco Labs – Semester 4 – Wide-Area Networking
LAB 13.2 – WAN WEB RESEARCH – OVERVIEW
(Estimated time: 60 minutes)

Objectives:
- Explore Semester 4 WAN technologies further
- Investigate other WAN and networking technologies
- Use the World Wide Web as a research tool
- Put together a brief presentation for the class on a WAN-related topic

Background:
A tremendous amount of information is available on the web related to networking in general and wide-area networking in particular. The purpose of this lab is to begin to use the web as a research tool to expand your knowledge of the basic WAN technologies covered in these Semester 4 labs. You also can investigate a number of other WAN technologies in use. When you become aware of a new WAN technology, term, or acronym during a conversation or in your reading, you can research it with several web-based tools to help increase your understanding of it. In this lab, you will select one or more topics or terms to research, and then document your findings. The goals for this lab are to become more familiar with some of the web-based research tools available and to use the information you have collected to put together a brief presentation for the class on a WAN-related topic of interest to you.

Tools/Preparation:
Before you start the lab, the teacher or lab assistant should have a PC with web access and PowerPoint available. The following is a list of resources required. Use PowerPoint or a similar tool, if possible, to develop your presentation. The presentation should not be more than three to five pages long and should not last more than 10 minutes, with 5 minutes for questions and answers.

Resource Required:
- Workstation with browser (Internet Explorer or Netscape) and PowerPoint software installed

Web Site Resources:
- **Terms and acronyms** – http://www.cisco.com/univercd/cc/td/doc/cisintwk/ita/index.htm
- **Introduction to WAN technologies** – http://www.cisco.com/univercd/cc/td/doc/cisintwk/ito_doc/introwan.htm
- **Cisco web site search engine** – http://www.cisco.com (select tech docs or products)
- **Networking terminology definitions and web links** – http://www.whatis.com
- **Networking terminology definitions and web links** – http://www.webopeida .com
- **Networking concepts search engine** – http://www.google.com

Notes:

_____

_____

_____

Cisco Labs – Semester 4 – Wide-Area Networking
LAB 13.2 – WAN WEB RESEARCH – WORKSHEET

Step 1. Select your research term or networking concept from the list in Lab 8.2, "WAN Acronyms," or pick your own. Choose terms and concepts that you are interested in or that you feel are important in this industry. Then use the web-based tools listed in the "Web Site Resources" section of this lab to find out more information on the topic(s) you have selected.

Term/Concept	Web Site Researched	Findings

Cisco Labs – Semester 4 – Wide-Area Networking
LAB 13.3 – PRACTICAL FINAL PREPARATION – OVERVIEW
(Estimated time: 60 minutes)

Router Name - LAB A
Router Type - 2514
E 0 = 192.5.5.1
E 1 = 205.7.5.1
S 0 = 201.100.11.1
SM = 255.255.255.0

Router Name - LAB B
Router Type - 2503
E 0 = 219.17.100.1
S 0 = 199.6.13.1
S 1 = 201.100.11.2
SM = 255.255.255.0

Router Name - LAB C
Router Type - 2503
E 0 = 223.8.151.1
S 0 = 204.204.7.1
S 1 = 199.6.13.2
SM = 255.255.255.0

Router Name - LAB D
Router Type - 2501
E 0 = 210.93.105.1
S 1 = 204.204.7.2
SM = 255.255.255.0

Router Name - LAB E
Router Type - 2501
E 0 = 210.93.105.2
SM = 255.255.255.0

LEGEND

= ROUTER   User Exec Password = cisco

= HUB   Enable Secret Exec Password = class

= LAN SWITCH   Terminal vty Password = cisco

= CONSOLE CABLE

Objectives:
- Analyze the requirements for integrating a router into an existing network
- Practice configuring routers given specific requirements
- Help prepare for the Semester 3/4 Skills-Based Assessment (SBA) practical final exam

Background:
With this lab, you are a network administrator for one of your company's remote sites, which is connected to the central corporate offices though a wide-area network (WAN) T1 link. Your assignment is to configure your router from scratch based on some specific requirements and corporate guidelines. Your site must connect to the corporate router that is already configured. Your site also must adapt to the IP addressing scheme and protocols being used at the corporate location because you will have no control over the corporate router. In addition, you will create an access control list (ACL) to prevent a certain type of access from your remote site to the corporate location. This lab will help prepare you for the hands-on Semester 4 Skill-Based Assessment final exam. You will work in teams, with one team setting up the corporate router and the other team configuring the remote router to connect to it.

Cisco Labs – Semester 4 – Wide-Area Networking
LAB 13.3 – PRACTICAL FINAL PREPARATION – OVERVIEW

Tools/Preparation:

Before you start the lab, the teacher or lab assistant should have two routers available with a WAN link, such as routers Lab-A and Lab-B (one for the remote site and one for the corporate site). Your team should be able to configure your router from scratch using the setup configuration utility, or preferably from the command line. You should try to do this lab without looking at your notes and using only the command-line help facility.

Before beginning this lab, you should review the *Cisco Networking Academy Program: Second-Year Companion Guide* chapters on basic router EXEC mode IOS configuration commands, subnet masking, WAN encapsulation, and extended ACLs. You should also review the corresponding online chapters. Work in teams of three or more. One team is responsible for configuring the corporate router, and the other team is responsible for configuring the remote router. The corporate router team members can look at the answers to ensure that it is configured properly. The remote router team members can ask questions of the corporate team members but should not see the actual configuration of the corporate router. They can use only the information given for the corporate router in the worksheet section of the lab.

Resources Required:

- Two routers with IOS 11.2 or later ("remote" router and "corporate" router)
- WAN cable link between them, with the corporate router providing the DCE clocking
- Remote router connected to an Ethernet LAN
- Workstation connected to the remote router's console port and the Ethernet LAN
- Corporate router should not be accessible except through the WAN link

Web Site Resources:

- **Routing basics** – http://www.cisco.com/univercd/cc/td/doc/cisintwk/ito_doc/routing.htm
- **General information on routers** – http://www.cisco.com/univercd/cc/td/doc/pcat/#2
- **2500 series routers** –http://www.cisco.com/warp/public/cc/cisco/mkt/access/2500/index.shtml
- **1600 series routers** – http://www.cisco.com/warp/public/cc/cisco/mkt/access/1600/index.shtml
- **Terms and acronyms** –http://www.cisco.com/univercd/cc/td/doc/cisintwk/ita/index.htm
- **IP routing protocol IOS command summary** –
  http://www.cisco.com/univercd/cc/td/doc/product/software/ios120/12cgcr/rbkixol.htm
- **Introduction to WAN technologies** –
  http://www.cisco.com/univercd/cc/td/doc/cisintwk/ito_doc/introwan.htm

Cisco Labs – Semester 4 – Wide-Area Networking
LAB 13.3 – PRACTICAL FINAL PREPARATION – WORKSHEET

Step 1. Verify the WAN physical connection between the routers.
Verify that the DCE cable is attached to the corporate router and that the DTE cable is attached to the remote router. Check the physical cables, each of which should be labeled as either DCE or DTE.

Step 2. Erase the startup configuration file for the remote router.
The router startup configuration file may have already been erased, but it is useful to go through the process for practice. If the Remote router configuration file has been erased, you should see a message saying "Notice: NVRAM invalid, possibly due to write erase" when the router is powered on. If the router is already on and the prompt is Router>, then the startup configuration file has probably been erased. Verify this by entering privileged EXEC mode with the **enable** command. If the configuration is blank, you will not be prompted for a password. If you issue the **show run** command, none of the interfaces will be configured.

Erase the NVRAM startup configuration file as follows:

Router>enable (There is no configuration, so you will not be prompted for a password.)

Router# erase start
Erasing the nvram filesystem will remove all files! Continue? [confirm]
[OK]
Erase of nvram: complete

Router# reload
Proceed with reload? [confirm]
00:09:30: %SYS-5-RELOAD: Reload requested
System Bootstrap, Version 11.0(10c), SOFTWARE
Copyright (c) 1986-1996 by cisco Systems
2500 processor with 6144 Kbytes of main memory
Notice: NVRAM invalid, possibly due to write erase.

System configuration has been modified. Save? [yes/no]: NO

---- System Configuration Dialog ----
Would you like to enter the initial configuration dialog? [yes/no]: NO

Notes: You may run the configuration (setup) dialog, but you will be prompted for configuration parameters. You should be able to configure the router using only the command line to demonstrate your understanding of router IOS commands and to help build your confidence. In practice, you will store the configuration files on a workstation with a console connection and HyperTerminal or on a TFTP server.

Would you like to terminate autoinstall? [yes]: YES
(Do not allow autoinstall to run, and do not enter management configuration mode if prompted.)

Cisco Labs – Semester 4 – Wide-Area Networking
LAB 13.3 – PRACTICAL FINAL PREPARATION – WORKSHEET

Step 3. Verify/configure the corporate router.
The corporate router configuration team or lab assistant/instructor should use the startup configuration file shown in the answers section to verify that it is configured correctly before the remote router team tries to configure the remote router. **Note: The remote team should also review this section carefully because it gives information that will be needed to configure the remote router later.** The corporate router should be configured as follows:

1. The router host name is "corporate."
2. Configure the enable secret password to be "class."
3. Configure the password to be "cisco" when someone tries to log in from the console port.
4. Configure the password to be "cisco" when someone tries to Telnet into the router.
5. Configure WAN interface S1:
    a. The WAN subnetwork address is one subnet of a Class B network address.
    b. The S1 interface address is 172.16.1.1. (This is already set.)
    c. What is the S1 interface subnet mask? _____ (There are 512 subnets total.)
    d. The S1 interface is providing the DCE clocking at 56000. Add a description to the S1 interface describing the link: _____
    e. Configure a static host name mapping for the remote router.
    f. Add IGRP routing and appropriate network numbers to the router. The AS number is 287.
6. Between the corporate router and remote router, use PPP encapsulation.

Step 4. Configure the remote router.
The remote router configuration team should configure the remote router as follows:

7. The router host name is "remote."
8. Configure the enable secret password to be "class."
9. Configure the password to be "cisco" when someone tries to log in from the console port.
10. Configure the password to be "cisco" when someone tries to Telnet into the router.
11. Configure WAN interface S0:
    a. The WAN subnetwork address is one subnet of a Class B network address.
    b. What is the S0 interface address?_____ (This must be compatible with the corporate router.)
    c. What is the S0 interface subnet mask? _____ (There are 512 subnets total.)
    d. Add a description to the S0 interface describing the link: _____
12. Configure LAN interface E0:
    a. Must be on a valid subnet of the Class B corporate network address.
    b. What is the subnet address for the LAN? _____
    c. What is the E0 interface address? _____
    d. What is the E0 interface subnet mask? _____
    e. Add a description to the E0 interface describing the link: _____
13. Configure a static host name mapping for the corporate router.
14. Add IGRP routing and appropriate network numbers to the router. The AS number is 287
15. Between the corporate router and the remote router, use PPP encapsulation.
16. Add an access control list (ACL) that will prevent Telnet from workstations on the LAN attached to the remote router from getting to the corporate network. All other traffic is permitted.
17. Enter the command here to apply the ACL to the correct interface and in the correct direction:

_____

Cisco Labs – Semester 4 – Wide-Area Networking
LAB 13.3 – PRACTICAL FINAL PREPARATION – WORKSHEET

Step 5. Configure the LAN workstation.
The remote configuration team should configure the workstation that is attached to the LAN as follows:

18. Configure the workstation IP address: _____
    (The workstation IP address must be compatible with the E0 interface of the remote router.)
19. Configure the workstation subnet mask: _____
    (This must be compatible with the E0 interface of the remote router.)
20. Configure the workstation default gateway: _____

(Reboot the workstation as necessary after making TCP/IP configuration changes)

Step 6. Ping from the remote router to the corporate router.
Ping from the remote router to the S1 interface of the corporate router.
21. Was the ping successful? _____   Why or why not? _____

Step 7. Ping from the workstation to the corporate router.
Ping from the LAN workstation (from the DOS prompt) to the S1 interface of the corporate router.
22. Was the ping successful? _____   Why or why not? _____

Step 8. Telnet from the remote router to the corporate router using the IP address.
Telnet from the remote router to the S1 interface of the corporate router.
23. Was the Telnet successful? _____   Why or why not? _____

Step 9. Telnet from the remote router to the corporate router using the hostname
Telnet from the remote router to the host name of the corporate router.
24. Was the Telnet successful? _____   Why or why not? _____

Step 10. Telnet from the workstation to the corporate router.
Telnet from the LAN workstation (from the DOS prompt) to the S1 interface of the corporate router.
25. Was the Telnet successful? _____   Why or why not? _____

LAB 13.3 – PRACTICAL FINAL PREPARATION –ANSWERS

Step 3. Verify/configure the corporate router.

The corporate router configuration team or lab assistant/instructor should use the startup configuration file shown in the answers section to verify that it is configured correctly before trying to configure the remote router. The corporate router should be configured as follows:

1. The router host name is "corporate."
2. Configure the enable secret password to be "class."
3. Configure the password to be "cisco" when someone tries to log in from the console port.
4. Configure the password to be "cisco" when someone tries to telnet into the router.
5. Configure WAN interface S1:
    a. The WAN subnetwork address is one subnet of a Class B network address.
    b. The S1 interface address is 172.16.1.1. (This is already set.)
    c. What is the S1 interface subnet mask is? **255.255.255.128** (There are 512 subnets total.)
    d. The S1 interface is providing the DCE clocking at 56000. Add a description to the S1 interface describing the link: **56K WAN link to remote**
    e. Configure a static host name mapping for the remote router.
    f. Add IGRP routing and appropriate network numbers to the router. The AS number is 287.
6. Between the corporate router and remote router, use PPP encapsulation.

IOS Configuration Commands for the Corporate Router

```
hostname Corporate
enable secret class
!
interface Ethernet0
 no ip address
 shutdown
interface Serial0
 no ip address
 shutdown
interface Serial1
 description 56K WAN link to Remote
 ip address  172.16.1.1  255.255.255.128
 clock rate 56000
 encapsulation ppp
 no shutdown
!
router igrp 287
  network 172.16.1.0
!
ip host remote  172.16.1.2
line con 0
 password cisco
 login
line aux 0
line vty 0 4
 password cisco
 login
```

Cisco Labs – Semester 4 – Wide-Area Networking
LAB 13.3 – PRACTICAL FINAL PREPARATION – ANSWERS

show running-config Results for Corporate Router (Cisco 2514 with IOS 12.0.9)

```
Current configuration:
!
version 12.0
service timestamps debug uptime
service timestamps log uptime
no service password-encryption
!
hostname Corporate
enable secret 5 $1$zFmB$ruP4x4IubsWCmm1r.Gnr..
!
ip subnet-zero
ip host remote 172.16.1.2
!
interface Ethernet0
 no ip address
 no ip directed-broadcast
 shutdown
!
interface Serial0
 no ip address
 no ip directed-broadcast
 no ip mroute-cache
 shutdown
!
interface Serial1
 description 56K WAN link to Remote
 ip address 172.16.1.1 255.255.255.128
 no ip directed-broadcast
 encapsulation ppp
 clockrate 56000
!
router igrp 287
 network 172.16.0.0
!
ip classless
!
line con 0
 password cisco
 login
 transport input none
line aux 0
line vty 0 4
 password cisco
 login
!
end
```

Cisco Labs – Semester 4 – Wide-Area Networking
LAB 13.3 – PRACTICAL FINAL PREPARATION – ANSWERS

Step 4. Configure the remote router.

The remote router configuration team should configure the remote router as follows:

7.   The router host name is "remote."
8.   Configure the enable secret password to be "class."
9.   Configure the password to be "cisco" when someone tries to log in from the console port.
10. Configure the password to be "cisco" when someone tries to Telnet into the router.
11. Configure WAN interface S0:
     a.   The WAN subnetwork address is one subnet of a Class B network address.
     b.   What is the S0 interface address? **172.16.1.2** (This must be compatible with the corporate router.)
     c.   What is the S0 interface subnet mask? **255.255.255.128** (There are 512 subnets total.)
     d.   Add a description to the S0 interface describing the link: **56K WAN link to remote**
12. Configure LAN interface E0:
     a.   Must be on a valid subnet of the Class B corporate network address.
     b.   What is the subnet address for the LAN? **172.16.2.0**
     c.   What is the E0 interface address? **172.16.2.1**
     d.   What is the E0 interface subnet mask? **255.255.255.128**
     e.   Add a description to the E0 interface describing the link: **Link to remote LAN**
13. Configure a static host name mapping for the corporate router.
14. Add IGRP routing and appropriate network numbers to the router. The AS number is 287.
15. Between the corporate router and the remote router, use PPP encapsulation.
16. Add an access control list (ACL) that will prevent Telnet from workstations on the LAN attached to the remote router from getting to the corporate network. All other traffic is permitted.
17. Enter the command here to apply the ACL to the correct interface and in the correct direction:
     Remote(config-if)# ip access list 101 in (applies ACL to remote router; interface E0 for incoming packets)

IOS Configuration Commands for the Remote Router

```
hostname Remote
enable secret class
!
interface Ethernet0
 description Connected to remote LAN
 ip address  172.16.2.1  255.255.255.128
 no shutdown
!
interface Serial0
 description 56K WAN link to Corporate
 ip address  172.16.1.2  255.255.255.128
 encapsulation ppp
 no shutdown
!
interface Serial1
 no ip address
 shutdown
```

LAB 13.3 – PRACTICAL FINAL PREPARATION – ANSWERS

```
router igrp 287
 network 172.16.1.0
 network 172.16.2.0
!
ip host corporate 172.16.1.1
!
access-list 101 deny tcp any 172.16.1.0  0.0.0.255 eq telnet
access-list 101 permit ip any any
!
line con 0
 password cisco
 login
line aux 0
line vty 0 4
 password cisco
 login
```

show running-config results for Remote Router (Cisco 2501 with IOS 12.0.9)

```
Current configuration:
!
version 12.0
service timestamps debug uptime
service timestamps log uptime
no service password-encryption
!
hostname Remote
!
enable secret 5 $1$ErKy$WZbdn2B7HkDBfLb/xhwRt0
!
ip subnet-zero
ip host corporate 172.16.1.1
!
interface Ethernet0
 description Connected to remote LAN
 ip address 172.16.2.1 255.255.255.128
 no ip directed-broadcast
!
interface Ethernet1
 no ip address
 no ip directed-broadcast
 shutdown
!
interface Serial0
 description 56K WAN link to Corporate router
 ip address 172.16.1.2 255.255.255.128
 no ip directed-broadcast
 encapsulation ppp
```

LAB 13.3 – PRACTICAL FINAL PREPARATION – ANSWERS

```
 no ip mroute-cache
no fair-queue
!
interface Serial1
 no ip address
 no ip directed-broadcast
 shutdown
!
router igrp 287
 network 172.16.0.0
!
ip classless
!
access-list 101 deny   tcp any 172.16.1.0 0.0.0.255 eq telnet
access-list 101 permit ip any any
!
line con 0
 password cisco
 login
 transport input none
line aux 0
line vty 0 4
 password cisco
 login
!
end
```

Step 5. Configure the LAN workstation.
The remote configuration team should configure the workstation that is attached to the LAN as follows:

18. Configure the workstation IP address: **172.16.2.2**
    (The workstation IP address must be compatible with the E0 interface of the remote router.)
19. Configure the workstation subnet mask: **255.255.255.128**
    (This must be compatible with the E0 interface of the remote router.)
20. Configure the workstation default gateway: **172.16.2.1 (IP address near-side router interface)**

Step 6. Ping from the remote router to the corporate router.
Ping from the remote router to the S1 interface of the corporate router.
21. Was the ping successful? **Yes**   Why or why not? **This is the WAN link and should ping okay.**

Step 7. Ping from the workstation to the corporate router.
Ping from the LAN workstation (from the DOS prompt) to the S1 interface of the corporate router.
22. Was the ping successful? **Yes**   Why or why not? **Ping is not blocked with the ACL (only Telnet).**

Cisco Labs – Semester 4 – Wide-Area Networking
LAB 13.3 – PRACTICAL FINAL PREPARATION – ANSWERS

Step 8. Telnet from the remote router to the corporate router using the IP address.
Telnet from the remote router to the S1 interface of the corporate router.
23. Was the Telnet successful? **Yes**   Why or why not? **Telnet is blocked only from the workstation.**

Step 9. Telnet from the remote router to the corporate router using the host name.
Telnet from the remote router to the host name of the corporate router.
24. Was the Telnet successful? **Yes**   Why or why not? **Host name entry will translate name to IP.**

Step 10. Telnet from the workstation to the corporate router.
Telnet from the LAN workstation (from the DOS prompt) to the S1 interface of the corporate router.
25. Was the Telnet successful? **No**   Why or why not? **Telnet should be blocked from the workstation.**

Notes

Notes

Notes

Notes